THE GOOD NEWS—A

A corporate leader goes a
product that makes his c
does the same thing with ~~another product~~—and winds
up with a fabulously costly failure. The man: Akio
Morita of Sony.

A company rises to utter dominance in its industry. It
then moves to expand its position—and has its market
share shredded. The company: IBM.

A man takes control of a famous auto company near
ruin. He restores it to its former glory. It then goes on
the skids again. The man and the car: John Egan and
Jaguar.

These are only a few of the many recent business-world
success stories and cautionary tales that vividly illustrate
the do's and the don'ts that Robert Heller explores in
the high-stakes world of—

THE DECISION MAKERS

ROBERT HELLER was the first U.S. correspondent
for the *Financial Times* of London: was business editor
of the *Observer*; and for twenty years was editor of
Britain's leading business publication, *Management
Today*. He is the author of *The Supermanagers, The Supermarketers,* and, recently, *The Age of the Common Millionaire*.
He lives and writes in London.

RECENT BOOKS BY ROBERT HELLER

The Supermarketers
The Supermanagers
The Pocket Manager
The Naked Manager
The Age of the Common Millionaire

THE
DECISION
MAKERS

The Men and the Million-Dollar Moves Behind
Today's Great Corporate Success Stories

ROBERT
HELLER

T·T

TRUMAN TALLEY BOOKS/PLUME
NEW YORK

PLUME
Published by the Penguin Group
Penguin Books USA Inc., 375 Hudson Street, New York, New York 10014,
U.S.A.
Penguin Books Ltd, 27 Wrights Lane, London W8 5TZ, England
Penguin Books Australia Ltd, Ringwood, Victoria, Australia
Penguin Books Canada Ltd, 2801 John Street, Markham, Ontario, Canada L3R 1B4
Penguin Books (N.Z.) Ltd, 182-190 Wairau Road, Auckland 10, New Zealand

Penguin Books Ltd, Registered Offices: Harmondsworth, Middlesex, England

Published by Truman Talley Books/Plume, an imprint of New American
Library, a division of Penguin Books USA Inc. Previously published in a
Truman Talley Books/Dutton edition.

First Truman Talley Books/Plume Printing, January, 1991
10 9 8 7 6 5 4 3 2 1

Grateful acknowledgment is given for permission to quote from the following
works:

Breakthroughs! by P. Ranganath Nayak and John M. Ketteringham. Copyright
© 1986 by Arthur D. Little, Inc. Reprinted with permission of Rawson
Associates, an imprint of Macmillan Publishing Company.

Made in Japan: Akio Morita and Sony by Akio Morita with Edwin M. Reingold
and Mitsuko Shimomura. Copyright © 1986 by E. P. Dutton, a division of New
American Library. Reprinted by permission of the publisher, E. P. Dutton, a
division of Penguin Books USA Inc.

 REGISTERED TRADEMARK—MARCA REGISTRADA

Library of Congress Cataloging-in-Publication Data

Heller, Robert, 1932-
    The decision makers : the men and the million-dollar moves behind
today's great corporate success stories / Robert Heller.
        p.   cm.
    Reprint. Originally published: New York : E.P. Dutton, c1989.
    Includes bibliographical references and index.
    ISBN 0-525-24798-X : $22.50
    1. Businessmen—Biography.   2. Decision-making.   3. Industrtial
management.   I. Title.
HC29.H45   1991
338.7′4′092273—dc20   90-45433
[B]   CIP

Original hardcover design by Earl Tidwell
Printed in the United States of America

to Angela

CONTENTS

CONTENTS

CONTENTS

THE
DECISION
MAKERS

Introduction

THE BIG DECIDERS— RIGHT AND WRONG

Nelson Bunker Hunt, bucking the accepted view of the oil industry, decided to search for oil in Libya. He made a find so fabulous that (as he devoutly intended) his wealth grew to billions that exceeded even those of his unbelievable two-family father, H. L. Hunt. One brave decision had created the world's largest private fortune: when Libya nationalized his oil, Hunt was worth, at the highest estimate, $16 billion.

Nelson Bunker Hunt, bucking the accepted view of the metals markets, decided that silver was due for a spectacular rise: when the advance failed to match his expectations, Hunt decided to force events to follow his plan by cornering the market. The collapse of his attempt sent Hunt into court, his main oil company into Chapter 11, and his billions tumbling into millions.

William T. Ylvisaker decided to build Gould Inc. into a much larger conglomerate by adding other, largely low-technology companies to the base of its revitalized battery-making operations: the decision was triumphal. Gould grew into a $2 billion corporation with an enviable record of expanding earnings from the disregarded smokestack industry.

William T. Ylvisaker decided that rapid growth could no longer be found in low-tech businesses. He took his total of acquisitions to over sixty and divestments to more than seventy as he converted Gould into a high-tech electronics company. By 1988 he had lost his job, Nippon Mining had bought a shrunken Gould for $1.1 million—and smokestack, rustbelt businesses were booming all over America.

Marc Rich and Pincus ("Pinky") Green decided to leave Philipp Brothers after a dispute over their bonus payments. They set up their own commodities trading business, which from 1974 expanded with unprecedented speed. The partners' earnings soared to some $300 million in 1980 as they developed their techniques for low-risk, high-volume trading on which the profits were assured.

Marc Rich and Pinky Green decided to engage in doubtful activities that raised their sales while lowering their taxes. The dubious courses led to federal charges of racketeering, fraud, tax evasion in the sum of $45 million, and illegal trading with Iran. Rich, Green, and their company remained enormously wealthy, despite paying a record corporate fine; but the pair were still wanted by the Feds, with a $500,000 price on their heads, and had to be awfully careful where they set foot.

Henry Wendt was high in the SmithKline French management team, which, seeing the prospect of a successful new ulcer treatment in a discovery by its British scientists, decided to go for broke and invest $10 million in a factory in Cork. The investment outdid every expectation and every other pharmaceutical: Tagamet became the world's first billion-dollar drug.

Henry Wendt, as chief executive, decided to use the Tagamet profits to buy Beckman Instruments for $1 billion so as to lessen the company's dependence on the wonder drug. The market for Beckman's products slumped after the acquisition.

So did SmithKline's share of the ulcer therapy market as Zantac took advantage of its competitor's vulnerable points; alarmingly, the company's profits slumped, too.

Daniel K. Ludwig decided that growing world demand for oil presented an irresistible opportunity to anybody who obtained a charter to transport the commodity, used the charter as collateral for a loan, used the loan to build a tanker to transport the oil, and then did it all over again. Acting on his decision, Ludwig became a double billionaire in shipping and real estate.

Daniel K. Ludwig decided that the Brazilian economy offered the next exciting opportunity in the industrial world, and that the way to exploit that promise, and to utilize his own wealth, was to establish a new industrial complex in the Amazon jungle; fourteen years later, he withdrew from the project after spending $1 billion—twice the value of all Ludwig's U.S. investments in 1986.

Akio Morita decided that, since Sony's technology made it possible to manufacture a miniaturized, portable, personal hi-fi, the company should put such a product on the market: although nearly everybody else at Sony objected to the proposal, and to the proposed low price, Morita took personal responsibility for the project—and the Walkman became one of Sony's great money-spinning innovations in the mass market.

Akio Morita decided that, having perfected the world's first videocassette recorder, capable of recording and playing back TV programs and films, Sony should keep a stranglehold on the technology. That allowed JVC, exploiting the technology of a product that had a longer playing time, to corral the other Japanese manufacturers into the VHS format, which stole virtually the entire market that Sony had made.

John R. Opel, as chief executive of IBM, decided to back the marketing of a personal computer and to entrust its production and marketing to an independent group empowered to short-circuit company rules in order to rush the PC on to the market in the shortest possible time: the PC vastly expanded total personal computer sales, took IBM to an overwhelming lead, and changed the whole strategy of a corporation that had previously thought almost entirely in terms of mainframes.

John R. Opel, in deciding to approve the PC plan, went along with the policy of making IBM the industry standard by having the technology so open that all software companies would write programs for the PC. But IBM's openness also left the door ajar for rival manufacturers. Some 300 of them proceeded to bring out "clones" that undercut the IBM product's price and cut its business market share from 86 percent to 23 percent.

Fred Smith decided while still at Yale that the right way to run an air freight company was on a "hub and spokes" system, with trucks coming along the spokes to the aircraft at the center, and with overnight delivery guaranteed. Returning from the Vietnam war, after an apprenticeship in corporate jets, Smith launched Federal Express in 1972; despite terrible early troubles, it became one of American business's fastest-growing successes.

Fred Smith decided that the next stage in communications was an electronic mail-delivery service. Launched under the name ZapMail, the Federal Express project ran into a number of technical difficulties. It was finally perfected just in time to be overtaken by the growth of facsimile, which needed no intermediary: after terrible early troubles, ZapMail was totally zapped.

Malcolm McLean in the late 1950s decided to start transporting goods in steel boxes called containers—generating an economic revolution with epoch-making results. His Sea-Land Corporation prospered so greatly with the container boom that McLean pocketed $157 million on its sale in 1969.

Malcolm McLean, after purchasing United States Lines,

decided to buy a dozen extralarge supertankers for $570 million, confident that rising oil prices would yield superprofits: oil prices collapsed, so did oil charters, and in 1986 McLean's fleet went under, with debts close to $1.3 billion.

F. Ross Johnson decided as chief executive to embark on two large mergers, first of Standard Brands with Nabisco, then of Nabisco with R. J. Reynolds. In the process he thrashed Procter & Gamble in the Great Cookie Wars and snatched the top spot in a $16 billion food and tobacco giant with matchless brand strengths.

F. Ross Johnson as chief executive of RJR Nabisco decided in short order to launch a new smokeless cigarette, and to propose a massive management buyout that stood to enrich him personally. The offer was topped by buyout specialists Kohlberg, Kravis, Roberts; Johnson lost his board's support, and eventually his job. The smokeless smoke flopped for a loss of at least $500 million.

Anthony Berry, taking over a private company for $500,000, decided to sell everything else and concentrate on its employment agency business: going public in 1984, Blue Arrow in three years grew to approaching $600 million in value by brilliantly executed acquisitions—and thanks to a sevenfold rise in the company's shares.

Anthony Berry decided to bid for Mitchell Fromstein's Manpower Inc., twice Blue Arrow's size. To win, he raised £837 million in new equity—just before the 1987 crash: the shares lost half their value, and finally Berry lost his chief executive job—to Fromstein, who he had only just dismissed.

Carlo de Benedetti decided in 1978 to invest $17 million of his own money to buy 20 percent of Olivetti and take over as its chief executive: within five years sales had increased 250 percent, losses of $6 million a month had turned to annual profits of $177.5 million, and de Benedetti, vastly wealthy, had twice been elected European Businessman of the Year.

Carlo de Benedetti decided in 1988 to capture the Belgian

conglomerate Société Générale and create a trans-European financial conglomerate: his failure left his plan in ruins at a moment when Olivetti, after sharp falls in profits for two years running, was in urgent need of reorganization itself.

J. Peter Grace as CEO decided to take an old family shipping business, W. R. Grace, away from shipping and into chemicals and other diversifications. Between 1960 and 1980, Grace's acquisitions, joint ventures, and start-ups totaled 275, hoisting the group to among the fifty largest U.S. companies, with sales of $6.7 billion in 1984.

J. Peter Grace, with earnings no higher in 1984 than ten years previously, decided to divest W. R. Grace of some of the 216 acquisitions that largely achieved his ambitious diversifying. The divestments finally came to between 65 and 70 percent of the buys: Grace's total sales fell to $4.5 billion in 1987, a decline of 41 percent from the previous year.

Great people and great companies can afford to make great mistakes in their decisions. This is fortunate because their batting average may be no better than that of other mortals. The mistaken decisions, too, flow from the same causes as all human error, from which it follows that so do the decisions that leave other mortals around the wrong side of the bend. The same person makes the great decision and the great mistake. In some circumstances, true, advancing years mean that internal changes, ranging from unnatural arrogance to natural senility, contribute to the gross external error. But even if the personality changes, the principles of sound decision breached by the self-made megalomaniac or old-age nonpensioner do not.

Their fundamental breach is often to assume that, because so many decisions have spun up heads, the next spin of the coin is certain to repeat the magic. To have confidence in your decisions is essential. To believe that they are invariably, necessarily right is lethal. All decisions are steps into the unknown. Decision makers at all levels choose or refuse a plan of action, a job candidate, an investment, or anything else in the light of their understanding of the chosen option and their knowledge of the circumstances that currently exist, together with their view of future circumstances, their experience of the past, and their extrapolation of the consequences of the choice. At all stages, it is extremely easy to be utterly wrong.

To start with, there may be better choices that you have not considered. Second, your information about the apparent options may be imperfect. Third, so may your knowledge of existing circumstances. Fourth, your experience of the past may be irrelevant. Fifth, your prediction of the future may be grievously wide of the mark: all predictions, forecasts, scenarios are subject to wide margins of error, and the further the gaze into the future, the wider the margin. Sixth, chains of cause and effect are also forecasts, and subject to the same high probability of error—only more so, because unforeseen side effects may prove more crucial than the accurately foreseen direct effects.

The examples jump out from the cases above. The Hunts would have multiplied their billions, instead of losing them, had they stuck to oil, an industry they understood, instead of venturing into trading in precious metals, of which they knew nothing. Ludwig acted in imperfect knowledge of the present difficulties he would encounter in building his Brazilian industrial empire. Morita misread the present circumstances when he tried to overexploit Sony's monopoly in video recording. Smith didn't foresee that the advent of facsimile would dramatically change the future environment for mailless mail. IBM didn't see that a side effect of its strategy in personal computers would lead to wholesale and unstoppable imitation. Yet in all these cases the same people and companies had shown, some of them many times, the ability to seize unhesitat-ingly on the best option—often a choice that had never crossed another mind; to do so with an unerringly accurate grasp of all the current facts about the option and the environment of the decision; to use experience brilliantly to move with assurance into an uncannily read future; and to maintain complete con-trol of the unfolding chain of cause, effect, and side effect.

Those excellent decisions are what number their makers and takers among today's shapers—the innovators who win the world with new goods and services; the expansionists who build empires; the improvers who take the given and turn it into a new creation; the planners who design a better future; the salvationists who make successes out of the failures of the past; the competitors who, in the end-century struggle for mar-ket position, lead the way in the face of constant challenge. This book is about how the good decisions and the bad are made, how the bad can be turned into good, and what distinguishes the great decision makers from the runners-up. It isn't that good guys finish last. It's that good decision makers finish first. This is how to join them.

I

THE TRUTH
ABOUT
DECISIONS

1. THE FORK IN THE JUNGLE

Here is a famous problem to test the powers of any decision maker. You are deep in the jungle. You come upon a fork in your perilous path. One fork, you have been told, leads to cannibals, man-eating tigers, poisonous swamps, crocodiles, and certain death—if not from one cause then from another. The other fork leads to the perfect safety of Jesuit missionaries and well-armed troops. But you lack one essential piece of data: Which fork is which?

Fortunately, there is an Indian standing at the junction. Unfortunately, there are two tribes of Indians in the vicinity: one invariably tells the truth, the other as invariably lies. Your decision thus couldn't be simpler (for there are only two choices) or weightier (for this is literally a matter of life or death).

Six explorers come, one after the other, to this fork in the road. The first is not a man to waste time. He knows that the odds are even in most human choices. "Nothing ventured, nothing gained," he says, without asking the Indian for guidance, and plunges down the right-hand path.

The man-eating tigers can hardly believe their luck.

The second explorer prides himself on the strength of his hunches, his "gut feeling": he asks the Indian the way, but without much interest, before following his hunch. He, too, takes the right-hand path.

The cannibals have his gut, and its feeling, as an entrée.

The third explorer is a student of human nature. He realizes that the Indian holds the key to his survival, and asks him "Do you tell the truth?" even though he is sure to get the answer "Yes"—because the liar will lie, and the truthful one won't. But the explorer studies the dark brown eyes and the nonverbal communications of the Indian with great care while asking the way. Convinced that he has been told the truth, he heads down the right-hand path.

The swamp claims him in precisely 7.6 seconds.

The fourth explorer has been thinking about the problem while hacking his way through the jungle. By the time he reaches the fork, he knows which question to ask the Indian. He gets the only possible answer, and therefore knows beyond any doubt which path to take.

He turns left and becomes president of the Royal Geographical Society.

The fifth explorer knows more jungle lore than all the others put together. Examining the trail, his expert eye finds four sets of recent tracks. He notes that three of his fellow explorers have turned right and only one left. Reassured, he takes the Indian's advice and goes with the crowd.

Very briefly, he learns more about the eating habits of the crocodile than he ever wanted to know.

The sixth explorer is the last to emerge from the jungle. He asks the Indian the way, but that, of course, doesn't help. He sets off along the left-hand path, stops, changes his mind, and returns to take the right-hand route. He stops again, dithers again, and returns to the fork. Then he sits down by a tree. The Indian watches him with contempt, congratulates him on the excellent safe spot he has chosen (which is, of course, a lie), and leaves the explorer sitting by his tree.

If the malaria, the snakes, or starvation haven't got him, he is there to this day.

2. THE TOUGH DECISIONS THAT WEREN'T

The six explorers in the preceding fable represent six principal types of decision maker. The first decides blindly, impulsively. Since the odds on human success really do seem to be about even, he sometimes lands on the right decision. His average, however, will be much lower than one in two, even if the evens rule is true, because other, shrewder, better decision makers will shift the odds in their own favor.

The second explorer, who relies on hunch, is wiser, since the feeling gut is actually the sensing subconscious: the geniuses of this genre may appear to have greater intuition, just as a lovely woman may seem to have natural beauty. Both may work at their strengths harder than you imagine. But many hunches are wrong, and many intuitive successes often make decisions that are indubitably bad. The problem is to know when the gut is telling the truth. Typically, the entrepreneur fits into this class.

The third explorer knows that decisions are better for being founded on fact, analysis, and interpretation. He doesn't know (though he should) that if any of the three are inaccurate, he is no better off than the blind decision maker. The majority of poor corporate decisions come under this heading: managers don't gather the right information, don't subject it to rigorous analysis, draw the wrong conclusions, and fail.

The fourth explorer is the hero of the management text-books, the ideal decision maker. He gets it right every time by anticipating the future decision point and working through the evidence and the alternatives to arrive at the infallibly correct conclusion (which, then, of course, must be translated into infallibly correct action). This hero is a mythical beast. Infallibility is not given to man: only sometimes will the solution be as logically clear as that which faced the six explorers.

The fifth explorer could come from any of the previous types. Whether he approaches the decision impulsively, intuitively, inaccurately, or analytically, he finds safety and comfort in numbers—not the numbers of calculation, which are indispensable, but the numbers in the crowd. Nearly all decision makers are likewise overinfluenced by accepted views, conventional wisdom, and crowded bandwagons. This is why so many make the same mistakes.

The only true path is that of the fourth explorer. But the ideal decision-making process needs to be backed by the second explorer's intuition, by much of the first explorer's readiness to act, by a good dose of the third explorer's concern with human judgment, by something of the fifth explorer's careful observation of the crowd, and by nothing of the sixth explorer's inability to take any decision at all—not even his caution. Judicious care, the intelligent weighing of risk, and waiting for the time to ripen are part of the ideal process. Letting "I dare not" wait upon "I would" is a mug's game, and those who play it usually get mugged.

The explorers are a good guide to general principles, but their particular problem is not—though you wouldn't think so to read most books on decision making and decision makers. The impression created is usually of a world in which forked paths and forked-tongued Indians occur all the time. In real life, though, problems hardly ever appear in the form of conundrums needing subtle solutions.

That to the two-forks problem, for what it's worth, is to ask the Indian the following question: "If I were to ask you which path was safe, which one would you point to?" The inveterate liar, asked which path is safe, would point to certain death; but if he were now to point in that direction he would be telling the truth—so he must lie and point to safety, which is where the truthful Indian will invariably point.

The story is, of course, ridiculous: nobody lies all the time, nor do many people always tell the truth, and the real-life liar might send you to certain death even if it meant telling you the truth—also, he might not understand the subtleties of the subjunctive. . . . But the absurdity runs deeper. Why are decisions, especially in business management, treated so ponderously, as if they belonged to this theater of the absurd? It's clear that many decisions lack all subtlety: in some, for example, the outcome of choosing one of two forks in the road is absolutely certain.

During the last war, a ship was torpedoed in the Pacific. The survivors, women and children among them, huddled in a crowded boat. The ship's medical officer weighed up the grim situation, said "There are too many of us in this boat," and went overboard. In making that decision, rightly or wrongly, he chose the certain death of a brilliant young medico and sportsman to improve the chances of survival of those left in the boat. He didn't know that they would survive, of course. But his was a logical sacrifice—if, that is, there really was one person too many in that boat.

In business, similar situations of absolute certainty occur surprisingly often. For instance, every car manufacturer knows, as divine and unassailable fact, that, if the company invests less, proportionately speaking, in new models and productive efficiency than its rivals, it will lose market share, profits, and long-term viability. There's no possible argument on this score: the most conspicuous evidence comes from the company known in mid-1988 as Rover Group, which initially encompassed most well-known brands (or marques) in the history of the British-owned car industry.

By that date, as the result of a policy of malign neglect, all brands save Rover had practically gone—Wolseley, Riley, MG, Morris, Austin, Triumph, Standard; Jaguar and Daimler survived, but in a different, independent company. It had risen from the cellar into the sunlight by acting on a wholly opposed policy, founded on heavy investment in product and process, which applied precisely the obvious decisions its former parents had so conspicuously ignored.

If this sounds like an example of charmingly destructive British eccentricity, the American giants (General Motors, Ford, and Chrysler) were no better. They also underinvested, leaving it to the Japanese to crack the American market with smaller cars that were initially inferior to models made by the Americans' very own subsidiaries in Europe. The panjandrums of Detroit can't have been ignorant of the appeal of small cars to the American motorist: Volkswagen, with the Beetle, had long before become the fourth-largest-selling car in the entire U.S. market. Yet the Americans chose to dive overboard into a sea infested by Japanese sharks.

Why people knowingly take the fork that leads to certain death is another question. But in these cases, the decision maker is better placed than the jungle explorer: he knows which path is which. To be specific, and to take another aspect of the decision to underinvest, GM had been alerted by the successful attacks of Ralph Nader, and Ford by its expensive incineration of Pinto drivers, to the gross dangers of inferior quality. The Toyota production system, which dated back to the 1950s, could have eliminated the Americans' grievous problems. Yet they chose not to adopt the Toyota principles, or didn't choose to adopt them, which comes to the same awful result.

Sometimes, though, decisions of certainty are deliberate

rather than inadvertent. In 1988, *Fortune* magazine asked eight of "tomorrow's chief executives" to name their "toughest business decision." The men and their answers make a fascinating collection:

"Closing manufacturing plants and laying off workers": Gerald Greenwald (Chrysler)

"Eliminating 24,000 jobs in the Information Systems Division in 1983, even though it saved several hundred million dollars": Robert E. Allen (AT&T)

"Restructuring the headquarters division of Rank Xerox in London. That was an organization I had built up, and I was forced to reduce the staff by 40 percent": Paul A. Allaire (Xerox)

"The people-related decisions after the merger with Gulf: deciding which offices to shut down, and which jobs to eliminate": Kenneth T. Derr (Chevron)

"Making large-scale layoffs as part of the turnaround at Kentucky Fried Chicken, which was losing several million dollars a year": Michael A. Miles (Kraft)

"Cutting jobs when Deere restructured during the agricultural downturn of the 1980s, because so many capable individuals were affected": Hans W. Becherer (Deere & Co.)

"The first time I fired a manager. That was one skill I wasn't sure I had": Jerry O. Williams (AM International)

"Making a major commitment to the consumer banking business in the late 1970s when it was losing money": Thomas G. Labrecque (Chase Manhattan Bank)

The stunning reality of those "toughest" decisions is that all save the last are (1) negative and (2) not decisions at all—in all but one case, the decisions had *already* been taken to close the plants, eliminate the jobs, fire the manager, restructure the headquarters, implement the merger, lay off the surplus workers, restructure the company. Nor can these decisions have been *intellectually* "tough." If a company is losing millions of dollars, or incurring unnecessary costs in the hundreds of millions, or reeling under the threat of bankruptcy and only being kept alive by federally guaranteed loans, there are no alternatives. The action must be taken, and the only problem—again intellectually—is to make the right moves in the hierarchy of decisions that must follow.

"Toughness" to these powerful and successful men has an emotional meaning: the relatively easy decision has hard and painful consequences—but for other people. The real tough time was had by those who lost their jobs through no fault of their own, maybe because of old, bad, voluntary decisions taken by managers who had long since vanished themselves, but in the end because of later, compulsory decisions. At Rank Xerox, Allaire was confronted with competition from the Japanese, who were undercutting his prices and outdistancing his technology, entirely because of slow and misguided responses by the parent company to the competitive thrust from the East. In those circumstances, the $200 million of costs Allaire decided to save were essential to creating a future for the employees who remained.

For Allaire personally, the future after that tough decision included the presidency of the parent and plenty of income with which to pursue his hobby of fox hunting. But what would have been his future had he balked at the 40 percent reduction in his staff or executed it (and them) badly? The answer is obvious.

This hard fact doesn't in any way impugn the motives of Allaire or the other six men who were in the same genuinely unhappy position. No decent person likes hurting other human beings, whether they come singly (the manager who has to be sacked) or in battalions. Near to his death, Field Marshal Montgomery worried how he would be received, on "crossing over Jordan," by the soldiers he had sent to their deaths. A friend and disciple comforted him about the heavenly response of his dead; but, of course, El Alamein couldn't have been won without British soldiers falling.

The really tough decisions taken by Montgomery included fighting the purely defensive action at Alam Halfa that halted Rommel in his tracks, and the refusal, against heavy pressure from Churchill, to launch El Alamein until the Eighth Army was very good and very ready. By the same token, the only truly tough decision among the eight above was that of banker Thomas Labrecque. If he had been wrong in committing the Chase heavily to consumer banking, the subsequent enormous losses would have ruined his career and done the bank several powers of no good at an already delicate and dangerous moment in its history.

That tough decision, however, didn't hurt people—no doubt hundreds of consumer banking executives, and thousands of their staff, have every reason to bless the fact that this man, known, says *Fortune*, "for consuming reams of data before making decisions," consumed and decided as he did. That was a true decision of uncertainty. The other class of decision—the path of certainty—presents no problems, except for those who are too squeamish, or humane, to do what must be done, or for those who cannot afford (unlike Detroit, which had all the resources needed to beat out the Japanese) to take the known, correct fork.

3. THE WARS WITH THE MINERS

The path of certainty has much in common with a second category: where (as in the stories of the self-immolating medico and the closed plants and offices) the choice is irrevocable, but where the outcome is unknown. War provides classic examples. Once General Eisenhower had taken his lonely decision to launch the delayed invasion of Europe, he couldn't change his mind: he couldn't say, "Sorry, fellers, it was all a mistake," and call back the ships, the troops, and the planes. If his meteorological advice had been wrong, and the brief window of good weather had slammed shut, Ike would have made one of the world's worst decisions. Its history might have been stained with blood (and not just of the invasion's dead) for years after 1944.

By D day, Eisenhower was running out of options. A no-go decision would have risked losing any chance of invading Fortress Europe that year. Any new delay would have demoralized the invasion force, dangerously risked the security of an operation that depended partly on surprise, and made Eisenhower appear to be weak and vacillating. The pressures were all pushing him in the same direction. While his decision triumphed, Ike had been boxed into a position where he had little or no alternative. That didn't matter, partly because the weather held, and partly because the invasion had been meticulously and brilliantly planned; thus the Allies could survive the inevitable but terrible errors—such as the paratroopers dropped in swamps and the Americans landed on the wrong beaches.

This teaches two crucial lessons about decisions: the quality of preparation has a fundamental effect on the outcome; and the larger the room for error, the better the chances that the decision will succeed. The chastening experience of the British prime minister Edward Heath in the winter of 1973/74 tells what happens if the D-day lessons are ignored, demonstrating the perils of getting boxed in with inadequate preparation and no margin for mistakes.

Faced with a stupendous wage claim from the National Union of Mineworkers, Heath built an elaborate trap for himself. First, it had to be victory or nothing—no compromise. Result: the miners went on strike. Second, with Britain's businesses forced by energy shortages to work a three-day week, Heath decided to threaten the use of his heaviest weapon, a general election. Result: he marched his Conservative troops up the hill—and then, like the noble Duke of York in the nursery rhyme, marched them down again. Third, when the last effort to negotiate unconditional surrender failed, he was trapped between the choice of an election or defeat; he no longer had any real alternative. The election, as Heath's opponent, Harold Wilson, correctly foresaw, revolved around other issues, not just the striking miners, and Heath lost a war that he could have won.

The next Tory prime minister, Margaret Thatcher, made no mistakes. The level of coal stocks in Britain was built up as massively as Montgomery's tanks or Eisenhower's invasion forces. The labor laws were reformed to strengthen her government's hand. At the same time, the cabinet ostensibly sat in the rear, like Roosevelt and Churchill on D day, while the commanders in the coalfields fought what was by then a far more militant National Union of Mineworkers. Thatcher allowed her opponent, the Marxist Arthur Scargill, to imitate Heath and box himself in: the strike was called at the worst time of year and on the kind of issue (nonwage) that historically has hardly ever led to success in a major industrial dispute on either side of the Atlantic.

It was a brilliant operation. Thatcher was implacably determined to defeat Scargill, but she avoided (as he did not) any material loss of her ability to control events. There are sometimes situations in the life of every person and organization when events do take over, when the dreaded TINA (There Is No Alternative—a favorite phrase of Thatcher's, incidentally, when defending policies that not only had plenty of alternatives but that she quite often changed anyway) takes charge.

TINA situations have no place in a book about decision

making and decision makers. If there truly is no alternative, no decision needs to be made. For decisions are choices. The act of decision presupposes that alternatives exist. Yet in real life, the availability of options is restricted by factors which may be as irrelevant as some of those that led to the downfall of Edward Heath. Thus, the key decisions in most people's lives are the choice of a career, a mate, and a house. Just as a computer can only say on or off, so the brain says only yes or no on these life moves—as if the choices offered were the only ones in the world.

The same process occurs, most of the time, when managements decide on acquisitions. They may or may not have screened all manner of alternative purchases before deciding on this particular buy, but the final decision becomes a simple yes or no, without any consideration of the immediate alternatives—small wonder that at least half of all acquisitions misfire.

It's a valid objection that in the end yes/no decisions can't be avoided. That's perfectly true: the art of the great decision maker is to reduce the alternatives to the point of total simplicity. The reduction, however, will be too simple if the decision maker hasn't begun by thoroughly exploring the alternatives and finished by establishing the criteria against which the choice must be made. The objective is paradoxical: to reach the position of the bad decision maker, in which there is no alternative, but this time purely because all others have been eliminated, leaving only the obviously and indisputably best.

To write of decisions in such terms, though, is to imply that all choices are vital and that life, especially organizational life, consists of moving from one decision to another—like a train that stops at station after station, except that, at each halt, a choice between tracks has to be made. The reality is much closer to a normal train journey. For most of the time, the company proceeds on a fixed track. Very likely the distribution in Pareto's Law applies: for 80 percent of the time, what happens inside an organization, and what it does outside, are predetermined. Only for a fifth of the time do conscious decisions actually influence outcomes.

The built-in stabilizers explain the stasis, the resistance to change, that is the bane of corporate life (or should be). The organization's self-declared decision makers want to achieve change, but they preside over an institution that is dead set on continuing along the same track. The great, the true decision makers include those who refuse to accept stasis and deliberately decide to institutionalize change. Their examples show the decisive power of decision. Those who wield it, though, are not powerful because they can decide but because they can act.

This distinction wasn't appreciated by the trade unions of Europe, which in the 1960s and early 1970s demanded a say in the decision making or taking of the corporations that employed their members. The decisions the union leaders had in mind were those affecting employment: they didn't want action but inaction—no layoffs of superfluous workers, no closures of uneconomic plants or (like Scargill later) loss-making mines. Giving unions these powers often caused more economic harm than good, not only by putting off the evil day until it was worse still, but, far more evilly, postponing the benevolent hour when German, Dutch, and other plants could compete on equal terms with the Japanese.

But whatever the rights and wrongs, the unions came nowhere near exercising, or even helping to exercise, the decisions that truly determine the destiny of the corporation. There are such decisions, but the decision makers themselves may well not realize that the great moment, and the momentous decision, have arrived. Sony was unblissfully ignorant that by opting for a one-hour tape and laying down take-it-or-leave-it terms for would-be licensees, it was throwing away the market in videocassette recorders. IBM didn't appreciate that, by flinging open the door to its PC technology, it would let in a legion of clones and weaken one of the greatest brand names ever created.

These are negative examples. But by the same token, Britain's Rank Organization had no means of knowing the importance of the decision to buy, for a pittance, 51 percent of the rights to the infant technology of xerography outside the United States. By definition, backing the new and the untried rests on incalculable decisions. They may have more profound implications for the future than any decisions that can be tabulated by the mind of man, or by the massed powers of every supercomputer he has made. But being incalculable doesn't mean that calculation has no role. It does—and that role should literally be decisive.

4. THE REVERSE ORDER OF PEPSICO

Calculating the incalculable is an unavoidable management paradox. But one astonishing commentary on the difficulty of applying logical thought to problematical business decisions is the way that every major electronic, business equipment, and electrical company, with only one exception, made a mess of exploiting one of the century's supreme inventions: the digital computer.

Where IBM led, the others sought to follow: GE, Burroughs, RCA, Honeywell, Machines Bull, Siemens, Philips, and so on, and so on, all with no clear-cut or lasting success—even though, no doubt, all their calculations showed that this was a market that would grow very rapidly, where the technological barriers were not forbidding, and where they had every right to expect the significant share that (again, no doubt) they included in their sums.

In most cases, these were in the class of optional decisions—decisions that do not have to be taken, where no is as acceptable as yes (on the argument that regretting the fish that got away is far less painful than counting the cost of the poisoned mackerel you ate). Often, these options are presented as necessities: thus, Xerox justified its disastrous buy of Scientific Data Systems on the grounds that it needed computer capacity (so it did, later on—the SDS catastrophe probably helped to delay and confuse Xerox's response when the time truly came).

It's clear that good decisions can't be made without efficient preliminary analysis of what kind of decision is on the table. The analysis should place decisions in one of five categories.

1. *Unavoidable.* These subdivide into decisions where there are no options (and that, remember, are therefore not decisions) and those where choices do exist.

2. *Desirable.* These decisions are those that, if they succeed, will have significant beneficial effect on the organization but that are not imperative.

3. *Passive.* Decisions that are not taken—for instance, you don't decide on, or even think about, an overhaul of the sales organization—are decisions none the less. All companies run largely on passive decisions, which may well explain why they run badly—or less well than anybody would like.

4. *Active.* When you take an initiative in the continuing business of the company—say, revamping that sales organization or raising a price.

5. *Reactive.* When you respond to somebody else's initiative—when they raise a price, say. Managers don't always realize that (as with the passive variety) doing nothing is a decision: for instance, not following a rival's price lead is a decision to cut your own *relative* price (which is the only significant price).

The basis of proper calculation, not in the mathematical sense (though math will definitely be essential), but in the archaic definition of "thinking out," starts with the above analysis. The basic question is: What kind of decision am I considering? With that answer in hand, at least fifteen other critical questions follow:

1. What decisions am I, consciously or unconsciously, not taking that I ought to take?
2. (*Very important*) What is the question that this decision will answer?
3. How many realistic alternatives are there as answers to the question?
4. Does this decision have to be taken at all?
5. If it is not taken, what consequences will follow?
6. What objective is the decision intended to achieve?
7. What results if that aim is not achieved?
8. What is the perfect information that will enable the decision to be taken in perfect confidence?
9. How near can I get to that perfect information?
10. Is the degree of imperfection so great as to undermine the basis for rational decision?
11. How is the decision to be executed? By whom? Monitored in what way and against what criteria?
12. What can go wrong?
13. In the event that Murphy's Law operates, and what can go wrong does, what will be the response?
14. What can go too well?
15. If the results of this decision flow broadly to plan, what further decisions will have to be taken—and when?

The last five questions are all concerned with action, and rightly so, since a decision that isn't converted into deeds is merely conversation. The pivotal difference between the great decision makers and the mass isn't only that the great have the imagination and the courage to see an opportunity and decide to seize their chance; they are also people of action. They may be prepared to wait years for the call to arms, but they spring into battle the moment the bugle sounds.

Far more often, there is no time lag. To decide, for these maestros, is to do: and to do is to carry out your decision—the decision, the whole decision, and nothing but the decision. They act, in a word, decisively. The semantics have become a little muddled here, for the noun *decision* in the context of decision making has come to embrace deliberation and careful consideration of alternatives—the kind of process embodied in the questions just listed. The adjective *decisive*, with its roots in the Latin for "to cut," expresses clarity, speed, and firmness of action.

In my book *The Supermarketers*, I quoted with some approval the way in which D. Wayne Calloway, chief executive of PepsiCo, had reversed the normal order of things to "ready, fire, aim." This placing of speed over deliberation may or may not be a major explanation of PepsiCo's humbling sales lead over Coca-Cola: $11.5 billion of total sales in 1987 against Coke's $7.7 billion. Three years previously, the gap had been only a billion dollars. While Coke still led PepsiCo handsomely in return on sales and assets in 1987, that had more to do with far greater dependence on soft drinks—and there, in the intervening years, Coke had suffered a famous defeat.

Reading Pepsi-Cola's president Roger Enrico's account, *The Other Guy Blinked*, the reason "Pepsi won the cola wars" (to quote the subtitle) sounds like a clash between overcalculation and swift, decisive response. Coca-Cola entered into the fateful launch of New Coke from a negative platform: chairman Roberto Goizueta decided that something had to be done because "the product and the brand had a declining share in a shrinking segment of the market." The decision to act dramatically was based on numbers: the statistics that showed some preference for the tasty new recipe over the one that had served

Coke so nobly for ninety-nine years. But it missed Enrico's simple intuition: he spotted at once that Coke, the world's largest-selling soft drink, *had been withdrawn from its own domestic market.*

Enrico's reaction is an object lesson in where "ready, fire, aim" pays off. He shot into Calloway's office and got the extra millions he needed for an "offensive program": more advertising, more Pepsi in the stores, more merchandising, more incentives to convert the customers. For the customers disliked New Coke—or rather, which came to the same thing, they disliked losing the old. Enrico wonders why it took his rival so long to respond to the brand's swan dive, and he probably has the right answer: the calculators "were *still* looking at research and sales projections—at numbers."

Goizueta's decision to give America back the original Coke was a true TINA; there was no alternative, no need of further calculation, but also no hope of easily reversing a defeat that left Pepsi outselling the renamed Classic Coke and the weak New Coke brand put together. The Coca-Cola decision makers had only succeeded in accentuating the slide from which their wrongly calculated decision had sprung. But was the decision really as calculated as it seemed? Had the fifteen questions been properly asked and correctly answered?

Evidently they hadn't. All the signs point toward an emotional commitment by Coca-Cola's management, triggered by its inability to accept that the monotonous erosion of the brand resulted not from its taste but from monotonous marketing. The ready-fire-aim tactics of PepsiCo were simply more effective. It was *unavoidable* for Coca-Cola to tackle its declining market share, but the decision makers did have options other than New Coke. It would have been *desirable* to establish an entirely new, dynamic brand in old Coke's place. But it wasn't *imperative.*

The decision not to invest much more money and effort in old Coke was a *passive* decision of greater importance than the launch of New Coke—though it's doubtful if the decision makers at Coca-Cola realized that truth. New Coke was an *active* decision, which foundered in part on failure to anticipate the effectiveness of the *reactive* decisions taken by PepsiCo. Goizueta and his cohorts were led down these ways of uncertainty solely because they took the wrong path through the jungle at the very outset. They relied excessively on the research data because it seemed to confirm a decision that, emotionally, they had already taken.

Coca-Cola merely set up PepsiCo for a series of reactive decisions for which its shoot-from-the-hip style was perfectly adapted. As the results showed, there's much in its favor. The idea of the decision as a cutting stroke, like that of Alexander through the Gordian Knot, needs to be preserved. The great decisions are swords. Only little ones revolve around pinpoints—whether to accept this or that fractionally higher bid for this or that currency, or share, or commodity. The bolder the colors, the bigger the margins; the larger the potential payoff, the easier it is for decision to lead to triumph.

It follows that the process of reaching a decision should not be a long-winded debate in which pros and cons are bandied about before the matter is put to a vote. The great decision makers follow the Lincoln principle: if the president's was the only vote in favor, the ayes had it. Corporations in the West suffer, as the Japanese do not, from the illusion of collective and collegial decision making. It is illusory because all members of the college do not contribute equally—the dominant (in terms of status) tend to dominate. It is illusory because, while two heads may well be better than one, the benefits by no means increase with every added head.

On the contrary, the process that Robert Waterman, Jr., calls *group-think* in his book *The Renewal Factor*, can easily take over. Nobody expresses his own opinion, but instead mouths his understanding or version of what he believes the group view to be. This explains how groups of apparently intelligent people can arrive at asinine decisions that, as individuals, they would never have countenanced. Would any lone ranger of normal sense, knowing anything or nothing of the soft drink industry, have tampered with the world's best-selling brand?

Other people's arguments are enormously valuable, provided that they are (1) based on fact and (2) expressed vigorously, clearly, and frankly; and that (3) somebody has the power, after listening to all the fact-based opinions, to make the final decision, and (4) everybody else accepts that power and the decision to which it gives birth. If these conditions are not met, effective decision making is vitiated. Instead, managements often choose, unwittingly, to be hanged together, rather than to risk being hanged separately—all or any of them.

That is the fate of the Japanese president whose decisions damage the long-term survival and success of the corporation. But there's been no evidence that fear for their personal responsibility has hung over Japanese heads like a sword of Damocles, paralyzing their powers. The reverse has been true. Excessive caution damages the future just as surely as excessive ambition. In Japanese corporation after corporation, president after president has shown a capacity for adventurous, realistic decision making that has gone far beyond the prowess of all but the very best Western managements.

The West shouldn't be dismayed by this success. It proves that organizations can make decisions (or, rather, that decisions can be made inside organizations) as effectively as the powerful, freewheeling, freebooting individuals whose decisions sometimes shake the world. All it takes is the ability to decide to be decisive—to make decisions in the best possible way, and to expect, and only to be satisfied with, the best possible results.

II

JUDGES, JURIES, AND JAPANESE

1. THE EXECUTIVES IN THE DOCK

Great men, like those whose rights and wrongs are featured in the Introduction, bungle great decisions, as noted there, for the same reasons as lesser men. Their errors, like their successes, are exceptional, because their nature is to think big and they act in large dimensions—millions and billions instead of hundreds and thousands. Occasionally, the error is so gross that the decision is ruinous. More often, the folly is swallowed up in the results of the previous brilliance—because follies tend to be one-shot calamities, closed down and buried (from sight if possible, from memory for almost certain) at a finite cost.

The correct decisions, on the other hand, go on bearing ripe fruit for decades. From this observation, two conclusions are obvious. In making decisions, think big; having made them, follow an old stock-market adage—cut your losses and let your profits run. Unambitious decisions lead to unambitious results. If the decision, ambitious or not, proves wrong, it compounds the error to invest still more time, emotion, money, and thought in trying to turn mistakes into miracles.

As some of the cases in this book show, such miracles can be made—sometimes. But that depends on two principles. First, you make a clean start. You come at the problem afresh, as if the decision were totally new—and so it is, because the failure to date has itself changed the situation. Much better, it has added painfully but considerably to your information—and the more *relevant* information the decision maker possesses, the greater the chances of making the right, the marvelous decision.

Given perfect information, perfectly analyzed and interpreted, perfect decisions are bound to follow. That never happens. Decisions are taken today, on information gathered yesterday, with results that you hope will appear tomorrow. You're therefore acting on out-of-date knowledge on the basis of uncertain predictions. This alone is enough to explain failed decisions. But there are plenty of other causes. Prime among them is the fact that, although decisions are not like judgments in a courtroom, many decision makers act as if they were.

The judge and jury decide on the guilt of the accused; the judge decides, within narrow and prescribed limits, on the sentence, and passes it—and from that point judge and jury have no function. The black cap is put on, and the condemned man is led away for execution. There are no doubts. The hanging will only be prevented by a successful appeal—that is, a higher decision-making authority has made the decision all over again, and its decision, to uphold or reverse, will again be executed automatically. *Executed* is the cardinal word. This book should perhaps be called *The Execution Makers*, for those who make decisions are increasingly unlikely to carry them out personally as the scale of the decisions mounts. The power of their decisions thus increasingly depends on their ability to call forth efficient execution.

But this, too, rarely resembles carrying out a judicial sentence. The execution isn't cut and dried. All strategies are conditional, and all tactics are provisional. Indeed, tactics can be viewed as a series of interactive decisions, some prejudged, some improvised. The preplanned or fixed elements include the organizational setup and the resources put in place. Here, the original decision maker can be deeply involved. But there are obvious limits to the strategist's ability to manage the tactics.

These are elementary observations, but they still have to be stressed, because corporate decision makers in particular ignore elementary principles—which is why they make elementary errors. Their original sin is to act as if they really are judges. Decisions are brought to the board of directors or executive committee as if they were tribunals. The "evidence" is presented by the management, whose darling plan it is, and after due deliberation, the "verdict" is given and "sentence" is passed. You don't have to be an authority on management systems to see the defects in these mock trials or to understand why so many corporate decisions—maybe the majority—are of poor quality.

First, the prisoners at the bar, the executives in the dock, will do their utmost to ensure that they win a favorable verdict. That means not only presenting the evidence in the most flattering light possible, but also only advancing proposals that have a strong chance of being approved—that is, the board or the chief executive will be told, by and large, what their managers *think* they want to hear. The mind reading may be quite wrong—but the gap between perception and reality explains why top management is always urging its subordinates to take risks, be innovative, strike out in new and ambitious directions—when, notoriously, the underlings won't.

They play safe because it *is* safe. Nobody wants to have a project torn to pieces in front of his peers or, still worse, his own subordinates. The atmosphere of a trial emerges clearly

35

from detailed studies undertaken by researchers at the London Business School of decision making in several companies: the subordinates in these cases come across as supplicants, petitioners to the royal court, if not prisoners before the legal tribunal. The latter is the better metaphor, because the judges also act as prosecutors—possibly with help from a corporate planning department. It's very easy, reading the accounts of such proceedings, to forget that these guys are supposed to be on the same side.

They often don't appear to be on the same side in the case histories of successful innovation described in the absorbing book *Breakthroughs!* by P. R. Nayak and J. M. Ketteringham. Whether it's Post-it adhesive Note Pads at 3M or microwave ovens at Raytheon (and there are countless other examples), the innovator has to fight *against* the organization to implement a decision that he, and he alone (and often lonely), has made.

Gifford Pinchot III, in his definitive study titled *Intrapreneuring*, tells the tale of an electronic device under development at Hewlett-Packard. The great Dave Packard himself made an on-the-spot decision that all work on the device should cease. The intrapreneurs cunningly ignored the order by sticking to the letter of the great decision maker's words—that he didn't want to see the product in the lab when he came around in a year's time. So they finished the work, to Hewlett-Packard's considerable profit, within twelve months.

In the case of Raytheon's microwave oven, the entire board turned up for a demonstration before making its judge-and-jury decision. The innovator demonstrated the prowess of microwave technology by splattering the directors with an exploded egg. That served them right, but all that kept the project alive was the chief executive's (or chief justice's) unexplained reluctance to let the project die.

The cases above surely raise the question of whether these judges have the credentials to sit in doom on their subordinates.

A brilliant study by Michael E. Porter, published in the spring of 1987 in the *Harvard Business Review*, gives some idea of the answer. He looked at thirty-three leading U.S. companies, including such paradigms as 3M, Procter & Gamble, and General Electric, as well as the notorious buy-of-the-month brigades such as ITT and W. R. Grace: in the years 1950 through 1980, they had collectively decided to make 3,788 diversifications. (That's 114.8 bites per biter, a truly gargantuan feast.) Of these, 2,644 were entries into new industries, of which 70.3 percent were acquisitions, 7.9 percent joint ventures, and 21.8 percent start-ups.

The proportions were much the same for "new industries that represented entirely new fields": here start-ups were higher, though, at 25.9 percent. The 2,021 new industry acquisitions had exactly the fate a cynic would expect: over half were later divested. The new fields were even less green: over 60 percent of the buys were divested—70 percent in the sorry case of W. R. Grace. But pride of place (if that's the phrase) must go to Xerox and GE, which disposed of 100 percent of their "new field" acquisitions and kept only a minor proportion of the new industries.

Across the creaking board, three-quarters of all decisions to enter unrelated businesses flopped, on the evidence of later divestment decisions. The hasty conclusion would be to take these figures as mere confirmation that acquisitions are mantraps—and the more, the less merry. But that would be over-hasty: half the much smaller number of joint ventures were also divested. There is a glimmer of light with start-up decisions: 59.1 percent of ventures begun by 1975 survived, and 56 percent of the pre-1980 generation also remained in the land of the living. But that slight edge may only mean that managements are more reluctant to slaughter their own children. However you look at Porter's statistics, you can't escape his description of the picture of these thirty-three top decision makers at work as "sobering."

Think of just some of the people who handed down the verdicts in those thirty-three corporate courts in those twenty years: Harry S. Gray of United Technologies, Nathan Cumming (Consolidated Foods, which, hosts of divestments later, became Sara Lee), J. Peter Grace (W. R. Grace), Charles H. Bluhdorn (Gulf + Western), Reginald Jones (General Electric), Crawford Greenewalt (Du Pont), Harold S. Geneen (ITT), William S. Paley. The last-named, the fabled head of CBS, presided over one of the worst offenders: little more than a tenth of its diversifications survived.

Even the best of them, like Gray, saw one in four acquisitions fail. As a bunch, their record is indefensible. After all, if the thirty-three decision-making bodies had merely had a coin tossed by the office boy, they would have been right as often. Most of their decisions must have failed Porter's three equally sobering tests: "attractiveness" (meaning that decision makers should only diversify into industries that are "structurally attractive or capable of being made attractive"; "better-off" (either the new unit gets competitive advantage from its links with you or vice versa); and "cost-of-entry" (which must not be so high that it capitalizes all future profits).

The tests induce sobriety because many of these 3,788 top management decisions must have been taken without proper thought for such commonsense banalities—though the first two tests do have a hole in the middle. Beauty and synergy are both in the eye of the beholder; those making decisions to diversify nearly always believe fondly, and however foolishly, that they will benefit from both.

The third test, though, is objective acid. To quote Porter: "Philip Morris paid more than four times book value for Seven-Up. . . . Simple arithmetic meant that profits had to more than quadruple to sustain the preacquisition ROI." Since this return on investment was far beyond even the marketing skills of the men who brought you Marlboro cigarettes, the later decision to sell Seven-Up was as inevitable as the purchase decision was poor. Nor is there much comfort when Porter turns from his saddening statistics to look at four conventional strategic concepts (portfolio management, restructuring, transferring skills, sharing activities). He finds enough serious "common pitfalls" to scare any would-be corporate wanderer into making just one decision: to stay at home.

Staying at home, or near to it, is a substantial element in Porter's gospel. First look for the new growth opportunities inside the company, get your core businesses in the finest fettle, cross-fertilize between cores and business units; only then can you gingerly test the waters of external diversification—but never in unrelated fields. Despite its apparent soundness, confirmed by the evidence of countless duff, unrelated acquisitions or diversifications, the gospel has continued to fall on stone-deaf ears. To take just two multibillion-dollar examples of deafness, Eastman Kodak had as much relation to Sterling Drug as ethical pharmaceuticals do to color film: none. Britain's Grand Metropolitan sought to maintain that its pubs had a close relationship to Pillsbury's Burger King: nobody believed it.

And so the music continues to go around and around. In pursuing their own projects, and doubtless when judging those of their subordinates, top decision makers plainly dance to tunes other than the desire to create value for the shareholder, which Porter puts forward as the obvious objective. There must be a better method than unqualified judges sitting with subservient juries to try fearful executives—and the Japanese have shown all too powerfully what it is.

2. WHY TOSHIBA
TROUNCED RAYTHEON

The microwave oven, Raytheon's most innovative diversification, was unrelated to the company's main lines of defense business, but it otherwise met the Michael E. Porter criteria well: it was an internal growth opportunity, cross-fertilizing from military technology into civil. Yet no clear-cut decision was made on the project until many years into its life, when the languishing oven was dumped, metaphorically speaking, into the lap of an experienced consumer durables hand—and maybe that long yawn of indecision explains why the Japanese left Raytheon and the rest of American industry near the starting gate, in microwaves as in far too many consumer products.

Since the Japanese have made a crippling (for their competition) series of correct decisions, superior in number, quality, and execution to those of rivals in the West, there's a prima facie case for believing that their decision-making process must be superior, too.

It has distinct cultural peculiarities, which at first sight provide bad excuses for shrugging off the whole issue, as if, like the No plays or sumo wrestling, Japanese decision making is something that you not only can't translate into Western practice but wouldn't want to. And it is true that the *ringi* method of consensus decision making reads like some elaborate, unaccountable ritual dance in which the performers may understand what they are doing but nobody else does, and that lasts so long that all sense of purpose seems to be dissipated.

Yet that cannot be: otherwise such triumphs of technology combined with market penetration as the Toyota production system, the fully automated camera, the pocket calculator, and the facsimile machine could not have been achieved—or the mass-market microwave. The small Japanese company that achieved this breakthrough, New Japan Radio Corporation, did so by deciding that the Raytheon technology, derived from the wartime invention of radar, was too cumbersome. NJRC's engineering genius, Keishi Ogura, decided to reinvent the vital component, the magnetron—in the words of *Breakthroughs!*: "to disregard the elements of the past to focus on the functions of the present."

This involved deciding on nine precise objectives for technical sophistication, design simplicity, easy manufacture, cost, stability in performance, longer tube life, instant heating, voltage requirement, and energy efficiency. In the end, the company succeeded all too well. As the volume of microwave sales mounted steeply, far larger firms that sold the entire appliance moved downstream and undercut the cost: with Toshiba manufacturing at $7 (the cheapest Raytheon ever managed was $125), the innovator couldn't compete and vanished from the scene.

NJRC hadn't reached the correct decision on how to stay in the game once larger players were involved—as JVC did when making its VHS technology available to other manufacturers on generous terms that ensured its continued place in a rising sun. These contrasting tales demonstrate that Japanese decision makers are, of course, fallible: they are, after all, human beings. This being so, the principles of their decision making, with its evidently higher batting average, must be accessible; behind the ritual dance must lie clear and effective principles.

Ringiseido (a system of reverential inquiry about a superior's intentions) works broadly like this: the problem on which a decision is required is tackled down the line by the people— *all* the people—concerned with and well placed to grapple with the issue. Their written solution is passed back up the hierarchy, receiving at each level the seal of approval—literally. Each executive stamps the proposal (the *ringi-sho*) all the way to the top, from which the project may actually have originated.

Naturally, all Japanese decisions aren't and can't be reached in this laborious manner. The powers of the Japanese president are at least as great as those of a Harry Gray, a Hal Geneen, or any other dominating Western CEO. At the apex of any effective decision-making pyramid, there must be a single, clear, unambiguous, truly decisive voice. But it is a pyramid. Even in the most hierarchical Western corporation, with the least genuine delegation of power and influence, the lower strata have more effect on the quality of decision and execution than the almighty judge at the summit may realize. The *ringi* system consolidates this reality and seeks to convert it into a strength.

In the process, the judge and jury, prosecution and defense system are eradicated. At each level of decision, more information accumulates and a new participant engages, not in judging the proposal but in confirming its form. By the time the decision reaches the top, it has, in effect, made itself. More important, however, is the fact that *ringi* and its variants eliminate another insidious weakness of the Western tribunal system: that execution is separate from the judgment (or decision).

In the West, the judges cannot (by the very nature of business management) be certain that the execution will be properly performed—for a start, very few of those to be involved later on will know even the first thing about the plan at its inception. This produces a sharp contrast in the curve of decision. The Western curve moves rapidly to the point of decision in principle, but then levels off and lengthens as the messy details of execution and timing are hammered out. The slow phase of the Japanese curve comes before the decision in principle, but the latter is the same as the decision in practice— the company is ready to go, with a speed and decisiveness that often astound Western partners who are still stuck back down the curve.

Decisions involve an investment of time, thought, emotion, and money—and that is more or less the correct order. Time generally equals information, which requires painstaking collection; in its absence, thought is mere speculation. Armed with information, the decision maker has the tools and tests for thought; at that point, the emotional drive of the organization and the individual can be harnessed to making the decision work—which will invariably cost money, and more time, and more thought, and more emotion, and still more money.

One Western project can serve as a how-not-to exercise in non-Japanese decision making. The idea was launched without heraldry by the company's "research and development" department (really a new-product organization of sorts) at an informal meeting. The product area was one where the company had previously competed with unique success before selling out to a rival who now held a monopoly. Many of those with knowledge of the market were still in senior positions. There were no problems in devising a differentiated, better-quality competitor, although staffing the operation would present difficulties.

Without the advice of his experienced production supremo, the chief executive decided to close a money-losing operation and transfer the staff to this new and radically different venture. When finally taken out of the dark, the production expert objected, but far too late in the day to affect the decision, which was partly influenced by the desire to save redundancy costs. This was followed by the only formal meeting at which all the senior people with knowledge of the product were present.

The meeting was dominated by a presentation from the director who had most knowledge of the market and the previous, sold business. His logical and detailed argument established beyond any contradiction (or possibility of it) that, of two possible launch dates, the earlier was ruled out by industry practice and by a major, immovable time constraint on achieving the essential distribution.

The meeting ended in apparent consensus on the later date. Subsequently, the chief executive decided to launch at the earlier opportunity. His motive, never communicated, appeared in hindsight to be anxiety—fear that a very improbable, unidentified competitor would preempt the market opportunity if the company waited longer. In a crash program, the product design went ahead on schedule, as did the launch: its success was hard-won, since nearly all the staff who were supposed to transfer left the company, taking their redundancy pay, rather than work on what they saw as an uncongenial, alien activity.

For all that, the product was well received in the marketplace. But the strong warning sounded by the best-informed director at that sole full-scale meeting proved all too true. The distribution failed, through shortage of time; the trade was alienated; and long, painful months saw money lost in unplanned, large amounts while uphill efforts continued to convert the trade. The difficulties were compounded by vigorous, no-cost-spared counterattack from the former monopolist.

The pressures on the general manager of the venture inevitably mounted, but were intensified by two unnecessary factors: first, this major investment wasn't his sole responsibility; second, as the losses rose, so the detailed interference of the chief executive increased—until half the general manager's time was spent managing his superior (none too successfully) rather than the venture. Decision after decision was made by the chief executive, with little or no input from anybody else, in the vain effort to stop the large, but by no means critical, losses.

After only twelve months, again without consultation, he decided to cut the losses and close the project. Much later, hindsight made it clear that, disastrous as the initial timing had been, the decision to pull out was worse. But no long-term plan for managing the project into success existed, on or off paper, to act as a guidance system. So the hard-won, weak, but established market position was sacrificed at precisely the time when the distribution and the trade were at last swinging the company's way.

There's no point in enumerating the defects in this characteristic tale. But its strongly negative elements can be turned upside down to produce positive rules for decision makers who want to achieve opposite, excellent results.

1. Involve all relevant people from the start.

2. Have a single, fully-worked-out object in view—aim to kill one bird with many stones, not two birds with one.

3. Having obtained the best possible information and counsel in concert, act on it in concert.

4. Be governed by what you know rather than what you fear.

5. Embody the decisions in a comprehensive plan that everybody knows and that will cover the expected consequences of setback or success.

6. Entrust execution to competent people with no conflicting responsibilities.

7. Leave operational people to operate.

8. In the event of serious failure, start again to review and renew the decisions.

9. Only abandon the decision when it is plain to all that its objectives cannot be achieved.

These nine points bear very little resemblance to judge-and-jury decision making, Western style. They do, however, come much closer to a description of the *ringi* approach of Japan. It turns out that the Eastern method is founded on unassailable logic, which is comprehensible in any language and in any culture. It nearly always happens that, when Japanese management methods are investigated, their secret is found to lie not in esoteric mystery but in accessible and obvious common sense. More, the underlying principles are generally familiar in the West, and have often been pioneered there—only to be honored more in the foolish breach than the intelligent observance.

Of course, Japan has autocratic managers to whom all the

above means no more than it does to one Western tycoon. Cruising in his company jet, he was fed pieces of paper by a senior executive and reeled off a series of yes/no decisions. He then wheeled around to a guest and said, "That's how we make decisions in this company. What do you think of it?"—obviously craving an admiring answer.

But these decision hogs actually break fewer of the *ringi* rules than the judge-and-jury corpocrats—which is one powerful reason why the latter nearly always lose against tycoons. First, the moguls always involve all relevant people, because only one person qualifies: themselves. They characteristically concentrate on single, great objectives; they are fearless; they know exactly what they are doing and why; they automatically adapt and adjust to failure; they only persist with it up to the point of no return; if they still see the prospect of a ripe payoff, they stick octopuslike to their task.

In all this, because they follow no consensus save that inside their own heads, their actions, despite frequent appearances to the contrary, are generally coherent and clearly motivated. The one point of the nine that they consistently ignore is leaving operating people to operate. These decision makers interfere constantly, in fair weather and foul. Their whole method presupposes underlings who will do only one thing: what they are told. At this point, tycoonery and judge-and-jury methods come together. Like the legal judge, the tycoon depends on the warders and hangman to obey his orders in utterly predictable conformity. So he needs predictable conformists without imagination, independence, or pride.

That need explains why the giants of commerce are so often served by mediocrities. Clever, independent, proud, self-motivating people won't serve such masters in the first place; in the second, they would get in the way. To be served by relatively stupid managers sounds like a highway to catastrophe. With the masters of this style, it isn't, simply because they have genius, for which there are no rules. But there are rules for managers who lack that quality—which means nearly all corpocrats.

For their decisions to be right and to be executed aright, they need the ablest, most imaginative, and most effective associates they can find—and the ability to use such colleagues with the highest possible success. Judge-and-jury decision making might have been designed to achieve the opposite results. Only observe the comeuppance of ITT, the sprawling conglomerate that Harold S. Geneen, the arch-inquisitor, partly ran through a regular series of General Management Meetings (GMMs) that were sometimes a cross between the Spanish Inquisition and Stalinist show-trials.

Philip Crosby, formerly ITT vice president in charge of quality, author of *Quality Is Free* and *The Eternally Successful Organization*, gives a fascinating account in the latter book of what went on at Geneen's pet forum. The GMM lasted for three days. It took so long because, in Crosby's inelegant words, "no sparrow fell anywhere in the world of ITT that its autopsy was not reviewed in detail." But what was accomplished by the enormous expense, the presentations by each manager, and the public questioning, led by Geneen?

Crosby observes that "he didn't arrange all that for our benefit; he did it for himself. And I must say that it worked well, he seemed to know everything." Yet on the next page, Crosby remarks, surely correctly, that "even Geneen's 'system' produced only a small understanding of what those 400,000 people in 60 countries were doing with the assets and customers of the company." He goes on to say, "It may not be possible to know what is happening in any significant detail. Each company's GMM may be equivalent to only a gossip session."

As a forum for helping to make better decisions, ITT's GMM can fairly be judged by such crimes against the shareholder as the negative growth in earnings per share over the

1974/84 period. The conglomerate's sales actually slumped from $14 billion at the end of that decade to under $8.55 billion in 1986. That calamity followed from reversing, by divestment, over half of the 246 decisions to diversify taken between 1950 and 1980.

Japanese decision makers, with no similar calamities to answer for, don't rely on gossip sessions any more than on trial by judge and jury. By and large they make better decisions because they make them in better ways. To do likewise is the best decision any Westerner can make—and it should be one of the easiest. The following six parts look at the innovators, the expansionists, the improvers, the planners, the salvationists, and the competitors to see who took that decision and got it right—and who didn't.

III

THE INNOVATORS

The innovators come first because that's what they do—come first. Also, they have primacy in the minds of managers who have learned the salient truth about modern competition: victory goes to the innovative, defeat to the innovatory laggards. If the innovation is mighty enough, like Michael Milken's reinvention of the junk bond, the innovator will retain a leading position in the market even when (inevitably, in today's conditions) others leap onto the speeding bandwagon. The first two sections show how to find the priceless anomaly. That's only the beginning; but there's no better start—if you next follow the golden rules of exploitation.

Anomaly finders are brilliant at asking questions nobody else has asked. This is also the key to gathering crucial information on which successful innovation must hinge. You don't need only information, however—you need analysis, the ability to interpret the discovered data. One of the most innovative companies in Japan, Canon, sprang forward as its president acted on one broad perception based on analysis of the company's record on profits and innovation. The case tells how to find and act on information, both at the general level and in the detail from which general success can flow so abundantly.

Sometimes, though, the information from the market tells you nothing—the innovation itself creates a market that didn't exist before. In hindsight, technological triumphs like that of Tagamet, the antiulcer drug, look preordained. But the innovatory company of the 1990s can learn from that drug's unpredicted smash hit how markets and customers can and must be led by companies that take bold and big decisions. The fact that the most compelling force in the Tagamet case was dire necessity carries powerful lessons for the companies that want to avoid desperate need for new products. That's one ulcerous condition that's hard to heal and is far better averted.

But can new product successes themselves teach anything? The Ford Taurus and the Laser Tag may not seem to have anything in common, but there are common principles that underlie the selection of winning items or (more important, since there are far more of them) the decisions to back failures. The basic reason for the unacceptably high rate of new-product failure lies not in the external marketplace but is internal, in the company itself. This is the essence of the trouble: decisions are made to suit the business, not the market, and are made in ways that obstruct success. The evidence can't be ignored: the more innovation companies undertake, the better they become at the game. This is because they learn lessons that were always available—and much less expensively.

The crucial internal source isn't the company, its technological armory, or its production needs, but the brain of the decision maker. Innovation begins with ideas, and mental creativity is as manageable as any other brainwork. It doesn't drop down from heaven, but is always founded on earthly observation—as in the five cases of people, ranging from a man renting out his own house to the founder of a major company and industry, who solved tricky problems. They did so by finding eccentric solutions, based on what they saw, using familiar processes such as analogy, linear thought, and putting two and two together to achieve their winning answers. Organizations don't lack the same abilities: they simply don't apply them. That shortage of creativity and innovation is another problem that offbeat solutions can cure—and must.

1. THE QUESTION OF MIKE MILKEN

In 1977 a young man named Michael Milken graduated from the Wharton Business School and, like so many of the brightest and best of his generation, headed for Wall Street and its pots of gold. His chosen employer, Drexel Burnham Lambert, wasn't the most golden of houses on the Street, and it didn't give the young Milken the most golden of its businesses—it gave him *junk* to look after.

The term referred to bonds whose issuing companies, once able to command acceptable ratings from Standard and Poor's and Moody's, maybe even the paramount AAA, had slipped. When they fell into Milken's field of vision, the bonds were rated as below "investment grade"—meaning that there was a significant risk of default. It followed that the price of junk bonds had dropped along with the rating, so that the yields were much higher than those on investment-grade securities; that was some compensation. But how much?

Figuring out the answer to that little sum was Milken's task. Financial history was made, according to Edward Jay Epstein, writing in the London *Sunday Times*, when Milken's fertile mind ranged beyond this calculation. First, he noted that the "investment grade" rating rested on the past—the "historic balance sheet"; and only 600 to 700 major corporations had balance sheet totals large enough to pass muster. Second, of the 22,000 U.S. companies that flunked that test, many had cash flow, now and in the future, that was large and safe enough to cover lusher rates of interest than investment-grade bonds would grant.

Third, if fixed-interest investors, such as savings and loans, life insurance companies, and pension funds, could be persuaded that "junk" bonds were indeed sufficiently safe, the far higher yield (maybe 5 percent greater) would be irresistibly attractive. Why not issue such securities? Why not, indeed. Money flooded in: the total of junk bonds in issue soared phenomenally, and Drexel and Milken soared with it. Drexel's $1.5 billion of 1986 net income made it the richest investment bank on Wall Street, while Milken was very likely the richest employee—earning $10 million a week and worth well over a billion dollars, thanks in part to his personal and controversial share in the stupendous deals that Drexel had financed.

For Milken put a fourth card in play. His relationships with useful fixed-interest investors such as Saul Steinberg, Carl Lindner, and Victor Posner allied him with the more sharklike elements in the Wall Street ocean. The junk bond (and thus Drexel) became a crucial element in the financing of rapacious corporate raids. Milken's contrarian logic worked wonders again: since future cash flows were the key to servicing debt, why bother about a bidder's current financing ability; why not issue bonds to be financed not from what the issuer owned but from what he *would* own—if the bid succeeded?

Why not, again, indeed. A mere letter expressing Drexel's

confidence that it could thus finance a bid became a passport to daring raids and sweeping coups (and staggering fees for the investment bankers). From Sir James Goldsmith to Ronald Perelman, T. Boone Pickens to John Werner Kluge, a new generation of gunslinging financiers had as much reason as Milken to bless his discovery. So had the insider trader Ivan Boesky. His disgrace and intimate relations with Drexel cast a shadow over the bank and the vice president in charge of its Hollywood office, one Michael Milken. The investigators slowly closed in: in the late summer of 1988 the first ominous charges were duly filed.

Whatever the future held for Milken personally (for Drexel Burnham it held a $650 million settlement of criminal charges and the enforced loss of Milken's services), corporate finance in America would never be the same again; not because of Milken's fifteen-hour days ("I don't know if I am smarter than anyone else," he said, according to an Epstein quote, "but I can work twenty-five percent harder") but because he had asked what may be the most important question in decision making: Why not?

2. HUNTING THE ANOMALY

In the end, everybody in the investment world where Michael Milken made his amazing decisions follows the herd. That's because everybody *is* the herd. The gold that lies in anomalies can only be mined when other investors agree with the finder's discovery and make his fortune by backing his judgment. An anomaly that lies there gathering dust has no value; indeed, it hardly counts as an anomaly at all.

In accepted theory, stock-market anomalies should never occur. The widely beloved and believed efficient market hypothesis (EMH) holds that nobody can find stocks that will perform consistently better than the mass. It holds that, since the market (for which read "people feeding into the market") knows everything there is to know about every company, every share is always, except for the briefest possible periods, valued at exactly the right price. Therefore, nobody can beat the market, except by pure chance.

It's not necessary to tell that to the marines. Telling it to George Soros and Warren Buffett will do as nicely. From 1969 until the debacle of October 1987, Soros achieved a 350-times increase in the value of the Quantum Fund. His interview with *Fortune* in September 1987, just before the deluge, led the magazine to paraphrase his views: while bargains no longer predominated, "a search quickly turns up stocks selling for less than a company's breakup value." Soros is an explicit foe of the EMH; rather, he believes that something called "the theory of reflexivity" reigns—this theory says that the price of a stock is not the result of intelligent reaction to known information but the outcome of perceptions that are influenced by emotion as much as data.

That is plainly true, although knowing it makes the task of hunting the anomaly no easier. *Fortune* noted the skill of Soros in "detecting subtle shifts in investors' perceptions and delusions" during that 350-fold buildup of the Quantum Fund to a stupendous value of $2.5 billion; but not only did the maestro in 1987 invest in highly leveraged futures contracts that were no place to be on that October's Black Monday, he opined that the "perception value" had become so extended in Japan that "an orderly retreat seems impossible. There may be a crash coming." As it turned out, the Tokyo market proved by far the most resilient of the world's bourses in the wake of the 1987 crash, which (at least by its first anniversary) had entirely failed to trigger the Japanese "implosion" that Soros feared.

Anomaly hunters are best advised to avoid generalizations and concentrate on specifics—in the stock market or anywhere else. But there is one magic word on which the anomaly hunter homes: *value.* It is music to the ears and the money boxes of Buffett and the other disciples of the late Ben Graham. That great stock-market theorist, at whose feet the young Buffett sat, meant, by searching for "values," looking for companies whose businesses, for one bad reason or another, are intrinsically worth more than their stock-market price. By the same token, the great decision maker looks for situations in which he can create far more value than he puts in—because the decisive opportunity has not been widely spotted, if it has been spotted at all.

Junk bonds may well be the largest and richest anomaly in the history of financial markets, although the latter are always throwing up gaping holes. For instance, life insurance companies in Britain invested policyholders' money in equities, but the owners of the investments had no means of following their progress. That anomaly was gratefully seized by the future Sir Mark Weinberg, who made a fortune for ITT, and then for himself, by investing the policyholders' premiums directly into mutual funds whose performance (and cash-in value) was visible and palpable. In contrast, the decisions of virtually all major investment houses to turn themselves into financial supermarkets in the 1980s were doomed to disappointment precisely because virtually all of them were adopting the same policy.

Grahamites such as Warren Buffett, who are prepared to wait for a long time, doing nothing until a select, discrete, anomalous opportunity arises, would find such Gadarene decisions impossible. Their life in the 1980s was made much easier by the previous recession. As hyperinflation and the associated heaven-high interest rates devalued the market price of stocks, especially those of companies that had suffered most from the recession itself, the discount from underlying asset values became widespread and wide, often terribly so. Add to that the impact of changing technology and other topsy-turvy economic circumstances on corporate performance, and the resulting anomalies could be dazzling in their temptations.

No anomalies were greater than those in Fleet Street, home of a British newspaper industry that, because of the dominance of Mafia-style local print unions and a history of inept management, was held at arm's length from the offended nostrils of the nearby City of London. Nobody thought it at all odd, except for the supposed inordinate expense, when the heritage of the great Canadian wheeler-dealer Lord Beaverbrook, including three excellently established papers and some choice real estate, passed from the weak hands of his son into those of a property-based conglomerate called Trafalgar House. The tab was £15 million.

That pittance was exposed when the Reuters news agency suddenly blossomed forth as a world leader in the new industry of electronic dissemination of facts and figures (correcting another huge and handsome anomaly, the fact that a sophisticated financial industry relied on relatively primitive means of communicating vital data). The stake of the Express newspapers in Reuters proved to be worth no less than £100 million.

Nor was that all. The economic pressure on the print unions mounted to the point that, largely under Rupert Murdoch's massively and cunningly applied weight, the Mafia's resistance to new technology and reduction in members employed (many of whom did little or no honest toil) collapsed. Against that background, the next transfer price of the Beaverbrook legacy came much nearer to the old man's generally voracious ideas; it was sold for £370 million, a nearly twenty-five-fold increase, to a publisher of regional newspapers.

Anyone should have been able to spot that gross undervaluation at the beginning. Yet the accepted view, even in the media industry itself, was that Trafalgar had grossly overpaid for an unjustifiable indulgence of the personal tastes of its managing director. He did indeed become Lord Matthews as a result of the purchase (peerages are frequently part of the Fleet Street payoff), but he also made a tycoon-size personal profit on his shares. Matthews could not, and therefore did not, foresee exactly how events would unfold, but he certainly spotted and rejoiced in the original anomaly.

Such opportunities don't only exist on the stock market or in the buying and selling of companies. The middle-aged entrepreneur who noticed that undersize oranges were being thrown away as waste, and thereupon founded Tropicana and the frozen orange juice business, also discovered an anomaly (which was worth $1.2 billion to Seagrams in May 1988). So did Heinz Nordhoff of Volkswagen, when he saw GIs eagerly buying VW Beetles, and even shipping them back to the States, where no similar-size car was manufactured. So did the Apple founders when, having made the first personal computer, they found business users lapping up a product intended for domestic use.

Yet the rules for spotting the golden anomaly are the same in business (and other activities from politics to science) as in the stock market. First, keep your eyes open at all times for an incongruity—for a fact that doesn't fit into its context. It will fall into one of two categories, each leading to a different short, pregnant question: Why? or Why not? In a famous Buffett example, the great Omaha investor's hawkish eye saw that Walt Disney stock was selling at a price that placed its market value below that of its inventory of cartoon features such as *Snow White* and *Dumbo*. The question Why? produced no sensible answer. The efficient market had simply been inefficient. But the stock market, like all markets, tends to gravitate toward efficiency; so the anomaly was certain to be corrected—and faithfully following that principle explains much of Buffett's celebrated ability to grow his Berkshire Hathaway Company by 28 percent compounded year after year.

The Milken case, spotting that nobody was using junk

bonds to raise financing, or as a major investment medium, even though their default rate was perfectly acceptable and their yield remarkable, prompted (as noted) the question Why not? Again, there was no sensible answer. Again, the market would, if pushed by Drexel Burnham, gravitate in the direction of a more efficient solution. Because Milken's venture required marketing to investors, the complications of turning vision into billions, and the amount of information required to support the decision, were incomparably greater than the simple purchase of, say, Disney shares in the stock market. Milken had to answer a much more difficult question: How?

Why? and Why not? are themselves only straightforward when the reason, as in those two cases, lies in the conventional wisdom. While rarely right, it isn't always wrong. But far more money stands to be made by going against the accepted view— by being a "contrarian"—than by following where everybody else has been led. If the answer is "You can't do that in this business" or "If the idea's that good, somebody else would have tried it" or "Everybody knows that's nonsense," the odds are overwhelming that you're talking to the wrong (very wrong) kind of people. They're the type who probably told Buffett that Disney shares were only cheap because the management was terrible (it was no great shakes, at that), or assured Milken that thrift company investors would never put depositors' savings into bonds that ranked below investment grade.

Disdain and disregard are signposts for anomalies. So is cheapness. There can also be expensive anomalies, however, where the purchaser is thought to have paid dearly for his acquisition (a statement that applies to almost any real estate purchase in metropolitan downtown areas in recent years); yet subsequent, sometimes almost simultaneous, events prove the buy to be cheap. It might seem to be a latter-day expression of the potent selling line that Lord Duveen would use to American multimillionaires who were jibbing at his extravagant prices for Old Masters: "If you're buying the priceless, you're getting it cheap."

If anybody had said that to purchasers of real estate in downtown Dallas and Houston, where values were shattered by the oil slump, he is no doubt still running. Expensive anomalies should be hunted with extreme caution. Lesser mortals, financially speaking, are likely to do better by concentrating on simple, cheap anomalies and obeying simple rules of decision.

1. Don't be put off by the fact that the anomaly sticks out like the sorest of thumbs—that's what makes it anomalous.

2. Don't take any notice of the prevailing climate of opinion that has created the anomaly—test it, rigorously and without fear.

3. Practice anomaly hunting all the time, in the stock market and everywhere else; practice makes perfect, and the Golden Fleeces of anomaly are few and far between.

4. Finally, if the anomaly passes the test, grab it as eagerly and vigorously as if you will never have the same opportunity again. You may not.

3. THE CUNNING OF CANON

Good information is essential to good, rational decisions. Lack of information about the whereabouts of the last American aircraft carriers in the Pacific led the Japanese commanders at Midway into decisions so bad that they caused catastrophe—despite overwhelming superiority in numbers. The Japanese tried hard enough to locate the U.S. ships, for the whole national method, in business as in war, revolves around painstaking collection and analysis of all available information. Through misfortune (mostly with the weather) and mismanagement (proceeding without full knowledge of indispensable facts), the Japanese plucked defeat out of victory.

At Midway, fortune, known facts, and their interpretation

favored the Americans. In postwar world markets, the Japanese have rarely made the Midway mistake: they have helped to make their own good fortune through the decisive power of the fact. Japanese decision makers operate in the absolute belief that the greater the quantity of what you know, the better the quality of the information on which your decisions are based. The more sources of information you tap, moreover, the more you will find out.

The following list of questions was assembled by Frederick D. Buggie, chairman of Strategic Innovations International. Are you:

1. Tracking the technical literature (if any) in your field?
2. Examining competitors' displays at trade fairs and exhibitions?
3. Keeping a close watch on any legislation anywhere that might affect your business via new rules and regulations?
4. Listening hard to what salesmen report back from the front line?
5. Analyzing broad swings in costs that have a bearing on your business?
6. Attending selected conferences, seminars, and symposia?
7. Watching what's happening in California?
8. Subscribing to specific intelligence reports?
9. Keeping an eye on do-it-yourself enthusiasts to see what ideas they're coming up with?
10. Exposing yourself to authorities and experts?
11. Checking what social rebels are doing with their money?
12. Finding out what prostitutes are wearing?

Those who can answer yes to all dozen questions (especially the twelfth) are very rare innovative decision makers indeed. But a dozen nos, while a much more common result, are as dangerous as the affirmative answers are valuable. All the questions point toward heightening awareness of changes and developments that could shorten or lengthen the lives of products or services; just as important, if their life is drawing to a close, such questions indicate where new offerings can be found to take up the fight—so that, like Canon in the U.S. camera market, you win your peacetime Midways.

When a new boss took over Canon in the United States in the early 1970s, the company's camera sales were lagging behind not only its other products on the American market but also the cameras of its main competitor, Minolta. According to Johny K. Johansson and Ikijuro Nonaka, writing in the *Harvard Business Review*, the Canon man made a brilliantly simple decision: to seek so-called soft data from the trade—from dealers—in exactly the spirit of the Buggie questions. He "himself spent almost six weeks in 1972 visiting camera stores and other retail outlets across the United States." From talks with store owners, he learned that "U.S. dealers weren't giving Canon much support because its sales forces were too small." He also found out what kinds of cameras and promotional support would get the stores on his side. The Canon man's technique is worth study and imitation for its own sweet sake.

1. Go into the shop as if you are a browsing customer, but keep an acute eye on how all the X goods are displayed and how customers are served.

2. Ask "What Xs do you stock?" This establishes (a) how keen (or otherwise) the dealer is on your wonder product and (b) how knowledgeable the staff are about the products in question.

3. Only then identify yourself to the manager and invite him to lunch to discuss the product and whatever else he chooses to mention.

4. Use this contact as the basis for a lasting relationship with individual retailers.

The hard results from the soft data are impressive. The trade inquiries led the Canon softie to decide on dealing exclusively through specialist outlets with products aimed a notch below Nikon at the top of the market. Market leader Minolta, which relied on discount and drugstores, was ousted. Of course, Canon also required a highly salable product. In these terms, the key to its success was the AE-1 range of cameras, which led the world in automatic, programmed exposure. The resulting lead in the marketplace lasted until Canon missed the next change in single-lens reflex technology—autofocus. The company that was first in this field had obviously learned its lessons from Canon's example. The new product swept into the lead, a notch below Nikon, selling through the specialist outlets. It was the Magnum—and it was made, of course, by Minolta.

4. ACTING ON INFORMATION

The questions in the previous section, as noted, were assembled by Frederick D. Buggie, chairman of Strategic Innovations International, whose game is helping people identify new business opportunities, and then dream up ideal new products, with Japanese-style thoroughness. As Buggie points out: "Timing is crucial. You've simply got to start developing your new product early enough so that it will pick up the slack in profits before your current product falls down dead." That means "you must start *before* you notice the first signs of the inexorable tailing-off of your current product life-cycle curve. By then it is too late."

These words, from the U.S. magazine *Chief Executive*, are wise and worth any decision maker's weight in gold. But just how inexorable is that life cycle? For instance, Shredded Wheat was invented on March 1, 1893. Plenty of other food products can boast long lineages—Ovaltine, Kellogg's Corn Flakes, Carnation milk, and so on. What tastes good to one generation, and fits its nutritional needs, is more likely to satisfy the next generation than, say, a past clothing fashion. Even a literally durable wonder such as blue jeans (as Levi Strauss discovered to its sorry cost) can run out of steam as emphatically as it originally gathered speed.

Run out of innovatory steam and you also run out of corporate success. When Ryuzaburo Kaku, later president of Canon, was a young manager, he spotted the fact that the firm's profits had always moved sharply upward after new products were introduced. On taking the purple, he decided to make that observation the foundation of an extraordinarily successful strategy.

Since 1976 (when the strategy, labeled the Premier Company Plan, got under way), the spate of new products has been unending—cameras, videos, copiers, micrographics, laser beam printers, facsimile, electronic typewriters, semiconductor production equipment, medical equipment, and much else besides have all poured forth. Kaku's plan hinged vitally on sustaining a flow of research and development into this new-product cornucopia, through the manufacturing plants, and then out into the marketplace.

He decided to set up three "conceptual pillars," separate but interlinked systems, to do the trick. They ran (and still run) horizontally across the company and are known as CDS, CPS, and CMS—for Canon Development System, Canon Production System, and Canon Marketing System. CDS is charged with research into and creation of new products and technology, CPS with achieving optimum quality and rationalization in all the company's plants, and CMS with operating what the company calls "a scientific and systematic marketing plan to provide personalized service to every Canon customer."

The three pillars support the three product groups: cameras, business machines, and optical products. Each of these in turn is organized into specialized divisions (such as video products, business systems, or broadcast equipment), and each of those operates as an independent vertical profit center. Although Canon constantly modifies its internal structure, it prides itself on the stability and the achievement of this "unique" matrix organization. Certainly the matrix has served well in the company's advance, through the objective of "premier Japanese company" to the next ambition on which Kaku has decided: "premier global corporation."

For all its progress, by the standards of today's global giants Canon is not especially large. All the same, 1987 sales of 976 billion yen ($7.7 billion) are impressive enough, especially against the 196 billion yen of 1977. Over the first decade of the plan, profits grew twenty-two times, and sales eightfold, which is convincing testimony to the rightness of Kaku's observation about the correlation between innovation and profit, and to the efficiency with which precept was turned into practice.

You don't get surging expansion like Canon's unless all decisions are founded on (1) ensuring that the company has all the physical resources (technological, human, financial, logistical) that the innovatory strategy requires; (2) arranging the resources, like Canon's, in an organizational format that will enable the resource to be fully used; and (3) bending the efforts of everybody in the company to the same end—constant renewal and extension of the company's products—at the same, right time.

Moreover, you won't get that expansionary surge, either, without continual awareness that nothing lasts and that all products, and all markets, are subject to change, sometimes slow, sometimes fast, but equally inevitable in either case. The great decision maker looks carefully at the product that supplies his livelihood and assesses whether it's vulnerable to obsolescence—and, if so, where the threat is likely to come from, and when. And threats, according to Buggie, are universal, omnipresent.

THE INNOVATORS

If your pride is in the category of *fashion goods*, the trend-setters will determine its fate. Do you know who they are? Are you watching what trends they are setting? If *cosmetics* are involved, consumer demand is fickle. If manufacturers don't monitor what's happening in the shops, they can lose a great deal more than face, so to speak.

The problem in dry *packaged foods* is competition. The average life expectancy of a new grocery product in the United States has come down from two or three years to a mere six months; competition for launches is now so intense that some supermarket chains have actually been charging anybody wanting to launch a new product for shelf space. Plainly, this situation puts a premium on keeping the appeal of an existing product fresh and strong. What are you doing (1) to make that happen and (2) to find out for sure that it is happening?

In *toys and games*, while some (such as Lego) seem to go on forever, others have at most one season's life—and those butterflies must be far more numerous. The problem is to maximize supply to meet the maximum demand. The decisive questions here are: What forecasting system do you employ? and How great a degree of production flexibility have you built into the business? If the toy or game is based on *electronics*, the problem, as with every product under that heading (especially for business use), is to keep up with changing technology. And do you have adequate R & D to capitalize on innovations when the time is ripe?

There's a technological threat with *chemical-based products*, too, but that's associated with a threat of legal or consumer action that may at worst remove the product from the market altogether. Are you prepared for this possibility—and watching out for it with acute attention?

The trouble with *materials-based products* is the economic trade-off; that is, something else does the job better, or cheaper, or both. An example is the threat of plastic pipes to the clay product for buildings.

Finally, there's *capital goods*. The threat here is: What do you do for an encore? Every hospital that can afford one has a body scanner, for instance; that market will never repeat its one-time boom.

Reading this list of threats might seem enough to deter the would-be entrepreneur from starting at all. But the reality is that some threats don't become destructive for generations, while others can be forestalled by the intelligent questioning and questing that are the foundation of good decisions. Take the last two threats: if a management can answer enough of the dozen Buggie questions in the previous section in the affirmative, it will surely know about the possibility that alternative products may take over the market for a materials-based product, or the certainty that the saturation point will be reached. It can then act to ensure that the business has a bridgehead (something much more than a toehold) in alternative supplies or markets.

As for capital goods, if he's making, say, onetime products with a long lead time to compete for a market composed of few purchasers, the right-minded decision maker might simultaneously be developing or looking for a related product (related to his real capabilities, that is) with utterly different characteristics—repetitive production, a multitude of customers, and rapid turnover.

Before deciding that the product portfolio does need body-building, the runes of the product life cycle must be read. The information from the past will chart the sales of each product against the profits. Leveling off indicates that the life cycle has passed its peak—and, as the Canon story shows, the company should *already* have started doing something about it; in the autofocus case, Canon may well not have done enough, or done it soon enough.

Second, the decision maker operates on the principle of balance (see the discussion of capital goods above). If the bulk of the profits comes from one particular operation, he looks for a contrasting business to offset its characteristics—for instance, in a publishing operation, if all the income derives from advertising sales, the logical thrust should be into businesses where the revenue comes largely from subscriptions. (The nonoptional extra is to ensure that the firm is not jumping out of the single-market frying pan into the multimarket fire by buying or starting a dumb diversification.)

Third, the decision maker concentrates great attention on renewing the appeal of the existing line by improvement, extension, innovation, better marketing, and so forth. Neglect these essentials and you will create a product death cycle, as sure as death and taxes. Force wheatflakes were once as popular as cornflakes or Shredded Wheat. The popularity didn't last because the management copped or dropped out of its basic business: the appeal must be kept *fresh and strong*.

Fourth, don't forget the time lags. To quote Buggie: "If it takes you eighteen months to develop a new product, and your product life is only fourteen months, you'd better have the successor already in the hopper when you launch the latest 'state of the art,' or else you'd better shorten your new product development time to about ten months." Significantly, the struggling General Motors in 1988 charged a bright young executive thing with getting down the lead time in launching a new model from forty months to the Honda standard of thirty-six, which is much tougher than it sounds.

The worst sin against time, though, is to watch your market disappearing from under you and to do nothing. Levi Strauss took far too long to develop alternative garments to replace the blue jeans boom. It took too many years before the Swiss watch industry, battered into total disarray by the Japanese, pulled itself together and came up with Swatch timepieces (this is discussed later, in the section titled "The Sultan of Swatch"). Yet often competitors will kindly give you the one thing in their power that is rarely in yours—time. In the British banking market, the Midland introduced free banking, abolishing transaction charges for private customers. The other banks thought it wouldn't work, and said so. Six months later, when they were all clambering on the bandwagon, the Midland had picked up half a million new customers. Be ready to move decisively at all times—and move when you have to.

Finally, take a long, hard look at the business to see if it displays the Buggie Bugbears; if it does, eradicate them.

1. *Chauvinism.* The "my company, right or wrong" approach tries (but fails) to cover up its stupidity by arguing that whatever is actually being done is by definition right because the company is doing it.

2. *Loyalty.* This touching but misplaced faith in the present product is summed up in the hilarious idea that everything the company (and its sales literature) says about the thing is true.

3. *Reverence for precedent.* "That's the way we've always done things" and "You can't argue with success."

There's the vital clue: *always* argue with success—that's how to make the decisions that will prolong and reproduce market leadership. And there's another. Seek success, and make decisions, without fear.

In 1933 some young Japanese enthusiasts had the ridiculously bold, or boldly ridiculous, idea of making a 35-mm camera that would stand comparison with Germany's fabled Leica. They could and did—and that's how Canon was born. Three decades later Canon had the even more ridiculous notion that it could compete in office copiers with the fabled Xerox. It could and did—and without that fearless decision, Kaku's plan for Canon would have taken far longer, if not forever, to raise the company to premier status.

Like perfect love, the perfect innovative decision casts out fear. But that also works the other way around.

5. THE TAKEOFF OF TAGAMET

In the early 1970s, the Philadelphia pharmaceutical company Smith Kline French, which became SmithKline Beckman, had little going for it—apart from some aging and declining products and some unproved research in Welwyn Garden City, England. The Welwyn work, into which $2.5 million a year was being sunk, had been generated by a genius named James Black. He believed that the secretion of gastric acid (the villain of the ulcer) could be blocked in much the same way as antihistamines inhibited the secretion of mucus in the nose.

Black and two other world-class researchers, all hired away from Imperial Chemical Industries (ICI), formed a team that was, in effect, given its head. Although Philadelphia was also working on ulcer therapy, top management was unaware that, 3,000 miles away in Welwyn, Black was following an entirely different and highly speculative line of research. Still, that needn't have grieved them; for hadn't Black, hired in 1963, promised in the following summer that SmithKline would have a successful compound by the coming Christmas?

In reality, the research breakthrough didn't come until 1968. Four years later, when Black (now Sir James) quit for a professorship, SmithKline still had no marketable product. It was a dozen years after his bold promise of Christmas delivery that Tagamet finally went on sale. From one angle, the perseverance of SmithKline's management might seem worthy of great congratulation—in any business, management has to be patient to reap the rewards of innovation; and in pharmaceuticals you have to be abnormally patient. But according to the book *Breakthroughs!,* the "very far away" managers in Philadelphia "didn't really understand" how Black was spending their millions.

Since his project might have involved testing 30 billion different compounds (meaning forty years' work for 18 million scientists), their ignorance was quite fortunate. Yet the research also made no sense in relation to the existing market. The sums then spent by ulcer sufferers on prescription drugs were small—only $100 million a year. Still worse, 700 compounds had been tested unsuccessfully. But then one of the team members discovered a basic flaw in the test method. Going back to the very beginning, the corrected approach proved that, four years before, Black had been absolutely right: a compound could have been found by that early Christmas.

There were still slips between cups and lips—the first successful compound had unacceptable side effects and had to be urgently replaced. Yet SmithKline's managers took two far-reaching, all but farfetched, decisions. First, they decided to put a full-scale marketing operation in place before the launch—drawing on past experience with Thorazine, their last best-seller, the potential of which hadn't been fully exploited in the psychiatric market because of an inadequate marketing setup.

Second, and even braver, before the directors were sure exactly what they were going to sell, and before they had any idea how much of it could be sold, SmithKline started the construction of a $10 million plant in Cork that would have been utterly useless if the drug had flopped. It was the best decision any of them would ever make: Tagamet became the first drug ever to top $1 billion in annual sales, and the only problem at Cork was how to cope with the relentlessly escalating demand. The plant boss's orders are worth noting. "Money is no issue," he was told. "Make as much as you can." Which is what SmithKline did with its antiulcer miracle—and could

73

never have done without its two brave, bold, and correct decisions.

6. BACKING THE BREAKTHROUGH

No decision in business provides greater potential for the creation of wealth (or its destruction, come to think of it) than the choice of which innovation to back. *Breakthroughs!* lists a dozen along with Tagamet, including 3M's little yellow Post-it Note Pads, Nike jogging shoes, JVC's videocassette recorder, the Nautilus gym machine, the Sony Walkman, the microwave oven, and so on. Any one of them is enough to create a billionaire—and studying the whole collection should surely provide some invaluable clues on how to make decisions on innovation.

So it does, up to a point. For a start, the book, instigated by the Arthur D. Little consultancy, destroys four false ideas:

Myth 1. Tread where no man has trod before. In reality, the far better course is to look for your novelty not among total unknowns but among ideas other people *have* had before—but haven't used properly. Breakthroughs don't come from outer space but from exploiting what's already been discovered by some other sucker. Tagamet sprang from an abandoned concept about blocking the formation of gastric acid (just as video recording was a well-established professional technology before it was adapted for the home—and so, for that matter, was sound tape recording).

Myth 2. Just find your genius and back him to the hilt. In reality, innovation never relies on one clever individual—a genius such as Sir James Black, the Tagamet inventor, will need backing up by others. The talents have got to cover manufacture and marketing as well as technology (it took three key men in three different firms to produce the microwave takeoff).

Myth 3. Build a better mousetrap and the world will beat a path to your door (one of the oldest, most repeated pieces of rubbish). As SmithKline had fortunately learned from its earlier experience, you cannot rely on an innovation, however wonderful, to sell itself. The Post-it pioneers had terrible trouble selling their idea, especially within 3M; the key (as with the first Sony tape recorder) was to have people use the product, in the Post-it case, both inside and outside the firm.

Myth 4. God is on the side of the big battalions. Not in the matter of breakthroughs. In half of the dozen Little cases, small outfits produced the innovation. In others, true, big resources were essential—but it's more important by far to concentrate the effort and the money on the projects likely to succeed. SmithKline was a second-division drug company, and Welwyn wasn't even its main lab; but the antiulcer project absorbed more and more of that lab's resources, and that proved crucial.

Myth destruction is a valuable start on the way to making the right innovatory decisions. But it is by no means enough. Good decisions, like good shots in golf, depend heavily on the stance the player adopts. In decision plays, the good manager of innovation:

1. Sees his main role as generating new ideas from other people—not having brain waves himself.

2. Encourages the formation of small, tight-knit, innovative teams.

3. Creates an atmosphere in which new ideas are applauded.

4. Leads from the front, getting personally involved in the innovatory effort.

5. Asks a lot of questions, all the time.

6. Allows for eccentric behavior.

There were convincing examples of most of these six elements in the Tagamet saga. But the (truly) decisive fact in the SmithKline stance was more negative than positive. The driving force was a measure of desperation. A company that hadn't produced a major new drug for the best part of two decades was doomed without a significant success. And Black's baby was the only research project in the corporation that offered any major prospect of any kind.

It is, of course, rank bad management to get boxed into a corner in such a way. But often the actions a management takes when it has no choice show with stark clarity how to manage when options do exist. Having chosen one, you go with the decision, the chosen option, with the sum of your forces, and all the way.

This was among the classic maxims of war laid down by the Prussian master strategist Karl von Clausewitz. The principle was demonstrated in the 1980s by a team of star Rugby football players drawn from New Zealand, Australia, and South Africa. Although they had mostly never played together, had hardly met, and were never to play together again, the fifteen men gave one of the best coordinated, most powerful, and most irresistible team performances ever staged. Yet teamwork is supposed to evolve only by constant practice and long association. What was the secret?

It had two parts:

1. The players had supreme individual skills and knowledge, so they knew what to decide on in any given situation—and exactly how to do it.

2. Having in a split second picked the right decision by instinct (which is the sum of experience and talent), they performed it instantly with maximum commitment and force—in a word, decisively.

Go back to that Cork plant on which SmithKline gambled its entire future, and remember the extraordinary orders given to the plant manager: "Money is no issue; make as much as you can." This is the same quality of decisive action that the football team exemplified. The SmithKline management, driven by one equation (no Tagamet equals no company), fully understood another: no plant equals no Tagamet.

It would thus be unfair to present the SmithKline decision makers as automatons driven by the consequences of the company's own past bungling down a road of which they had no understanding. They demonstrated, drawing on the past, great intelligence in handling the possibility (for this was no certainty) that with Tagamet they might win big. One member of management, in particular, believed that the existing size of the antiulcer market, woefully inadequate to support SmithKline's need for new sales, was no guide to the potential—that ulcer patients who currently coped by taking antacids, for instance, might come out of the closet for the new therapy.

In deciding on an innovation, the wise marketer bears in mind that a successful launch creates its own demand. The size of the previous market is no indicator of demand once the market has been changed by the advent of a major new entrant—IBM found this, to its great embarrassment, when it launched its personal computer and came nowhere near meeting the surge of orders. Four Tagamets a day were prescribed to people who had received no therapy before—and therefore didn't figure in the statistics.

Always have contingency plans against the possibility that you've grossly underestimated demand. It's too late to react when you're already swamped. SmithKline was just able to cope—but only just. Still, it emerged from the story not only immensely rich but with considerable management credit, even if the right behavior had been forced by wrong circumstances. The bad management medal goes not to SmithKline but to ICI.

Why did the Tagamet trio leave the latter company? Because ICI wouldn't allow Black to follow the line of thought that eventually produced Tagamet. The reasoning (if that's the word) was that Black had already produced a brilliant break-through—the beta-blockers that, by checking the secretion of adrenaline, stop concert pianists, or anybody else, from becoming overly nervous, and that, in 1988, won Black the Nobel Prize.

Although there's an analogy between beta-blockers and "H_2 antagonists," which refers to the action of Tagamet in checking the secretion of gastric acid, ICI preferred to follow the law of historical experience, which says that lightning never strikes twice in the same place or on the same inventor. Black had enjoyed his ration of spectacular success, and the odds were thus certainly against him. But you can't decide on the new by extrapolating from the old. Black was plainly a genius, and genius doesn't always obey the rules. ICI could (just about) afford to lose Tagamet. Most companies couldn't. And if ICI could have its decision rerun, you can bet its decision makers' lives that Black would have been given his head—and anything else he wanted.

7. THE TAURUS AND THE LASER TAG

Every year, every week, every day, maybe every hour, somebody, somewhere decides to launch a new product. The evidence says overwhelmingly that nearly all these decisions are wrong; the great majority of new products fail. Yet that knowledge will never stem the flow, any more than buyers of sweepstakes tickets are deterred by the certain knowledge that many bet but few win. The analogy is not farfetched: while few products win, those that do win big. But can the odds be swung in the innovator's favor? Does the study of winning products help in the struggle to avoid losers?

Hindsight is an uncertain guide, which too often leads to "me-too" products and follow-the-leader decisions to enter a marketplace where somebody else has mined the gold but where all too often, as in the efforts of telecommunications companies, from AT&T downward, to prosper in personal computers, nothing but dross can be found. Yet following the leader is not so disastrous a decision as it sounds—it can't be, given the success that the Japanese have won by waiting for others to blaze the trail and then taking the same road, preferably in overwhelming force.

The policy is partly a conditioned reflex, triggered by a pronounced national business characteristic: total inability to bear the contemplation of somebody else's success. But the Japanese are rarely so foolish that they stoop to impure imitation, nor so unprofessional that they fail to launch their late entry with the utmost rigor and determination. Rather, they concentrate all available resources, reducing the risk by using the experience of the leader to provide free market research, and the defects of his product and its method of delivery to guide them to a differentiated offering that serves the same market need, only more effectively.

Thus Canon, when left flat-footed by the Minolta innovation of an autofocus single-lens reflex camera, decided to stay out of the race until it could follow its leader with the technologically superior EOS solution. This policy is less "me too" than "me as well," and the disciplines brought to its execution are the same as those required by the original innovator—with one crucial difference. The follower knows that a rich market exists; the innovator can never be entirely sure.

When Minolta proved that the static SLR market could still be brought to life by technological innovation, its instant, sweeping success made far easier Canon's decision to proceed with expensive investment in a totally new product line. But does studying the nature of a product's success, as opposed to its specific market appeal, give any general guidance to the innovative decision maker? You wouldn't think so, to judge by the list of products that triumphed resoundingly enough in 1986 to attract the plaudits of *Fortune* and *Business Week*. The fourteen miracles, all consumer products, cover a bewildering range of human needs, fashions, and foibles, with hardly an overlap among them.

The *Fortune* editors settled on:

1. U.S. Mint gold coins.
2. The Hyundai Excel car from South Korea.
3. Eastman Kodak's lithium batteries.
4. The Polaroid Spectra camera.
5. Plax Dental Rinse.
6. Bruce Springsteen's five-record boxed set of concert recordings.
7. Azidothymidine (AZT): the AIDS inhibitor better known as Retrovir.
8. Laser Tag, the light-emitting toy gun.
9. Pepsi Slice soft drinks.
10. The Compaq Deskpro 386 personal computer.

Business Week saw eye-to-eye with *Fortune* on the Spectra and the Deskpro, but in a shorter list added:

11. The Ford Taurus/Mercury Sable cars.
12. Hepatitis B vaccine, marketed by Merck.
13. Ultra Pampers disposable diapers from Procter & Gamble.
14. The Copy-Jack pocket-camera-size copier.

No more than half of these products required the manufacturer to achieve major advances in new technology—but all of them could claim to be *new*, the word that, as all market researchers, advertisers, and wise decision makers know, is the one best calculated to succeed. The consequential advice—don't decide to launch a new product unless it is one—should be too obvious to be worth stating. Alas, many allegedly new products are about as fresh, in the immortal words of the song, as yesterday's mashed potato. But the less blatant lessons from this list are equally valuable—and just as easy to follow.

What are they?

8. SEVEN SATISFIERS OF SUCCESS

The starting point for finding the new has to be the old. All man's knowledge concerns what is and has been. Even his guesses about the future can only be constructed out of the materials of the present and the past. Sometimes the past itself may be the future—when a wave of nostalgia brings back replica Stutz Bearcats, or a tide of healthy eating restores whole-meal bread to the table. But even the newest fangled of devices embodies both technology and needs that are well established and well known, and have been for years.

The easiest way to extrapolate profitably into the future is to copy—for instance, from a geographical market that is leading the way. The United States has long served this function for European and Japanese entrepreneurs: in the immediate postwar years, when seekers still crossed the Atlantic by sea, the time lag was measured in years but the transfer was inexorable. In Britain, the Thorn lighting empire was built around the fluorescent lamp technology developed by Sylvania; several Britons exploited the revolutionary idea known as the supermarket; and nylon swept the European textile industry before Du Pont, its American progenitor, had placed a foot over the water.

Since the postwar paradise, the time lag has shrunk in most cases, though not all. Take the microwave oven. As described in *Breakthroughs!*, the first microwave patent was taken out by Raytheon in 1949. The biggest of the few customers was in Japan, where two manufacturers, Toshiba and Sanyo, jumped at the idea when Raytheon exhibited at an international trade show in 1960.

Within four years a Japanese company had vastly improved the basic magnetron, and its customers won a two-year lead over the Americans, who had invented the device in the first place. Two quotes from the book sum up the sobering story: "While America slept, the sun was dawning in the East" and (referring to the 1960s) "Although no one really knew it, time was running out in the United States." In other words, while the Japanese were decisive, the Americans were ruined by indecision—and decisiveness is the essence of innovation.

You don't have to rely on Japanese examples to prove the point. The majority of "America's fastest-growing companies," two dozen of them, as singled out by *Fortune* in May 1988, were innovators. Sun Microsystems has built the belief that fast decisions breed fast growth into its ethos—or rather its emotions. "We get all fired up," chief executive Scott McNealy told the magazine. "Our adrenaline gets going and we start knocking against walls. Our new microprocessor's success was 90% assumption and 10% fact." That sounds suspiciously like the explorer in the jungle who barged impulsively ahead—and got eaten. But McNealy is operating in a market where, as competitor Rod Canion of Compaq says, "one success is gone almost before it even happened." There's method in the mild madness that saw Sun launching both an extrapowerful workstation and its own Compaq-challenging personal computer in the same brief time span.

Led by such risk-taking decision makers, the diverse, enormously rich, progressive American market is still the likeliest source of new product ideas. Look back at those fourteen hits of 1986; only three (the Hyundai, AZT, and Copy-Jack) are non-American products. Even after allowing for a little local press chauvinism, it's evident that the inventive American marketing machine still leads the world. The blistering competitive pace in the United States, matched nowhere save in Japan, forces aware managements into the basic stance from which all innovation stems: asking questions.

To phrase it another way, you look at the present to find its defects—like a dentist probing teeth in search of cavities. What the probing decision maker seeks is evidence of:

1. Unfilled need.
2. Disadvantages in established products.
3. Gaps in otherwise well-served markets.
4. Extensions or new formats for proven lines.
5. Technological breakthroughs.
6. Transferable successes in other markets.
7. More economical ways of satisfying needs now being expensively met.

These Seven Satisfiers cover most successful innovations—and all but one of the fourteen hot products listed: the Laser Tag. There are no rules for toys or for other novelty trades such as fashion. But that didn't stop Toys 'R' Us from growing by an average 19 percent compounded between 1983 and 1987 to over $3 billion in sales. The company's boss, Charles Lazarus, neatly dodged the fashion problem: "We don't want to decide which toys you should buy. We offer everything."

That omnibus approach removed the risk from the fact that nobody could have predicted the Cabbage Patch Kids or known when the miniskirt would again (as you might say) ride high. That particular point was one that Liz Claiborne's co-founder, Jerry Chazen, got spectacularly wrong in the fall of 1987. His customers didn't want their skirts rising high. Chazen took the blame when talking to *Fortune*: "The working woman wants to be stylish, but she also wants to be dignified. It was the biggest boo-boo that I know of in my 35 years of business." Boo-boo or no, the company's rise to $1 billion in sales represented a 36 percent annual growth rate. Very few businesses are so utterly dominated by intuition, hunch, fortune, and luck—although all decision makers in the innovation game need their fair share of these things to achieve a record like Liz Claiborne's.

Above all, they need the questioning mind that led Liz Claiborne's founders to break convention by dispensing with both factories and salespeople on the road—with the crucial result of reducing overhead, which, at higher levels, would have given hemline boo-boos a crucifying impact. In clothing America's working women, moreover, they had discovered an *unfilled need*. In this case the need was real but not agonizing. Often the unfilled need is clearly indicated by public agony, never more conspicuous than in the case of AIDS. The Burroughs Wellcome researchers deliberately decided to concentrate on stopping the seemingly inexorable march of the virus—and AZT (plus two Nobel Prizes) was the result. In another, far less critical area, dental plaque, the makers of Plax followed precisely the same principle: where there's public anxiety, decide to market a product that will relieve its causes.

Disadvantages in established products are usually just as obvious. Instant cameras didn't take photographs that compared well enough with 35-mm shots, and the instant products didn't compare well as gadgets with the constantly improving 35-mm cameras. In batteries, the short life of the standard product is a major and irritating drawback. Reducing the first fault with the Polaroid Spectra restored life and profit to an instant-camera market that had declined by 60 percent from its peak; the longer life of the lithium battery promised Kodak a badly needed new line outside photography (as it happened, the promise hadn't been fulfilled by late 1988—innovation has few certainties).

You couldn't ask for more obviously *well served markets* than financial investment products or volume cars. But the politically enforced withdrawal of the South African Krugerrand left a beautiful gap for the U.S. Mint; and the price structure of the car market left a bottom space into which Hyundai could decide to drive an Excel smart enough to appeal to a record 50,000 motorists in its first year. In theory, there were enough suppliers of jogging shoes, including the innovative Nike, to cushion every interested pair of feet twice over; greater emphasis on style, reports *Fortune*, "brought Reebok 20 million customers that its competitors had overlooked" and raised sales from $13 million to $1.4 billion in four years.

Developments of *established successes* have something of the same decision flavor—or, in the case of Pepsi Slice, four flavors of fruit juice (lemon-lime, mandarin orange, cherry cola, and apple), which, when added to a soft drink in the proportions of one to nine, gave additional mileage to the Pepsi brand—just as the Springsteen boxed set was another way of selling the same music to the same customers, the fans, all over again. The same principle forces Compaq to replace its old models every nine months: the innovations not only extend the market but they keep the whole product image vitally fresh.

Technological breakthroughs are generally quite obvious: the amazing performance of the 80386 chip had been trumpeted by its manufacturer, Intel, and the first computer manufacturer to decide on its use (Compaq, almost inevitably) was bound to establish an immediate marketing advantage—which was equally certain to follow for a diaper that, because of a new superabsorbent polymer, resulted in drier babies. The Ford Taurus was partly a *transferable success*, taking an established European best-selling car and adapting it to the requirements of the American market: the reverse of the traditional flow described earlier, and one that Ford has now wisely decided to build into its worldwide design-and-engineering system.

There will be more such reverse flows, especially as the formidable Japanese competitive machine exploits all Seven Satisfiers. The technique of finding *smaller and/or cheaper* ways of meeting demand is all but unfailing. You can even undercut the undercutters, as Sol Price of San Diego undercut even Wal-Mart Stores, outgrowing Sam Walton's chain by 39 percent compounded against 28 percent in 1983–87 on the way to $3.3 billion in sales. Price's $25-a-year subscribers get their cases and cartons from cash-and-carry warehouses that concentrate solely on price (low, low) rather than choice.

Price competition, either by straight undercutting or by finding cheaper, smaller ways of satisfying demand currently met by larger and/or more expensive equipment, has brought Japanese companies great markets; copiers are a prominent example of the large, costly supplier (Xerox) savaged by a spate of more economical designs. It was inevitable that the smallest, cheapest, hand-held copier would come from the same Asian stable. The case of the microwave oven was no different. The Raytheon invention was refrigerator-size, needed 220 volts, and sold only 10,000 units in America in fourteen years: Toshiba sold a quarter of that number to a single customer, the Japanese National Railway, for use in its dining cars. The speed with which Toshiba seized on the restaurant market contrasts painfully with the cumbersome decision process of the Americans.

As *Breakthroughs!* describes that process, it went through the following stages:

1. In 1942 one Percy Spencer thinks of using radio waves for cooking.

2. Raytheon's board of directors decides to give Spencer some money (it comes to $5 million over ten years) to develop the product, since civilian goods are desperately needed to fill a deserted war products factory.

3. In 1953 the Radarange oven appears, and Tappan and Litton decide to manufacture with Raytheon technology—at automobile prices.

4. In 1960, at that fateful Japanese trade show, Toshiba

and Sanyo are alerted—and immediately decide to enter the market.

5. They also decide that the oven must be made smaller—and another Japanese company, New Japan Radio (one-third owned by Raytheon, oddly enough), decides to make a novel magnetron with the necessary improvements, succeeding by 1964.

6. In 1965 Raytheon buys Amana, and "after almost twenty years of muddling around with microwave ovens," the chairman, Charles F. Adams, finally makes a clear decision: "We'd give it one shot, and if it didn't work, then we'd forget it—put an end to it once and for all."

7. The Amana boss, George Foerstner, takes the Radarange over and makes another decision: a product of roughly the same size as an air conditioner should sell at an air-conditioner price—$499. With the implementation of that product, Raytheon finally gets a viable position in a market. That market proceeds to multiply twentyfold between 1975 and 1985. But which companies then dominated that 15-million-unit market? They were, of course, Japanese.

The microwave saga has several of the Seven Satisfiers at work: unfilled need, disadvantages of the established product, gaps in otherwise well-served markets, technological breakthrough, and transferable success. Raytheon's relative failure arose from making halfhearted decisions on the basis not of the market's need but of the company's. The Japanese, seeing at once that microwave cookery was ideal for the national staple foods of rice and saké, decided to meet that need, asked the right questions, and got the right answers at the right time. That's how product miracles are decided.

9. THE BEGINNING OF L. L. BEAN

Five very different businesspeople faced five very difficult decisions. Put yourself in their shoes and decide how you would have dealt with the situations they faced (in two of the cases, the shoes are literal).

Case 1. You want to buy a business from another company. Even though the desire of your heart is unrelated to the main activity of the company, the management refuses to sell. You can't appeal to the owners, going over the heads of the management, because the management owns half the stock. How can you get hold of your heart's desire without paying any more money—in fact, while paying *less*?

Case 2. You're having trouble getting going as a realtor. You go to a charity auction where there's champagne, dancing, a buffet dinner, and an auctioneer in a dinner jacket. Inside a couple of years, you're a rich man, thanks to selling 6,800 homes and business properties. What did you do after the charity affair to produce this amazing result?

Case 3. You rent your house to a TV production company that wants to make a commercial. You get other bookings from producers who find the house suitable, but you ardently wish you could rent the property more often: at $1,200 a day for ten hours, it's money for nothing. How do you increase your rentals to three days a week?

Case 4. You're bending down to tie your tennis shoe's lace when it breaks into two equal pieces. Neither piece is long enough to tie the shoe on its own. Without joining them together, how do you solve the immediate problem, and how does that lead to a business with $21 million in sales?

Case 5. You come back from a day in the country with soggy leather boots—and wet feet. You notice a pair of galoshes and wish somebody made them for boots. That gives you a different product idea—which starts you off toward the creation of a $250 million business. What's the big idea?

This is how the five real-life cases, as reported in the Bangkok magazine *Senior Management*, were solved to the great profit of those who saw and implemented the correct decisions. In case 1, the man launched an unprecedented hostile takeover bid for the company that wouldn't sell him its unrelated business. Nobody had ever been so stupid as to bid for a company when even as much as a fifth of the stock was tied up. Obviously, the bid couldn't win, but the bidder picked up a quarter of the shares, demanded and got a seat on the board, and, after making himself a nuisance, exchanged his shares for the part of the business his heart had desired all along—for a sum less than he had originally bid.

The case 2 solution is more obvious. The estate agent enrolled in a school that taught cattle auctioneering, and then opened for business as a full-time operation selling properties only by auction. The idea was an instant and understandable hit.

In the other property example, case 3, the owner converted the house to offer producers of TV commercials a choice of three different types of outdoor façades, with movable interior walls, furnishings, and fittings, enabling the $1,200-a-day tenants to choose whatever background they wanted. (The owners understandably moved out, but their daughter and son-in-law continued to live in this mini-studio lot).

In the shoelace situation in case 4, the amateur tennis player tied one of the half laces around the ball of his foot, the other around the instep. To his surprise, that foot felt much better while playing than the other, with the shoe tied in the normal way. He eventually patented a sports shoe design using two separate laces and launched his own company in 1975. It now markets a full range of sporting shoes—double-laced, of course. (He was, incidentally, a priest when his shoelace broke.)

The other footwear tale goes back a long time, to 1911, when the hero of case 5 had a hardware store in Maine. His idea for dealing with the soggy boot problem was to combine leather uppers with the galosh-type rubber feet to keep out the soggy, soggy wet. He then sold the product by mail order. The method, given the date, may be far more important than the inspiration. For the man with the wet feet was L. L. Bean. His double stroke of genius not only created a $250 million business in itself, but sparked off the specialty mail-order trade that is still minting money for other millionaires.

10. BEATING THE BLOCKAGE

The case of L. L. Bean, like the other four, stresses the crucial importance, in making the decisions that create business wealth, of never being afraid to think creatively. Creativity and innovation have plainly become more and more vital as the business world has become more competitive. Without deciding to seek, and getting, the winning edge—the difference in product or service that shifts the customer's preference—no company can be sure of sustaining its position, let alone improving its performance in the marketplace.

Thus, in the toughest of circumstances, innovation was the foundation of the 1980s counterattack of the Japanese against their own currency and the competitive effects of its inexorable rise. Yet, to take cars as the usual conspicuous example, Western firms have been slow to pick up the new challenge thrown down by such Eastern inventions as electronic ride control and four-wheel steering. Western managements pay plenty of lip service to creativity and imagination, but seem all too often to feel that these are God-given qualities.

Some wizard like Edwin Land or An Wang comes along,

and, hey presto, you've got a Polaroid or a magnetic memory. But it takes time: you have to wait for that unteachable quality of inspiration. Meanwhile you keep on badgering your research-and-development people and your new-product department (if any) in the hope that they will justify the appalling amount of money they cost. And it doesn't work.

In reality, creativity and innovation are as teachable as accountancy, and far more rewarding in terms of profitable corporate growth. Simon Majaro, the author of *The Creative Gap*, offers two basic definitions: creativity is the thinking process that helps to generate ideas; and innovation is the practical application of these ideas in meeting the organization's objectives more effectively. The important word in the first definition is *process*. It's possible to organize the search for innovation as thoroughly as any hunt for acquisition targets. Actually, that organized search is essential—for without innovation, as Majaro writes, "a firm simply continues to do what it has been doing in the past—a clear formula for stagnation, decay and ultimate death."

Just as many possible acquisitions are assayed but few are chosen, so with creative ideas: Majaro estimates that "on average, one needs sixty ideas for one successful innovation." Self-evidently, the decision maker must give his company a means of spouting ideas in profusion just to take advantage of this law of averages. That poses obvious demands on the culture, the climate: "Creativity can only survive in organizations in which the climate is empathetic to the whole process."

All experience shows that most companies fall at this first hurdle, that even companies with a high reputation for innovation, such as 3M and Hewlett-Packard, sometimes impose unendurable restraints and difficulties on their in-house pioneers (who should not, incidentally, be tucked away in seraglios labeled "new products"—innovation should be an integral part of the line manager's responsibility).

Majaro's real-life examples of how the climate can be

changed include an ethical drugs sales force. As part of the galvanizing process, the drug salesmen were given notepads labeled "My idea." Now, nobody claims that such devices will produce a silk-purse Edison out of a sow's-ear salesman, but Majaro says flatly: "I subscribe to the thesis that everybody is capable of being creative." The "psychology of the individual," as Jeeves demonstrates to Bertie Wooster in the P. G. Wodehouse stories, is the heart of the matter. How the decision maker uses the formidable powers of the brain, and how far he or she allows attitudes to restrain those powers, can ultimately determine the level of decisive creativity.

The shackles on corporate creativity can themselves only be removed by creative thinking. One decision maker, who had pondered profoundly over how to set the organization free from the chains of its reporting system, came up with a simple and arresting solution. He refused to look at the monthly financial reports. They were, of course, still scrutinized by his financial-control bean counters. But all the CEO wanted to know was whether current performance was "there or thereabouts." If it wasn't, the question became much harder and more insistent: Why hadn't he been told that things were going awry *before* the monthly figures made their routine appearance?

This radical management thinker continued to hold monthly meetings with his managers, but not for the usual hashing over of the historic figures. His questions were never about the past or the present but only about creating the future. How, he wanted to know, are you going to improve your business, area by area, and what will be the results if you do? The psychological pressure for business creativity was built into the process, for no manager was likely to admit to a lack of plans for improving the performance of his business.

The theory was thus as elegant as that of the system, blessed (or cursed) with the name of "management by objectives," or MBO, which seeks (or sought—it has lost popularity after numberless disappointments) to tie the corporate ambitions and individual performance into a seamless whole by the mechanisms of corporate planning, reports, and appraisal. Did that creative CEO's scheme work any better than MBO? He nearly doubled his market share (from II percent to 20 percent) and was able to increase his prices at the same time—for once, market share wasn't won at the expense of margins. Q.E.D.

But what exactly does this real-life experiment prove? The decision maker realized that nothing is to be gained from living in the past—even a past as recent as the previous month. Every top manager knows how, with the best will in the world, attempts to confine board or executive committee meetings to strategic and creative issues degenerate all too soon into the same old postmortem discussions, seeking explanations (and getting excuses) when targets are being missed, patting backs when the business is flooding in. The only way to avoid that trap—a lateral thought that would delight the founder of lateralism, Edward de Bono—is never to have the monthly figures on the table at all.

In a well-managed company, that can be done in near-perfect safety. An imperfectly run firm is another matter—but plainly there are faults other than one month's performance that need to be addressed, and that right soon. Forcing managers to look and think forward means that they will anticipate the future and, far more important, act to create it. The mechanics adopted by that crafty boss, though, aren't the only reason for his success.

All corporate systems give signals to those who inhabit them. In a strictly finance-controlled business, the chief executive may be burstingly keen on innovation, dynamic organic growth, and adventurous investment—and may even say so. But his people will react more strongly to action than words;

they feel the hot breath of the short-term figures down their necks, and they know why their colleagues get fired—for not making their numbers.

Moreover, just as managers told to report on what they are doing to improve the business won't want the embarrassment (let alone the pain) of saying and doing nothing, so those in tough financial regimes don't fancy putting forward plans that will be savaged by the accountants and by their superiors. There is nothing easier to savage than a new idea—because it rests on uncertain assumptions, and because nobody is likely to be blamed for stopping something. You may very well, however, be blamed for starting a venture that fails at the company's inordinate expense. So overcontrolled managers aim only for targets they can hit, which may be a far smaller ambition than the company actually needs to achieve, or than the manager is capable of reaching.

The right stuff is contained in a contrasting anecdote from the early career of James Burke, the chief executive of Johnson & Johnson; he was singled out by *Fortune* in June 1988 as a particular star among "The Innovators"—described as "America's most imaginative companies." At his start in 1953 Burke was much too imaginative for Johnson & Johnson. He lasted only a year because "the company was centralized and stifling, and I was bored." Also, the company didn't have a new-product department, which Burke had proposed as a better than good idea. After three weeks, however, he was asked back to head the very division he had suggested. He started to innovate—and his work resulted in an urgent invitation to the office of General Robert Wood Johnson, the company's awesome chairman.

The reason for the summons was self-evident. As *Fortune* tells it: "One of Burke's first stabs at innovation, a children's chest rub, had failed dismally." Fearing the ax, Burke was confronted by the general, who demanded, "Are you the one who just cost us all that money?" Burke admitted as much, only to be told: "Well, I just want to congratulate you. If you are making mistakes, that means you are making decisions and taking risks. And we won't grow unless you take risks." Burke told the magazine that thirty years later he and Johnson & Johnson were still living by that credo: "Any successful growth company is riddled with failure, and there's just not another way to do it."

A distinguished elder statesman of management who knew General Johnson well grinned when told this story and observed that, if Burke had laid another similar egg, his second stay at Johnson & Johnson would sure as hell have been shorter than his first. In fact, both principles are right: creativity demands that you risk failure; but if consistent failure is left to run on endlessly, the company itself will end.

The truly innovative decision maker only encourages faults, or rather failures, in the right direction. The essential is to remove the corporate obstacles to the right stuff, to prevent the knee-jerk reactions that will certainly mean that, if an L. L. Bean (or, for that matter, an Edwin Land), appears, he will be shown the door—and never, like Jim Burke, be invited back.

For a start, shun the "Yes, but . . ." responses, which really mean that the listener is putting up defenses against the very thing—a potentially valuable creative idea—that the organization's lip servers ostensibly desire. Most barriers to creativity revolve around the word *bureaucracy*, which is by no means a prerogative of large firms. The latter, however, are the most likely to fall into the "bean-counting" trap, in which accountancy definitions of profit rule the roost; after all, you require a fair number of departments before you can insist that "every department must become a profit center"—including R & D.

This insistence is fine, as far as it goes. But it doesn't go nearly far enough. Creativity and innovation cost money and entail more risk than counting beans, but they result, as Simon

Majaro writes, in "doing things differently, better, cheaper or more aesthetically": all of which in turn result in having far more beans to count in the future. Majaro puts forward the interesting idea of "creativity circles," a powerful development of the quality circle idea, as a way of breaking corporate log-jams such as bean counting. The new circles might well work, but they won't replace the existing technology of creativity and innovation, which has been around for a long time (and neglected for most of it), or methods such as problem solving, brainstorming, morphological analysis, scenarios, think tanks, and suggestion schemes.

  All these have their places. But the five cases in the previous section point to the most valuable methodology of all. Notice how often inspiration comes from a blockage. The first man *couldn't* buy the business he wanted. The second man *couldn't* break into estate agency on a major scale. The third *couldn't* rent his home for any more days as it was. The fourth *couldn't* tie his shoes in the orthodox manner. The fifth *couldn't* keep his feet dry while hunting—and, having come up with his solution, *couldn't* exploit it fully without selling beyond the confines of his single store in Maine.

  In each case, moreover, the decision was *unorthodox*. The five very winning answers involved doing something that nobody had ever done before. That is the way to achieve high and highly rewarding business creativity. Look for your blockages—what you wish you could do but can't because of some apparently insuperable barrier. Then search for an eccentric way over or around the obstacle—a solution that embodies a wholly new approach to the problem. Next, test the idea as best you can, in your head, on paper, or in practice if possible. Then comes the really difficult decision: to adopt the idea on a large and vigorous enough scale to make real money—and to sustain your drive for the long, long haul that may be needed before the full payoff.

The second part of Majaro's definition of creativity, meeting the organization's objectives more effectively, has to be achieved. The most important precondition by far is that the decision maker should be both thinker and doer. Too many managers don't recognize the need to do more thinking and less doing as their careers progress and their decisions grow more and more momentous: but the one without the other will not get creativity and innovation flowing through the organization into the marketplace. Here lies one of the world's rare generalized TINAs. There Is No Alternative to creativity and innovation: these days, obscurantism and conservatism will do for you every time.

To summarize some of the main points I've made about the innovators:

1. If you find anything that looks anomalous, ask Why? If you don't get a satisfactory answer, ask Why not?
2. Test the anomaly rigorously, without respect for prevailing opinion—and if it passes the test, grab it with both hands.
3. Always decide on the best information you can get—and look for information wherever it can be found.
4. Always argue with success—that's how to make the decisions that will prolong and reproduce it.
5. If you want to achieve big results, make big decisions.
6. Don't decide on the new by extrapolating from the old.
7. Make wholehearted decisions based on the market's need, not the company's.
8. Look for that need among unfilled wants, disadvantages in established products, gaps in otherwise well-served markets, and more economical ways of satisfying expensively met requirements.
9. Look for your blockages—what you want to achieve

97

but can't because of some apparently insuperable barrier—then go over or around it.

10. Make all your decisions in the knowledge that there is no alternative to creativity and innovation.

IV

THE
EXPANSIONISTS

As the 1980s unfolded, acquisition became more and more dominant as the prime means to every ambitious manager's end: expansion. The deals not only became vaster and vaster, graduating from hundreds of millions to tens of billions, but topsier and turvier—as tiny companies made titanic grabs for world class. The attacks by two lesser Britons on giants of American advertising and employment services, JWT and Manpower, owed a great deal to the now-exploded boom in stock markets and the eagerness of banks, flush with money and greed, to earn high interest and unprecedented fees. But the impudent assaults have lessons for opportunistic decision makers who will never make a bid, just as the defeat of the JWT and Manpower boards owed much to their own decisions— negative ones that made companies vulnerable that should never even have been biddable.

But mergers and acquisitions are the be-all and end-all only for those who make their fat livings from them. Most of the world's pacemaking decision makers are Japanese, and they rarely make acquisitions abroad and almost never at home. Examine the mind-boggling ascent and ascendancy of a business such as Nomura, Japan's leading securities house, and you discover that the springs of its megagrowth include an ability to think around corners, to seek out different methods—ones that differ not only from established market modes but from the company's own previous behavior. The whole heavy weight of typical Western hierarchies bears down upon internal subversives—people who want to challenge the norms to achieve abnormal results.

The great decision maker doesn't fear subversion: he encourages it. This may include making decisions that associates think to be utterly wrongheaded. Analyze the ways in which Sony achieved a unique position among the world's consumer electronics companies, and you find a repetitive pattern of right-angle turns away from the expected. That started with Akio Morita's very first decision to join forces with the struggling Masaru Ibuka rather than seek some surer opportunity elsewhere. Here, as in later decisions of steadily rising significance, Morita showed the true expansionist's surpassing ability to see not just the next move but the ones that lie ahead—sometimes far ahead. It isn't just a question of vision, but one of building long-range vision into immediate decisions.

This attribute is emphatically demonstrated by two long-running success stories, one American, one French, in wine and water. The striking similarities between the decisions of the Gallo brothers and Gustave Leven, the man behind Perrier, provide powerful guidance to businesses seeking growth of the kind that corpocratic managements have evidently found increasingly hard to achieve (hence the heaven-high prices being paid for "brands"—that is, the businesses built organically by some far more inspired predecessor). But inspiration is only part of the Gallo-Perrier formula: perfectionism and sheer perspiration are also needed to achieve such wondrous growth—

which, no doubt, is why lesser managements shy away from even trying.

Yet it's an illusion, exhaustively documented and known to every sentient manager, that management by merger is any easier. Maybe today's merger wave will avoid the fate of yesterday's, half of whose acquisitions failed. More likely, the result will be exactly the same. The conglomerates of the 1960s are riding high again in spirit, even as their earthly remains are being devoured by the new breed of predators. The decision to acquire can be triumphantly right, but not because of high-flown notions about transferring assets from weak hands to strong. As often as not, the strong hands are weakened by the acquisitions. The truth turns out to be that purchasing other companies isn't an alternative to organic growth. The former can't be effective unless it enhances the latter, which, again, is something that the true expansionists have always known—and shown.

1. THE TAKING OF J. WALTER THOMPSON

Sometimes the most crucial decisions in an organization's life are negative—to do nothing, to rest on the oars, to sit on one's laurels. That is especially tempting when the laurels are as old (123 years) and as heavily wreathed as they were on the brows of J. Walter Thompson (JWT), the world's most distinguished advertising agency. Impeccable in its manners, classy in its work, JWT seemed a cut or three above the faster-growing groups—above all, the thrusting Saatchi & Saatchi—whose ambitions were nakedly expansionist and whose hunger for profits and acquisitions was ravenous. In an increasingly ungentlemanly racket, JWT looked like a real gent.

True, JWT had followed the fashion for multinational agencies by becoming a publicly owned marketing services conglomerate, incorporating such optional extras as the large public relations firm of Hill and Knowlton and the market researchers of MRB. But the $4.5 billion group lacked financial dynamism: the profit margins on those high billings were low, the earnings record was poor, and the share price had deservedly languished, even in the hyperboom of 1987. Worse still, the gentlemanly image was disfigured by internal management squabbles. Yet JWT's negative decision was to carry on as if its world had not changed—though change it had.

In advertising, one of the agents of change was Martin Sorrell, a moneywise Briton who quit as financial director for the Saatchi brothers to build his own significant business in marketing services. That personal decision alone marked Sorrell's fitness for the brave new world: between March 1986 and the following summer, he aggrandized WPP, formerly a maker of supermarket baskets, by ten acquisitions in Britain and four in the United States. But nobody in advertising, least of all the squabbling directors of JWT, had reason to take much notice. After all, Sorrell's 1986 annual report had actually begun with two quotations pouring scorn on advertising.

True, Sorrell had decided to build a "dominant position" in Britain and the United States, but that was in other services to the world's marketers. Anyway, there was no chance of a British upstart bidding for an American leader whose market value was twice as high. Or was there? WPP had grown so vertically, multiplying sales sixfold and profits fourfold in 1986, that it was a darling child of the bull market. American corporate raiders had already shown that tiny attackers could win towering prizes by tapping Wall Street's ocean of finance. JWT was financially unloved, and, as a WPP man said, "We on the other hand were well placed to finance the acquisition. We could raise equity capital through our following in the City. So we went ahead."

The negative decisions of JWT were no match for the positive ones of Martin Sorrell. The centenarian agency, 150 percent larger than its upstart attacker, succumbed, despite the directors' hurt opposition, to a raised offer, $560 million, which Wall Street, in the run-up preceding the crash of 1987, wouldn't let them refuse.

The taking of JWT had important implications for an American made of sterner stuff than the admen, though he didn't yet know it. Mitchell S. Fromstein was the chief executive of Manpower Inc., whose U.S. and world lead was a more potent factor in employment services than JWT was in advertising or marketing. But Fromstein's firm had caught the fancy of another relatively young Briton, Tony Berry. Berry's Blue Arrow company, like Sorrell's WPP, was a relative newcomer: Berry had only moved into employment services five years before—after getting fired, with no explanation (either then or later), as boss of a contract cleaning business.

Fromstein's sales were two and a half times those of the interloper. But his strenuous efforts to avoid takeover fared no better than JWT's. Precisely the same forces favored Berry's bold decision. His plan had been to grow by more of the lesser acquisitions, six of them American, that had already taken Blue Arrow to a prebid market value of $680 million, and then to tackle Manpower when the British group was roughly its size. In the summer of 1987 Berry changed his mind and decided on immediate assault. This involved raising more additional equity than anybody had ever taken from the London stock market—a colossal £837 million, doubling Blue Arrow's value and making Sorrell's $310 million seem positively modest.

But Berry, too, was a darling of the greatest bull market. The links between the two cases are several, culminating with the megabids, and starting with the negative decisions of JWT and Manpower to think themselves invulnerable. Both Sorrell and Berry were experienced businessmen, but not owners, before they began their climb. Both bought into little-regarded companies, the public WPP for Sorrell, a private group for Berry, in deals that made them multimillionaires: Berry paid only half a million dollars to buy control of a business that, before the crash of 1987, was worth $1.7 billion.

Both used takeovers, none of them strikingly large, to supercharge their share prices onward and upward: Blue Arrow's equity had grown sevenfold in just three years, and that of WPP four times between Sorrell's 1985 arrival and the bid for JWT. Both had shown enough controlling and directing skills to make their many buys pay. Both chose a fleeting moment of decision. Black Monday slammed the window shut—and both equities tumbled thereafter. As late as the autumn of 1988, the two companies were worth substantially less in the market than the price of their impudent American buys, and both had worries. Sorrell survived the walkout of key directors from a smaller JWT agency, Lord Geller, and the subsequent loss of IBM's account—and survived strongly enough, what's more, to bid for and win another Madison Avenue Grand Old Agency, Ogilvy & Mather; but Berry, beset by disgruntled investors and franchisees and disappointing earnings from America, lost his chief executive job to a man he had just sacked from Manpower: none other than Mitchell Fromstein.

Without the boomtime lust for the shares shown by those same investors (Sorrell's price-earnings [P/E] ratio reached the unsupportable eighties), both megabids would have been still-born. But the share boom was only a precondition for the decision to attack such mighty targets—in what must have seemed to the victims, to paraphrase Oscar Wilde's crack about fox hunting, like the unthinkable chasing the impregnable. What decisions truly enabled the two British decision makers to catch their foxes—and eat them?

2. GREAT OBJECTS IN VIEW

Opportunity knocks all the time. It confronts the decision maker with two problems. Which opportunity to take? and

When? Both questions can paralyze the mind: like a greenhorn investor staring at all the prices listed on the New York Stock Exchange, you don't know where to start or whether tomorrow will be the next Black Monday. The miraculous French scientist Louis Pasteur had the answer to both problems (as to many other things): "Fortune," he wrote, "favors the prepared mind."

In business strategy, this means obeying three commandments.

1. Have a great object in view.
2. Prepare a base upon which you can climb.
3. Understand your environment as thoroughly as your business.

The mistake made by most entrepreneurs is to think small. Neither Berry nor Sorrell could have foreseen, at their minuscule starts, the precise moves that, in a handful of years, would convert dwarf companies into world-class Magogs. But both intended to become major forces in their chosen sectors; Sorrell had seen from the closest possible position the titanic practical power of Charles Saatchi's absurd ambition to control first Britain's and then the world's largest advertising-cum-consultancy empire.

The weak decision maker, seeing some such tumultuous success, enviously concludes that the door has slammed shut. It's a foolish conclusion—akin to that of the retailer who won't open next door to an established chain for fear of its competition: in fact, that is exactly the location to choose, because you know that it generates the required traffic. The trail that some other entrepreneur has blazed may well stay open—provided that circumstances haven't altered drastically since the trailblazing.

Sorrell thus used the same powerful technique that he had

perfected with the Saatchi brothers: buying up a business on the "earn-out" principle, offering high prices in two installments. The full cost is only paid if the purchased management hits high profit targets that in turn justify the high price. This in theory kills two birds with one stone (but see also the discussion on this subject in "How to Buy a Business," in Part V): you don't overpay, ultimately, and you keep and motivate an expert, experienced management, which spares you any operating worries.

Sorrell made his moves in a business tract that marched alongside that of the Saatchis, but without initially trampling on their territory. Marketing services, from below-the-line promotion to marketing incentives, are a distinct sector. But to seize his fullest opportunity, Sorrell's sights had to be set on direct competition with his former employers (and backers— the Saatchis owned 7 percent of WPP, and sold out, significantly after the JWT deal, for $12 million). Commissions of up to 15 percent, yielding sums that bear no direct relation to the services actually rendered, make advertising agencies by far the best-blessed consultants. Joining their number, and their golden stream of cash, was Sorrell's "great object in view," to use the phrase that, like so much sound management advice, comes from the Prussian military strategist Karl von Clausewitz.

The Saatchis began by purchasing advertising agencies and then added marketing and other management services: Sorrell simply reversed the order, deciding on a base that was (1) in an area he understood, (2) credible in the eyes of the City of London and Wall Street, and (3) abounding with takeover targets. In the very different field of employment services, Berry showed much the same precision. Having purchased his half-million-dollar company, he promptly sold off the unwanted subsidiary businesses—swiftly pocketing a half-million-dollar profit in the process.

Berry retained a small employment agency, for he had decided that this sector offered two kinds of opportunity. First, in the broad acres of this market, growth stretched ahead as far as any sensible eye could see. Second, despite the presence of powerful companies such as Manpower and Drake International, the industry was fragmented among a myriad of undersize businesses with geographical or other niches. Third, there was ease of entry and finance: employment agencies require little capital, but do generate healthy infusions of cash.

These characteristics also applied to the Saatchis' chosen field: they are essentials for anybody wanting to achieve great deeds with small means. Moreover, the nature of the business allowed Berry to structure the beanstalklike growth of Blue Arrow in much the same way as Sorrell's earn-outs. He divided the company into separate businesses, each with its own autonomous management, and thus freed himself from operational concerns.

The importance of this liberty is fundamental. The strategic opportunist must be free for what the eponymous hero of *The Education of Hyman Kaplan* called "dip thinking." Deep thinking comes hard to those who are immersed in operational detail and day-to-day anxieties. Deep thinking is essential for the third stage of strategic opportunism: after the big idea and the well-built base comes the understanding of the environment.

The economic ambience of the 1980s greased the fast-track progress of decision makers such as Berry and Sorrell the whole way along. Big ideas above your economic station have been encouraged by the same forces that made it possible to build medium-size companies from the ground in a great hurry, and that then enabled the middling creations to make their megabids for the big time.

The first of these forces was a bull market fed by an

overabundance of readily available capital: the bull market died, but the abundance didn't. The second was fierce competition (intensified after Black Monday) among financiers for corporate finance business. In an age when too much capital was chasing too few borrowers, that business was about the only rich source of income left. The third force was a breakdown of the old nexus between big money and big business—a breach brought about by the pressure on Wall Street and the City for performance, and by the fact that large, established, settled corporations nowadays generate less activity and profit for financiers than do the up-and-coming, ambitious firms: both factors continued to hold true after the 1987 crash.

Before those awful days of October 1987, these three powerful trends had combined to achieve conjurers' takeover victories—like that of Pantry Pride over the several times larger Revlon—which opened the door to Michael Milken's theater of the once-absurd: the proposition that a small company, by issuing vast quantities of debt or equity to purchase assets, could set its sights to any height it chose. The assets purchased would clear or finance the debt or the dividends, and at a stroke the opportunist could pocket the fruits of many working lifetimes.

It was also necessary for Sorrell and Berry to pick their moments. In the former case, the JWT management made it easy by combining a lackluster trading record with the boardroom split that ousted its chief executive. There couldn't have been a better time for Sorrell to swoop. Blue Arrow struck when Manpower's P/E ratio was far below its own. And both Brits used equity because, with the dollar weak, they could purchase American assets relatively cheaply, while also taking advantage of laxer British laws on accounting for mergers.

This bald description of the strategy and tactics ignores the dramas, the late-night bargaining, the transatlantic travels and traumas that were required before the megadeals were consummated. It goes without saying (though Lady Macbeth said it) that it's no use forming ambitions without the illness should attend them. The strategic opportunist must prepare his body and his will for the hard and maybe cruel demands of turning ideas into actuality. But Pasteur's preparation of the mind is the fundamental training. Without it, you are unlikely either to spot the opportunity (because you won't know what you're looking for) or to take it (because you won't have acquired the necessary weapons).

Opportunities like those that Sorrell seized and held with both fast hands are available right now for those who, like them, obey the four rules of opportunistic decision:

1. Prepare the mind—anything is impossible if you believe it to be.

2. Prepare the base—create a foundation for future expansion on any conceivable scale.

3. Prepare your intelligence—generate a deep knowledge of the environment and of those who can help you to exploit it.

4. Prepare yourself—be ready to take your main chance when it comes.

The moment for the great decision won't pass by those who live and work by just five words: *Think big and be prepared.*

3. THE BIG NUMBERS OF NOMURA

The largest securities firm in the world is not American, by a long shot—or, to be more precise, by $49 billion. That is the extent to which the value of Japan's Nomura Securities outran that of Citicorp; in mid-1988 it was twenty-one times that of Merrill Lynch. The so-called thundering herd is a dude ranch compared to the Japanese champion. Nomura has exploited its opportunities far more ably than the succession of highly paid executives who have decided the course of the prime American stockbrokers.

In the style natural to Japanese companies, Nomura has acted to implement umbrella decisions that govern all its activities. First, its immediate postwar president, Tsunao Okumura, decided that Nomura would emerge from military defeat as intact as possible and would immediately start rebuilding its position in the Japanese market for stocks and bonds: not exactly the most exciting opportunity around in the wake of Hiroshima and Nagasaki. The company's history says that Okumura "succeeded by means of procrastination, and in the face of threats of dismissal, in thwarting the strict orders of General MacArthur and protecting the valued name of Nomura."

Maybe this subversive postwar start set the tone for Nomura's early resumption of a second umbrella decision, originally formed before the first Wall Street crash, to become a leading global financial force. The overpowering wave that swept Nomura to success on both the domestic and international fronts was the industrial surge of the Japanese economy—the mighty tidal impetus that, to general surprise, turned Japan into the world's largest source of capital in the 1980s. Between the start of the decade and 1987, Japan's net purchase of foreign securities multiplied a fantastic twenty-two times. But no other Japanese securities house succeeded in riding this tidal wave so triumphantly—and at all stages Nomura's ride was powered by in-house, official "subversive" decisions.

To boost its business with individuals, Nomura took the weird decision (at least to Western eyes) to give away savings chests: door-to-door saleswomen held the keys and would place the saved contents in accounts with Nomura every month. The weirdness worked; according to *Time* magazine, over a million chests were distributed before a halt was called in 1962. The sales force, however, persists; it is now 2,600 strong and backed up by a computerized home investment service.

Second, forced by the authorities to invest in unpopular government bonds, Nomura decided to make the best of a bad job: placed in an investment trust with a low cost of entry, the unpopular bonds became a popular money spinner.

Third, making its play for a major position in Europe, Nomura decided to sell Eurobonds with warrants attached that enabled the purchaser to share painlessly in the Japanese equity boom. It also employed the traditional Japanese method of undercutting on price to force its way into the Eurobond lead, with a 1987 market share practically double that of the longtime leader, Crédit Suisse First Boston.

Thereby hangs another story. One of the partners in the beaten leader, First Boston (riven by a dispute over its own future direction), decided on a conservative course opposed by the two stars who had developed its merger-and-acquisition business into one of the hottest shops on Wall Street. Like many decisive, strong people before them (and many who will surely come after), the merger aces, Bruce Wasserstein and Joseph Perella, spat themselves out. Six months later (after their new firm had executed $19 billion of merger business), Nomura bought 20 percent of it for $100 million.

The decision to pay so enormous a sum for a stake in a business so young—and so dependent on two volatile talents—is another example of the Japanese giant's lissome ability to be unconventional, to subvert the established order so as to achieve its driving ambitions. That has become almost a pattern for Japanese invaders. Faced with any market, they act like renegades, challenging the established norms of price, distribution, and performance, burrowing away (like subversive moles) until they find the tunnel that undermines the opposition.

The technique has caught company after company in the West napping. That was their own doing as much as the invaders'. Often big companies perform badly because they smother the initiative and energy hidden inside their bulk. Often they only perform as well as they do because brave souls in their employ are prepared to think the unthinkable, decide the impossible, and (which has the ultimate importance) do the undoable.

4. SUBVERTING THE COMPANY

Few managers are more decisive, or have to be, than turnaround artists and company doctors. They only win their starring roles because their organizations are heading toward a final crash at high speed, with the terrified passengers clinging to the sides of the rickety coaches. One of those experts always followed a simple rule when moving into a beat-up company: whatever system he found operating, he changed it. If the workers were on incentives, he put them on straight wages. If straight pay was the rule, he moved them to incentives. If the selling was done through regional offices, he closed them and used centralized selling—and vice versa.

The logic wasn't the understandable idea that if a company is a mess the mess makers must have been universally inept. The relevant logic applies to good and bad businesses alike. People get locked into ideas and routines that stop them (or save them) from having to think. Change the system, compel them to act differently, and they begin to think differently. At the very least you achieve the same symbolic and physical recharging that, as experienced hands know, a mere change of offices usually generates.

Here's what happens, however, when the routines rule:
1. You order a manager to boost sales of an alternative product that is biting deep into your traditional line. But you

grudge him money, you don't authorize all the product variants he wants, and you decide that he must charge more for a product whose main advantage (and the reason that competitors have made inroads with this alternative) is that it's meant to be cheaper. Why all this nonsense? Because your systems and shibboleths are geared toward selling as much as possible of the traditional product line. . . .

2. One of your top people has a brain wave, a new retailing concept that, he is sure, will generate high sales. When results in the first of three proposed trial locations for the shops reach only half the promised sales, you decide against an increase in advertising; instead, you want it cut. Why? Because you run a tight ship, and you hate budgets' being missed. . . .

3. You have discovered that certain rules of thumb have worked in the past. So you make them guiding principles. Examples are: "Keep advertising at 4 percent of sales" or "Cut prices if you're converting less than one sales proposal in four into an order."

Rules of thumb are indispensable guides to good decision making, but they must not be sanctified or regarded as decisions in themselves. On the contrary, they need blasphemous reexamination from time to time, just in case the thumb has become master of the mind. All the above examples come from a *Harvard Business Review* article by Thomas V. Bonoma, who teaches at Harvard Business School and argues the case for "marketing subversives"—like the retailer in the second example of what happens when routines rule. This rebel with a cause was convinced that, unless the company spent much more on advertising (and lost much more money) in the first year, there wouldn't be a second, so he craftily and sharply boosted the advertising spending by diverting funds from other parts of the budget. It worked.

The "illegal" use of funds in large companies, which is far

more common than the textbooks (or the managements of the companies) would have you know, is a means of circumventing the corporate decision process. It's been seen in apparently small matters, such as the surreptitious purchase of Apple computers with which individual managers launched the PC revolution, and in relatively large affairs, such as the way in which Philips's managers, unable to get approval of badly needed new products from the notoriously slow and conservative head office in Eindhoven, Holland, developed and launched them all the same, under phony budget headings.

The compelling necessity was that, without the "illegal" innovation, their market share would deteriorate—which was something the Eindhoven controllers would immediately spot and excoriate. There are clear parallels here with the case of the Hewlett-Packard innovators, heroes of Gifford Pinchot's excellent book, *Intrapreneuring*, who defied their chief executive's order to cease work on a project from which the company eventually derived great profit. But relying on "subversives" to make their own decisions in spite of, or in opposition to, your own is a sloppy and uncertain way to run a business. These subordinates have to be subversive because their bosses are not. Great decision making hinges partly on building subversion into the whole corporation.

The generally accepted thesis is that the bigger they come, the harder it is for them to fall into this godly and goodly condition. Big companies run on conformity—and must, if their urban sprawl is to be controlled. It isn't just a question of the supercorporation's finding it difficult to formulate new initiatives: it will crush any that somehow arise, and sometimes do it inadvertently, like a large sow rolling over and squashing a piglet to death.

One such piglet was the Pontiac Fiero, a sporty two-seater that was once the public relations pride and joy of General Motors. The pride and pleasure stemmed from the Fiero's symbolic importance: it embodied the decision of the board to turn GM from lumbering mastodon into limber giant. The car not only represented "a revolutionary advancement in the technology of car building" but was manufactured by a dedicated team of Pontiac people operating independently of the GM machine, with results in productivity and sales that indicated that the board's dream of matching, even beating, Japanese rivals at their own efficient game might actually become a reality.

Unfortunately, reality and Fiero publicity were far apart on some key points. The car had design defects: the engine (which for cost reasons Pontiac had been forced to take from another GM line) was underpowered for a genuine sports car; that fortunately hadn't curbed sales, because young women had vigorously taken up the slack in demand—but they wanted power steering, and GM's hierarchy wouldn't allow the necessary investment. As one of the fathers of the Fiero tellingly lamented: "There were too many committees."

As underfinanced as it was underpowered, the Fiero sank into failure: 1987 sales were half those of 1984, and the next year the former pride and joy was sacrificed, along with its "revolutionary advancements" in car building and the 2,000-job plant where the abortive revolution had been staged. As a consultant pithily explained to the *International Herald Tribune*, the Fiero was viewed inside GM "as a renegade product that was made sort of outside the bureaucracy"—in another word, it was "subversive."

There are echoes here of the fate of the independent group that shattered IBM's norms in launching the PC "outside the bureaucracy." Just as enforced failure made the Fiero's renegades vulnerable, so success, sudden and of altogether uncovenanted scale, put the PC champions on the spot. Whatever the role of the IBM bureaucracy in the two subsequent flops (of the PC jr and the higher-powered AT), the subversives paid the price—the PC operation was sucked back into the mainstream of the corporation and into a competitive struggle in which IBM seemed unable to achieve a decisive winning edge.

That can't have surprised H. Ross Perot, the supersalesman who walked out of IBM when it rejected his subversive idea that the company, in addition to selling computers to people, should also sell them ways of actually using the machines. That bureaucratic knee jerk kicked Perot out of IBM and eventually into General Motors, after he sold GM his Electronic Data Systems for $2 billion. There his attempts to play the corporate gadfly, to sting the elephant into a new mode in which the Fiero fiasco would be impossible, produced a $700 million knee jerk: that being the cost to GM of eliminating Perot, subversive ideas and all, from the company.

As the sorry GM and IBM stories tell, though, the corpocrats can't rely on automatic response to squash subversion. The awkward new ideas will keep on surfacing, and the corpocrats must take difficult positive/negative decisions to subdue the renegades. No new engine for the Fiero; no investment in power steering; kill the car; close the plant. Even for committees these are big decisions, right or wrong. It follows, however, that the positive/negative decisions *could* have been wholly positive. There is no inherent reason why the subversives and the renegades should always be on the losing end.

Return to Bonoma's case of the frustrated retailer. He fully understood (as an advertising agent named Jack Wynne-Williams once admonished the mighty candy king, Forrest Mars) that "sometimes you have to spend money to defend money." The retailing subversive knew that if you pull your punches you don't hit the target hard enough. You don't, in other words, decide to reduce your planned investment because the losses are rising faster, or the venture is doing less well, than expected. If you do, the failure of the venture becomes certain: it's a self-fulfilling prophecy—a Fiero.

That leaves two big questions. First, how does that square with one of the oldest (and best) axioms in business: Abandon failure and reinforce success. Second, how far should the decision maker go in letting rebellious executives defy orders in pursuit of their own ideas?

The answers are linked. First, shun all shibboleths. The fact that the company does certain things in certain ways with certain set objectives (which will always be the case in any company) doesn't mean that the rules are unbreakable. You may break them—after reasoned discussion shows that you must.

That gets rid of "automatic" decisions. The other means of compulsion, the individual order-and-obey procedure of military fame, deserves no house-room in a modern organization. Operate on decisions reached collectively after (again) reasoned discussion. Note that a "decision reached collectively" doesn't mean the same thing as a "collective decision." A business isn't a debating society—but you must hear and air properly all the arguments and alternatives before doing the leader's duty, which is to decide.

If it's a good decision, people will for the most part travel along with it willingly, which is the only good way. That's where abandoning failure and reinforcing success come in. Before taking that kind of go/no-go decision, you must establish, beyond reasonable doubt, whether you have a failure or a success on your hands. This means comparing the original objectives with what has been achieved and analyzing the reasons for any discrepancy. It also means setting down what has been learned about the market since launching the venture— and that will always be plenty.

The next question is whether, had you known *then* what you know *now*, you would still have proceeded with the great enterprise. If the answer is no, there's a prima facie case for closure—but never make that no-go decision without first asking whether the venture can be "tweaked" or radically revised in any way that will achieve success. It's amazing how often happiness can be snatched out of the jaws of misery by a hard tweak.

Reverting to the retail case, the maverick's bosses had clearly not written off his store concept as a failure. But neither had they reasoned out a *strategic* response. That's why he had to implement his own strategic decision behind their backs. Conduct the business as recommended above and there should be no need for Bonoma's subversives. True, cases could still arise in which somebody has a dream that the decision maker doesn't share, based on arguments that he can't bring himself to accept. F. Ross Johnson, when CEO of RJR Nabisco, and billed by *Fortune* as "America's toughest marketing man," even shed a small tear over "one of the toughest things an executive has to do"—say no.

"You can't say yes to everybody," Johnson said. "Then nobody will need you. . . . You've got to keep your people coming in with ideas. You don't want to discourage them, but you have to say no. People have a project they have worked on for two weeks, and in my mighty position I tell them I don't think it's worth anything." As the victor over Procter & Gamble in the Great Cookie War; the man who, in three bites, removed 2,650 executives from the bureaucracy; and the CEO whose bid for his own company drove it into the hands of Kohlberg Kravis Roberts for $25 billion, Johnson is nothing if not decisive; but, of course, you don't say no just to remind people that you're there.

In an ideal world, all proposals brought to the chief executive would demand his yes, and get it. In the real world, the Johnsonian choice between discouragement and good decisions crops up continually. But always consider whether in these circumstances you can afford an *official* subversive—when the subordinate, say, believes in the project as strongly as Sony's

Akio Morita believed in the Walkman. If so, you make a three-part decision. First, to let the enthusiast go ahead, give him a budget, and tell him "on your own head be it" (that, as the next section recounts, being exactly where the far-from-subordinate Morita placed the Walkman responsibility). Second, to monitor progress as with any other project. Third, to bar corporate jealousies or any other irrelevant motives from interference with the full working out of the decision chain.

These three officially subversive rules apply whatever the size of the corporation: whether it's as big as GM and Nomura—or as small as an incipient retail chain of three stores run by a man who believes in his decisions, and whose bosses were wrong not to believe in him.

5. WHAT SONY TOLD BULOVA

Nothing is more crucial in decision making than simply being decisive. A turning point in the relentless rise of Sony in world consumer electronics arrived soon after the company, already a success in tape recorders at home, had created the first pocket transistor radio in 1957. The firm's cofounder Akio Morita took the new wonder over to the United States, and immediately struck pay dirt.

The then-great watch company, Bulova, came up with an order for 100,000 units. In the infant Sony's terms, the order was towering: "worth several times the total capital of our company," as Morita noted many years afterward. There was one important condition, though. The radios had to carry Bulova's name. Although his associates back in Tokyo had no objection, Morita wouldn't agree. The Bulova man was flabbergasted. "Our company is a famous brand name that has taken over fifty years to establish," he said. "Nobody has ever heard of your brand name. Why not take advantage of ours?"

To that Morita had a very Japanese answer. "Fifty years

ago your brand name must have been just as unknown as our name is today. I am here with a new product, and I am now taking the first step for the next fifty years of my company. Fifty years from now I promise you that our name will be just as famous as your company name is today."

Thirty years later, Sony is one of the premier multinational companies, with a brand name that, attached to any electronics product from a TV studio camera to a personal hi-fi, spells high enough quality to attract a premium price that may sometimes be slightly undeserved. Its market value in mid-1988 was nearly $10 billion. Bulova? Merely a cog in the $2 billion private empire of the Tisch brothers, and still famous just as a watch company, a brand in the crowd.

Akio Morita's shunning of the wonderful Bulova offer was the best decision he ever made—according to Morita himself. In latter days, many Japanese electronics firms have accepted huge orders from Western companies that, unable to compete, have had their branded consumer goods manufactured in the East. But by then most of the Eastern suppliers had already made their own names, establishing their own brands firmly in the world market. The Western offshore orders were simply a rich, easy source of fat, marginal profit.

In his very different position, nurturing a company that had no presence in world markets and not much at home, Morita was deciding to build his own business—and not somebody else's. As with all superbly correct decisions, Morita knew, then and there much as ball players know at the moment of impact that the bat hit the ball perfectly, that he was right, and why. But there is an equally profound aspect of the Bulova decision.

It was Morita's own. He was not afraid to be decisive, which is another way of saying that in shunning Bulova he didn't shun responsibility. Taking responsibility is the essence of making decisions. Much later on Morita very consciously demonstrated this truth in the debate over the Walkman personal hi-fi. In his book, *Made in Japan: Akio Morita and Sony*, he describes the Walkman as very much his own project: hardly anybody else in the company liked the idea of a tape recorder that couldn't record.

In forcing the project through against this united opposition, Morita made the statement—which in Japanese terms carries the weightiest possible implications—that he would "take personal responsibility" for proceeding. That included, after two meetings, "persuading" the young Walkman engineers to accept the initially money-losing price designed (wrongly, as it turned out) to reach the teenage market. The name Walkman, though, was picked by the young Sony people in Morita's absence. He ordered a change to Walking Stereo—and so it would have been, except that the boss had come back too late to change the decision. It was Morita, however, who rightly decided that the product should bear the disliked name worldwide. The whole of his career is an object lesson in making decisions that, like the Bulova and Walkman ones, have the future built in.

6. NINE MASTERPIECES OF MORITA

Great decision makers, like chess grand masters, don't make the move that yields the greatest immediate advantage but the move that, many steps later, will give them the best, the overwhelming, position. The history of any great entrepreneurial business consists of milestone decisions. There are specific points, clearly visible in hindsight, when a key decision (as Morita's on the Bulova brand name) must be made, when, by making the correct move, the entrepreneur has advanced significantly toward his winning endgame.

The essential attribute is to spot the critical moment, as Morita did, not in retrospect but in advance. Morita showed that talent—one beyond price—from the beginning, just after

Japan's cataclysm of 1945. The business he joined, at age twenty-four, was down, he says, "to a trickle of cash." But it was owned by a brilliant young engineer, Masaru Ibuka, whom Morita had met on a wartime project. Morita made a special journey to renew his acquaintance with this technical genius, and promptly decided that instead of joining his own family's brewery or becoming a full-time academic he would help his friend make shortwave radios. That was . . .

Decision 1. The partner you choose is as important as the business you select. Some people are able to dispense with the aid of equals. But everybody is stronger for the presence of the right associate, colleague, or friend.

The capital the partners scraped up, like the cash trickle, was hopelessly inadequate—a few hundred dollars. Fortunately, Morita was on good terms with his father, who kept the business going with loans and made no fuss about repayment. Morita decided to give his father shares in the company in return for his financial aid, and that resolved the financing difficulties.

Decision 2. You can't build a successful business hand to mouth. Finding a reliable and adequate source of financing is essential. If that means giving up a major portion of the equity at an early stage, so be it. The choice of the investor is almost as important as that of the partner—and full financing is far more valuable than full ownership. The availability of funds will not spare the entrepreneur from the usual struggle of small beginnings—and perhaps it shouldn't. These tough times anneal the entrepreneurial nerve—Morita even helped load the radios into a beat-up secondhand truck and then made the deliveries (he and his partner were the only people in the company with driving licenses). But the pair were already looking ahead. They wanted to produce something completely new—a consumer product, based on Ibuka's expertise, that would create its own market.

Decision 3. There's far less virtue in directly imitating

others than there is in a wholly original product or variant. Provided you've got the market right, you must then have a monopoly until, equally inevitably, the competition appears. But note, too, that this tiny company was already thinking about how to become a big one. *Think—and decide—big.*

The problem for the partners was to keep the business alive while they worked on those big, long-range ambitions. Ibuka put in a bid for some capital equipment, a one-shot job needed by a large customer. The bid won on cheapness and the quality of the technology. The skeptical executive who finally gave them the business "was puzzled by the fact that a small new company in a makeshift factory could produce such a high-technology product."

Decision 4. Playing to your strength is the most obvious and one of the most neglected strategies in business. The *only* strength Morita's company possessed was its technical ability. The partners made that the cornerstone not only of this first important order but of the culture, and thus the future, of their company. Note, however, that they took business that diverted energies away from the long-term project for the sake of the short term.

As luck would have it (and fortune always plays a big part in creating fortunes), Ibuka, while delivering that first crucial order, spotted an American machine that was exactly the type of tape recorder that he wanted for his winning consumer product. The two partners immediately decided—against the opposition of the administrative manager they had brought in, not to mention the clucking of their accountants—to plow money into this development. There are two lessons here.

Decision 5. Strengthen your management as soon as you have the resources to do so. If the business is going to be big, lay the groundwork for that future while it's small by bringing in people and systems that are bigger than your current needs. The head-shaking general manager freed Morita and Ibuka to build the company. To quote Morita himself: "In the long run . . . no matter how good or successful you are or how clever or crafty, your business and its future are in the hands of the people you hire. To put it a bit more dramatically, the fate of your business is actually in the hands of the youngest recruit on the staff." *There are no wiser management words.* But also note, too, how the American recorder opened the door for Sony.

The truly lucrative twist that Morita and Ibuka brought to the product was that it used a consumable item, tape—and they decided to make that as well. That's the old lesson of King C. Gillette, who made little profit from his razors but hundreds of millions of dollars from the blades. Sony's partners didn't then have either a marketable product or a consumable, but their thinking was impeccable. By deciding to make the consumable tape as well as the durable recorders, Morita showed a deep and instinctive grasp of business economics. All great engineering entrepreneurs, from Henry Ford onward, have instinctively risen vertically—allowing outsiders as little as possible of the final price paid by the ultimate user. The economic benefits are compounded when, as in Sony's case (or in the case of Kodak, which sells its camera buyers Kodak film), repetitive sales are added to the one-shot purchase of the equipment.

Decision 6. Looking for a model, a pattern, is far more common as a way to wealth than dreaming up a fully formed marvel in your head. Never be afraid to steal an idea. Just as the best inventions nearly always stem from seeking a solution to a problem, so the best businesses come mostly from developing a hint, found in somebody else's product or racket, that provides an intellectual base on which to build.

Decision 7. This move was closely linked, in Sony's case, with decision 6. It is: think and rethink the basic economics of the business. Decide when and where to take profits to maximize the ultimate return on sales and capital.

The besetting illusion of technological entrepreneurs, though, is that technological brilliance alone will sell their product. Morita made the embarrassing discovery that the new tape recorder "was not something people felt they needed. . . . I then realized that having unique technology and being able to make unique products are not enough to keep a business going. You have to sell the products, and to do that you have to show the potential buyer the real value of what you are selling." Morita saw that he had to become a marketing man: starting with a big public client (far from the mass consumer market he wanted), he demonstrated the recorder, and "sold twenty machines almost instantly"—to the Japanese supreme court.

Decision 8. Any successful business has to be marketing- or customer-oriented. Sometimes a product sells itself; but it will always sell better, especially in the long term, if it's sold well. Morita split the executive responsibility so that the genius Ibuka "could concentrate entirely on innovative product design and production while I learned the merchandising end of the business."

Within six years the partners were prospering enough for Ibuka to go over to the United States. There he found a new technology that offered wonderful possibilities for developing the product line beyond the existing machines—the transistor. The partners were inspired, not just to get a license for the technology but to look at the obviously far wider possibilities for selling to the United States and the world market.

Morita and Ibuka not only obtained the technology from Western Electric, they radically improved it over a long development period until it could supply the basis for an entire family of new products. By then Morita had decided to "abandon the clumsy company name and our brand name. That way we would not have to pay double the advertising cost to make both well known. We wanted a new name that could be recognized anywhere in the world, one that could be pronounced the same in any language."

Decision 9. At one bound Morita had made the intellectual jump from a modest, one-product, national business to one with a potential portfolio of products ready for the international big time.

The name the partners chose is far less important than the principle, although the tale of its selection is amusing enough. The path led from "sonus," meaning sound, to "sunny" and "sonny-boy." But "sonny," pronounced "sohn-nee" in Japan, means to lose money—take away one letter, however, and that's the name carried by the world's number-one brand in product after product launched since that first transistor radio of 1957.

The next thirty years saw many brilliant and decisive strikes, along with equally large errors—notably the fatal defect in the Betamax technology, its shorter recording time, which allowed VHS to scoop the pool in the VCR market that Sony had, as usual, pioneered. By that time Sony had grown arrogant—or, rather, the confident pride that ran through all those nine early decisions (ten, including Bulova) had swollen with success. A quite narrow line separates dangerous arrogance from proud confidence. But that is one of the vital ingredients of Sony-style decisions. Combine controlled Arrogance with Responsibility and Clarity and you get ARC—a light that both illuminates and creates a rich future.

7. THE SPARKLE IN PERRIER

"I decided I had to buy the business myself and never sell it again." Sometimes one decision is all it takes to create a lifetime success. The one in question was that of a Parisian stockbroker named Gustave Leven, and the business was the Perrier mineral water factory at Vergèze then owned by British investors.

Leven's father had asked him to find a buyer, and the young man approached a powerful acquaintance—the living legend, Sam Bronfman of Seagrams, who said, according to the *Financial Times*, "I will come in the fall, keep it for me."

Assuming that this was a conditional no, Leven a few months later visited the plant to find that "it was a shambles. There were broken bottles everywhere. Everything was done by hand. But I immediately thought this was a golden opportunity." The water simply bubbles out of the ground. It struck Leven at once that he could "sell it for more than the price of wine, milk, or for that matter oil," which he duly proceeded to do.

In hindsight, Leven hadn't stumbled across, but rather marched into one of the great postwar marketing opportunities. Perrier had everything: low cost, high prices, inexhaustible growth potential, and even (thanks to total accident) a unique marketing platform. That was the queerly shaped, immediately distinctive green bottle, which was a direct legacy from the English founder, Sir John Harmsworth. He was the brother of the newspaper magnate Lord Northcliffe (one of the few tycoons to have gone demonstrably mad). Harmsworth was introduced to the sparkling natural water by a Dr. Perrier, and started the business, modeling the now-famous bottle on the Indian clubs that kept him fit.

Neither at that point, nor when Leven and four friends took over the business in 1948, did anybody foresee the health-and-fitness movement that helped give Perrier its space-shot boost in the 1970s and 1980s. But the water's boom is far from being a Yuppie phenomenon: that was the second-stage rocket. In the first four years of Leven's ownership, Perrier multiplied output fifteenfold to 150 million bottles a year—almost entirely through sales in a French market that was then all but unique in its devotion to various bottled waters, allegedly good for the liver and other popular organs, but unquestionably safer than supplies from the tap.

Paradoxically, as tap water has become purer in country after country, so the growth in sales of bottled water has overtaken that of every other beverage, including booze and colas. But the surge of Perrier output to 1.2 billion bottles didn't come about by magic. It followed a second decision by the indefatigable Leven—one taken against all the advice he received. As he recounted to the *Financial Times*, "When I started looking at the American market in 1976/77, everyone told me it was madness. I paid consultants to prepare market studies, and all the conclusions were that it was not worth expanding in the United States."

In the land of the dry martini and the wet Coke, where tap water was safe, free, and served iced, it seemed logical to assume that, as the consultants insisted, the Americans would never pay money for a mineral water. But Leven still liked the prospects of an alternative to alcohol, soft drinks, and New York tap water (which to him tasted of disinfectant). "I concluded that there was clearly room for Perrier in the United States, whatever the consultants might have said."

Leven ended up with 85 percent of a market growing by 20 percent annually into the 1990s, as Americans, led by tastemakers on the West Coast, turned away from their three-martini lunches to "the champagne of table waters"—Leven's original slogan for his 1948 purchase. Many other watery buys have followed: all told, Perrier sells 4 billion bottles of its various waters a year to generate some 12 billion francs of sales worldwide, with $500 million coming from the United States. But for all the cascade of growth and wealth (profits of 312 million francs in 1986, four times the 1980 figure), and for all the marketing sophistication developed en route, one principle has remained intact ever since Leven visited that shambles of a bottling plant in 1946. "Decisions are taken in five minutes," he told his interviewer. "And no one spends any money without my approval."

8. GROWING À LA GALLO

The case of the septuagenarian Gustave Leven and his bottled, fizzy water has instructive parallels with that of the septuagenarian brothers Ernest and Julio Gallo. Both Leven and the Gallos, with an astounding dominance of American wine (a quarter of the entire market) that makes them the world's largest producers, have stuck to their liquid lasts with total tenacity to outdo hosts of competitors—any one of whom could, in theory, have created equal success. The basic decision was the same simple one in both cases: to build the strongest possible business on what initially was a weak foundation.

The Gallos' father actually committed suicide after his grape-growing business went bankrupt. Taking over, the brothers almost at once went downstream into wine production, heading toward the position Perrier already occupied—the point of maximum added value. As an excellent account in *Fortune* make evident, they shared with Leven three founding decisions:

    1. To have strong, controlled, swift decision making.

    2. To maximize sales volume.

    3. To add that maximum value—to keep as much as possible of the profit unto their own.

Since the Gallos came as a pair, those decisions (as at Sony) meant having clearly delineated spheres of interest. Julio would look exclusively after production. Ernest would run marketing, sales, and distribution—and did so with an equally iron hand. The only rivalry was that Julio tried to make more than his brother could sell, and vice versa. (Perrier, incidentally, has almost always been short of stock as sales growth has outstripped production.) Ernest showed his power of decision on receipt of the very first inquiry for their value-added down-stream product. He didn't write back, but paid a personal visit to Chicago and, traveling on eastward, didn't stop until the entire first year's production had been sold—at a substantial profit.

These were bulk sales, but, continuing the value-adding theme, the partners moved into selling under their own brand. The sales and the added value continued to grow until one of the variants struck liquid gold in the mass market as Thunder-bird: the partners promoted this low-priced product with heavy advertising. At last they were making money by the gallon (though at the cost of long-term damage to the marketing image).

Along the road, however, the brothers had made some basic business decisions that helped to launch them upward when market tastes moved in the same direction, far away from Thunderbird.

1. They would concentrate on the one basic business, in contrast to rivals who were part of diversified companies.

2. They would concentrate on building volume rather than margins.

3. They would go on vertically integrating; eventually, they could supply all their own needs in transportation, pack-aging, and so forth.

4. They would exert powerful, total control over their material suppliers, only accepting supplies that were up to Julio's high standards.

5. They would place their distributors in similar depen-dence, owning them wherever possible, but playing a decisive role in the distributor's business when not the owners (in con-trast to rivals who simply pushed out their products to inde-pendent distributors handling many competing lines).

6. They would develop and refine their sales techniques—finally the latter were enshrined in a 300-page manual, mandatory reading for every salesman in the company.

The powerful similarities between these foundations and the decisions with which Leven led the bottled-water revolution are not coincidental. Both display the same dedicated concentration: Perrier's only significant byway is the market (which again it leads) for the French blue cheeses of which Roquefort is king. Building volume was and is intrinsic to a product whose margins look after themselves. The vertical integration at Vergèze now extends right down to a glass-making plant—and heavy automation guarantees the high, unvarying quality on which Perrier's sparkling reputation rests.

As for the control over distribution and the refinement of sales techniques, the British operation is a model: sales boomed from a midget half-million bottles in 1972 to 80 million at the end of 1986 in response to Perrier's three-part formula:

1. Get your life-style right.
2. Get your advertising right.
3. Get your distribution right.

This means meticulous planning based on the detailed research that both the Gallos and Leven commission—though the decision makers will (as Leven did in America) override any research recommendation that doesn't fit their own interior view of the external market. It's tempting to conclude that the similar vision and trajectory of these very different people, the Italo-American grape growers and the Parisian stockbroker, must reflect some common principles that, if they don't apply to every business, certainly rule in the bottled-drinks market—and maybe in most markets for fast-moving consumer goods.

But an even more basic question arises. To what extent can the Perrier/Gallo principles be called decisions? Were there any moments, apart from Leven's original inspiration or Ernest Gallo's determination to press on eastward until he'd sold out, when yes/no choices were actually made—when the decision could have gone either way?

The answer goes to the heart of the difference between great decision makers and the also-rans. Leven's five-minute decisions flow from the accumulated workings of those basic principles over four decades. Decisions hardly ever have to be taken de novo, because the choice is already inherent in the decision maker's philosophy. Nor are decisions cramped by lack of resources, because the basic thrust of the decisions-in-principle gives the organization the practical strengths for swift and sure response. Finally, the principles predetermine most of the decisions—like nearly all the best decisions, they make themselves.

How this lucrative mechanism works can be seen by studying three more principles, shared by the liquid trio, in operation. Both Gallo and Perrier are heavyweight advertisers. But their strategy never relies on sheer weight of money: it is always forcefully directed to achieve specific purposes practically and effectively. Thus, using their mass-market muscle, the Gallos moved upmarket by striving for the highest available quality of materials and production, despite their huge output. But their advertising aimed less at marketing premium brands, more at improving the image of brands sold into the mass market—the arena in which they once relied on selling it cheap and piling it high. (Among the many money-making items of marketing lore gathered by the Gallos is the ideal shelf space to be occupied by their brands: seven feet on each of five shelves, that being, apparently, the largest area that the human eye can scan with ease.)

Over in Britain, Perrier followed the injunction to "get

your advertising right" to the letter. To start the water wagon rolling, the British management in 1977 decided on a campaign built around puns on the French for water: *par exemple*, "Eau la la." The puns were combined with seductive and striking images of that green Indian club bottle to get the widest possible market for a premium product necessarily sold at a premium price, the inevitable result of carting Perrier over in bottles from the South of France.

Advertising on TV met the target of widening the market beyond the Yuppies: the upper social sets in 1986 took only 37.4 percent of total British sales. In 1983, when the ads went national, Perrier abandoned the "eau" in favor of a drought-stricken man reaching a hotel in the desert and then crawling off again—because, natch, there was no Perrier. "It worked to the extent that we made it more accessible to more people, and sales went up," said the British managing director, Wenche Marshall Foster. Within a year, though, she said, "we were concerned that we might be losing the interest and ambience of the product." Research proved that "people wanted that bottle"—and it was given back to them. The "eau" continued to flow strongly; Perrier would change when "eau" is tired and stale, but only when research said so.

This intelligent, long-running use of advertising is an essential prop of another Gallo/Perrier principle: *never* to ignore any threat to market dominance. If a new product threatens to win significant sales, they rush out a rival—and they make sure that their contender wins. In wine coolers, joining late, the brothers Gallo rose swiftly to the top of more than one hundred contenders with Bartles & Jaymes, using their strengths (and brilliant advertising) to apply crushing pressure to the multitude. To quote the impact on one of the crushed, reported in *Fortune*: "We've had to double our ad spending and put our products on promotion a lot more often."

At Perrier, where the competitive threats are less complex,

the dominance has been reinforced by acquisition: Perrier has protected its flanks by buying springs in France, Britain, and the United States—though its attempt to oust Evian (one of the still waters that the French especially love) with a new product was one of Leven's rare marketing missteps.

Nobody is right all the time in consumer markets. But the odds on making the supremely right decisions will be skewed heavily in their maker's favor by getting nine yes answers to the following questions:

1. Are the key functions of the business clearly defined and just as clearly allocated?

2. Is it extracting the maximum added value from its markets?

3. Does it have a strong proprietary position, maintained by forceful branding and fully adequate promotion?

4. Is the management totally concentrated on its market?

5. Does it maximize sales by exploiting the distribution system to its best advantage?

6. Does it obtain the best possible VFM (value for money) from its suppliers (that is, the best quality for the best price and the best delivery performance)?

7. Does top management have total mastery of the know-how of the business (like that Gallo lore about supermarket shelves), and has that practical knowledge been communicated to, and understood by, all those with "need to know"?

8. Is the business moving upmarket as far as possible, maintaining volumes, but enhancing reputation and price by emphasis on quality and skillful promotion?

9. Does the company take seriously every threat and every opportunity—and insist, if it decides to react to threats or take opportunities, that it won't rest until it wins . . . and not even then?

The most important decision that anybody can make, though, is enshrined in those last four pregnant words: "and not even then." According to a quote in *Fortune*, the Gallo brothers follow a simple, clear, all-embracing credo: "a constant striving for perfection in every aspect of our business." Leven at Perrier would speak no differently. Decide that only the best—and not even that—is good enough, and many other decisions will fall perfectly into place, probably with near-perfect results.

But simple decisions don't mean easy execution. From their father's suicide in 1933, it took the Gallo brothers a quarter of a century before they hit the biggest time. From Gustave Leven's purchase of Perrier to the English-speaking breakthrough took longer—thirty years. Big and beautiful decisions can be taken in five minutes, but growing the backing strengths that potentiate the big decisions is measured in months, years—and decades.

9. THE CONGLOMERATES COME AGAIN

Toward the end of 1987, George Angus, the chairman of Unilever, decided to play white knight. His Anglo-Dutch consumer products combine would pay $3.1 billion to prevent the cherished brand names of Chesebrough-Pond's, including Vaseline, Q-tips, and Pond's cream itself, from falling into the hands of American Brands. Both white knight and black prince had made it clear, however, that some of the target's businesses wouldn't be retained: that meant, above all, Stauffer Chemical Co., acquired as recently as 1985 in what proved a forlorn effort to make Chesebrough indigestible. In June 1985, Angus decided to accept an offer for Stauffer from ICI—and Stauffer was moved on.

Denys Henderson, the chairman of ICI, had decided to

pay $1.9 billion for the bauble. A mere two weeks after taking possession of Stauffer, he sold its specialty chemicals business, for $650 million, to Akzo America. Just as Angus only wanted the skin-care, personal products, and food businesses, which Unilever hoped might at long last turn its North American interests into a durable, visible success, so Henderson was solely interested in agrochemicals. He wanted Stauffer as part of ICI's own clear and logical strategy of building world leadership in chosen sectors of the chemical industry. The Dutchmen of Akzo, in turn, had their own big ideas about specialty chemicals.

Compared to the notions of Donald P. Kelly, those of Akzo and ICI were penny-ante. In 1984 Kelly, then chief executive of Esmark, decided to sell the company to the fast-growing conglomerate Beatrice Foods for $2.7 billion. In 1986 he took a far greater stride, deciding to lead a buyout, the largest then completed, in order to take Beatrice private and break it up. For the stupendous sum of $8.2 billion, Kelly and his allies, the buyout kings Kohlberg Kravis Roberts (KKR), got the opportunity to take Beatrice to bits. Despite the untimely intervention of the October 1987 crash, by July 1988 sales to a clutch of buyers had totaled $6.9 billion; KKR investors were looking at a probable fourfold return on their money; Kelly was worth some $100 million—and Beatrice was still one of America's bigger food firms.

Jack Welch, the chairman of General Electric, had grander ideas than any of the above. He decided to raise GE to the largest market capitalization in America—bigger even than IBM and Exxon. To that somewhat remote end, he decided to pay $6.5 billion for RCA in 1986: a great leap forward that seemed somewhat negated by the end of the following year. By then Welch had sold or closed six of RCA's bigger businesses employing 41,000 people. But Welch-style decision makers buy and sell, sell and buy. His company's strategists decided some time ago that, unless a business held first or second place in its markets, it should be unceremoniously dumped.

Hence the RCA departures (including the radio network with which RCA's great history began): hence, in one and the same breath, Welch's decision to pick up the medical equipment business of France's Thomson, while offloading all production and marketing of domestic appliances (for which Ronald Reagan once made a mint as TV pitchman). The actions of other managers, like the quadripartite deal that dismembered Chesebrough-Pond's and Stauffer, likewise show that a new mood is governing big-time corporate decisions. In a world of global competition, so these decision makers believe, global presence is essential; building it by Japanese-style organic growth takes too long, so you either acquire the presence of another business, or feed some other management's ambitions by selling your own presence.

This raises in new form the old specter of 300 megacompanies dominating world business. They won't, in this scenario, dominate by virtue of monopolistic economies of scale (the old, exploded idea); instead, in one "core business" after another, leader and runner-up will crush the competition in key markets—and both will be owned and ultimately controlled by the relatively few supermanagements that possess the decisive purchasing power. There's at least one thing wrong with this picture. It sounds like a dead myth writ much, much larger: that of the conglomerates.

No management myth ever got exploded more rapidly and comprehensively than theirs. The conglomerators were supposed to be the dominant decision makers of the 1960s, reshaping and regenerating American business by the force with which they swept through its companies, buying and revamping those firms on which their inspired choices fell. Men such as Harold S. Geneen of ITT, Tex Thornton and Roy Ash of

Litton Industries, Fred Sullivan of Teledyne, and Charles H. Bluhdorn of Gulf + Western seemed to deserve a hall of fame all their own. But the fame fled as the performance waned—for example, as ITT, the largest hospital case, dropped from eighth largest U.S. corporation to forty-fifth.

By the late 1980s most of the conglomerates were either likewise diminished or had disappeared, often by takeover of the takers over. Two, Kidde and SCM, vanished into the stomach of Hanson Trust, a buyer that, in the fashion beloved of KKR and Kelly, likes to spit out, at great profit, what it doesn't want—a process perfectly suited to the Chesebrough-type reshuffling of corporate assets. Really, the engulf-and-devour boom of the Reagan years contained discouraging news for its participants. The dismemberment and subsequent divestment of previously failed merger creations are, or should be, like corpses on gibbets in medieval Europe: a gruesome warning to the boards whose buys have brought such joy to the pocketbooks of Wall Street investment bankers and arbitrageurs.

But megabuy breakup artists like Kelly and Hanson, as they prowl among the undervalued assets of previous mergers, are warehousing businesses for the new trend—the "strategic acquisition." (Somehow it sounds nobler with the adjective.) In any case, the buys fit neatly with the popular principle of splitting large, diverse companies into discrete operating businesses built around their markets, along the lines made famous by GE's "strategic business units." Welch has been combining this gambit with the neostrategic megamerger—meaning the hugely expensive acquisition, taking the corporation into a totally new market such as financial services or broadcasting, which was only made possible by the disappearance of antitrust policy under GE's former pitchman, Reagan.

The question is whether creations like Welch's can avoid the fate of the old-style conglomerates. Their superior general management skills, deployed by a central management team (supposed in the 1960s to be small, though some, like ITT's, were elephantine), were intended to make coherent, fast-expanding sense of great empires of extreme diversity. In real life, the now dead or moribund creations showed the convoy tendency to move at the speed of the slowest vehicle, which is why the parts of SCM or Kidde became worth more than the whole. Also, the whole theory of independent managers independently developing world-class businesses, both organically and by strategic acquisition, is contradicted if their horse is likely, at the decision of a Welch, to be shot or sold from under them.

Some of today's divisional chief executives in U.S. (and foreign) corporations have soldiered on through two, three, even four changes of ownership: Stauffer's executives in specialty chemicals had three owners in six months. It's impossible to believe that business decisions have been unaffected and businesses left undamaged, either directly or indirectly (or both), by all the consequent shifts of style, uncertainties, and reorganizations. Ownership is a significant factor in management performance, which is why the genuine management buyout can be so effective: although genuine (as opposed to Beatrice-style) buyouts are also ending often enough, and sometimes sadly enough, as somebody else's strategic acquisition.

The proprietors of these businesses are thus deprived of the chance to build the long-term value of their businesses along the trail blazed by companies such as IBM, Digital Equipment (DEC), and Hewlett-Packard, growing organically without benefit of any acquisitions, strategic or otherwise. Yet long-term worth must rest ultimately on long-term organic improvement in all sectors of the company. Are businesses to be regarded as the herrings in the Jewish story: not for eating (for which read managing), but just for buying and selling? And if they are so treated, will many of today's decisions work out any better than the conglomerate capers of yesteryear?

10. MAKING SENSE OF MERGERS

Do you agree with the following proposition? "Takeovers are good for the economy. They assure that a company's assets are controlled by the management that can use them most productively. They also enrich shareholders." Agreed? Then you must also presumably assent to the view that managers should have special financial inducements, such as the notorious American "golden parachutes," to forestall decisions "blocking takeovers to preserve their jobs." You do? Then how about this one: "Markets are efficient. Stock prices reflect all current information about a company's performance."

All three beliefs were attributed by *Business Week* in early 1988 to an economist named Michael C. Jensen, who was apparently "poised to shake up the Harvard Business School" with such "controversial" views. In fact, every grand master decision maker in the merger-and-acquisitions game has held the first article of faith, explicitly or implicitly. Successful bids allegedly transfer assets from the weak (the TWA board, say) to the strong (Carl Icahn) or (to take a highly contentious example) from H. Ross Perot (Electronic Data Systems [EDS]) to Roger B. Smith (General Motors). Perot served his prime economic function, in Jensen's theory, by persuading GM to price EDS in such a spectacular way.

Although the heftiest chunk of GM's $4.5 billion went to Perot (who got $700 million more on agreeing to disappear from the buyer's board), that doesn't settle the argument—indeed, it doesn't address the management issue at all. Without question, the overriding objective of corporate strategy must be to increase the real long-term worth of the corporation. The short-term price of the shares is relevant to that objective because it determines the cost of equity and sets the threshold over which a bidder, whether set on reversing the incumbent's strategy or not, must climb. All current bids, like all those before them, successful or unsuccessful, are pitched well above the levels achieved by the "efficient" market.

BAT Industries, for example, started by offering 36 percent more for Farmers Group in the United States than the previous market price: that was 17 percent more than even the precrash peak, and had to be handsomely exceeded to bring a fierce and complex resistance to its end. If bid prices are the criterion, the efficiency of the stock market's collective information stands condemned: no matter what the height of the indices, any board's perpetual complaint that shares are undervalued (only its own shares, of course) stands vindicated. What the stock market doesn't know (or isn't supposed to) is that some strong-handed fellow is willing to pay far more for the shares than they are apparently worth: someone like Edgar Bronfman of Seagrams.

The latter paid "three times the normal price" for Martell, said the cognac family's *chef,* holding back his tears on the way to the banque: and Bronfman himself confessed to the *Financial Times* that he couldn't justify his decision to pay a price of thirty-eight times the last year's earnings on short-term financial grounds. But long-term—ah, there the fit was perfect. That's the second leg of the takeover argument: if the decision doesn't make sense in the terms beloved of corporate raider Lord Hanson (a profit *and* your money back), it does in strategic ones. This line has become paramount among the bidders who, undeterred by the 1987 crash, became notably active on both sides of the Atlantic. Takeovers, said *Business Week*, have "become one of every corporation's strategic options."

There's an apparently logical explanation for this heroic confidence in the wake of an unprecedented, overnight collapse in the asset values on which capitalist prosperity is founded. For management, at least, the pricing of assets by the stock market never bears any relation to true value; therefore, the latter is unaffected by the booms or busts on the exchanges, and business can proceed as usual—with management itself deciding the value of corporate assets in the time-honored manner, by bids and deals, only more so.

The spate of acquisitions, both domestic and international, is plainly an economic and managerial development of greater significance than the 1987 crash, which the mergers-and-acquisitions movement bridged so effortlessly. Starting after the October catastrophe, two Wall Streeters named Bruce Wasserstein and Joseph Perella in six months did $19 billion of merger business and, as was noted earlier, in the section "The Big Numbers of Nomura," promptly had their firm valued at $500 million by Nomura's purchase of a 20 percent interest. The price is gigantic, but at two thousandths of the behemoth's value, the consideration must have seemed an infinitesimal entrance fee to a game in which the Japanese have virtually no experience but is one of the biggest in town.

The price decision, in other words, is irrelevant: only the strategic decision counts. The argument was put in truly heroic fashion by Eric Nicoll, head of United Biscuits Brands Division, who had just paid the dismemberers of Beatrice Foods £26 million for a confection called Callard & Bowser. In total, that's lemon drops beside the $3.7 billion bill paid by Nestlé for Rowntree Mackintosh. But proportionately United Brands far outstripped the Swiss—the price was *eighty-three times* earnings. In other words, the purchaser had to multiply the buy's profits nearly eightfold before the valuation came down to United Brands' own market level.

To give an idea of the mountain that must be climbed, United Brands only managed to treble its own pretax profits over the entire 1978 to 1987 decade. In that period, moreover, a widely praised management had taken the group to only a lowly 181st position out of 250 companies in the *Management Today* Growth League. But Nicoll, according to the *Financial Times*, "scoffed at the shrieks of horror roused by the apparently extravagant multiple paid. *'The measures applied to billion-dollar deals were not pertinent to small acquisitions,'* he said." Nicoll's words, which Nomura might well echo, are italicized because they go to the heart of the problem. Does it matter if decision makers ignore normal financial prudence because the sums involved are relative drops in their financial oceans?

In fact, Nicoll had it wrong from the start. Managements deciding in favor of billion-dollar deals at mind-boggling prices will argue, at the drop of a check, that the measures applied to small acquisitions aren't pertinent to them. Whichever end of the telescope is used, the proposition is the same: decisions that make no sense, or absolute nonsense, on traditional criteria are justified (1) because the strategic gains are worth the price and (2) because, anyway, the cost will be painlessly absorbed within the purchaser's financial bulk. The weakness in the proposition, however, is that the strategic benefits can't be worthwhile unless, sooner rather than later, they are reflected in a traditional payoff on financial criteria.

The insulation that large companies obtain from fat balance sheets is as much a delusion as the expert accountancy juggles that sweep acquisition costs under the financial carpet as if they had never been. The costs actually were incurred: real value passed in an exchange from one set of hands to another; those hands left holding the short end will do so forever. The permanent proof of this verity is the case of ITT. Under Harold S. Geneen's buy-of-the-month strategy, on his own admission, the archconglomerate nearly always paid the asking price for its buys, none of them especially vast. In the American corporate jungle, that's about as safe as lighting matches to look for a gas leak, and so it proved.

It's taken years post-Geneen, with scores of divestments, to raise ITT to a state of healthy mediocrity in which its once world-leading position in telecommunications (the old core) has evaporated during a long slide down the U.S. corporate scale. The key to success must be buying cheap and selling dear: there's no way in which the reverse policy can succeed, be the company never so big, or never so small.

Rupert Murdoch's sensational rise has been solidly based on picking up British properties at distress prices from distressed proprietors such as the British press barons. But the billions of market value thus created were used to underpin the financing for deals in which Murdoch paid well over, instead of several miles under, the odds.

His $3 billion purchase of Triangle Publications, the former Annenberg family fief that publishes *TV Guide*, represented fourteen or fifteen times current cash flow: even at the lower figure, that was roughly a quarter above the transfer fee in some other media deals. But why *current cash flow*? This concept has bobbed up simply because, in traditional methods of valuation, many media buys on both sides of the Atlantic would make even the Callard & Bowser deal seem reasonably sweet. The argument is that, if Murdoch had financed Triangle entirely in debt (which even his brave bankers wouldn't have stomached), the cash flow would have covered the interest costs—but only after two and a half years of normal growth.

On the face of it, that made little sense for shareholders. Once again, the strategic justification was trotted out. One suggestion was that *TV Guide* could lend succor to Murdoch's decision to build a fourth TV network around Fox— another of his expensive buys: Fox lost $80 million in 1987 and was heading for a further $30 million in 1988, scant reward for a buy in which $350 million represented just the previous owners' capital gain. But capital gain is where the financial circle gets squared: on the basis of return on capital or earnings per share, these over-the-market, sometimes over-the-top, purchase decisions may have no financial justification. But in a game of pass the corporate parcel, *the value of the dearly purchased asset to the next prospective purchaser will be much higher still.*

The secret, then, is not to buy cheap but to avoid passing on the parcel too soon, as Laurence Tisch did when selling a parcel of CBS magazines to the management for a sum that looked like pocket money after the deliriously happy buyout boys sold Diamandis to Hachette for $350 million more only months later. But those italicized words above have a familiar ring. It's the same justification that has underpinned every property boom in history. There's no more reason for the price of corporate assets, from candy brands such as Callard & Bowser to magazines such as *TV Guide*, to rise inexorably and eternally than there is for expecting a Dallas skyscraper to ignore the laws of financial gravity—or one in Tokyo or Manhattan, for that matter. At some point many managements will be left, like Geneen's successors at ITT, holding the parcel, and neither they nor the stock market will like what's inside.

Business Week's analysis of the postcrash merger boom went to the heart of the matter. "The biggest difference" (compared to the precrash mania) "may be that deals will be judged more on their business merits than the opportunity for financial legerdemain." The catch is well known and unarguable: while every merger is always justified strategically by those who perpetrate it, business merits only seem to appear in half the cases—and even then the relationship between the acquisition and the strategic success can be fuzzy. After a time, nobody can accurately assess the value of most acquisitions—or measure their contribution to any premium offered by some later bidder for the acquirer's shares.

The outcome only becomes incontrovertible when a clear strategy clearly misfires—as in the hundreds of divestments tabulated by Michael Porter and reported earlier in this book in "Judges, Juries, and Japanese." The flops, however, were a failure of strategy rather than of acquisition per se. The difficulty doesn't lie in determining whether a company is worth 16.1 times historic earnings to a cash bidder whose own P/E ratio is 9.8: any graduate from Jensen's Harvard classes can work out these sums. The problem is to ensure, first, that the decision points the bidder in the right direction and, second, that the bidding management has the power to exploit the strategic opportunity.

Perhaps paradoxically, this problem is most easily solved when the Bronfman contradiction does not exist, when the merger makes immense short-term financial sense and the long-term strategic vision can be left to look after itself. Thus raider Carl Icahn was widely believed to have ruptured himself, perhaps terminally, by buying 76 percent of TWA and ending up in inadvertent charge of its management. Icahn knew nothing about running an airline, but he did know the difference between an unprofitable route and a profitable one. Deciding to cut out twenty-four of the former and exploit thirty-one of the latter, along with $400 million of cost cutting, gave TWA $240.3 million in earnings in 1987—doubling the value of a now puny-looking investment of $310 million. The long-term future of TWA was left unsettled by this decisive action, but at least it now had a chance of a future.

The Icahn treatment also resolves the old difficulty, which has restrained the progress of many otherwise ambitious corporate decision makers, that good companies are too expensive and cheap ones are bad. The right-minded master touch can raise bad to mediocre fast enough to make Midas envious: Icahn also bought a railcar firm named ACF, and multiplied its earnings thirty-four times in three years by such means as axing one whole division of 173 finance people who were simply achieving no results, useful or otherwise. Lifting mediocre to magnificent is another, far harder matter, but it's nowhere near as difficult as elevating the already superb.

That should, however, be a rare problem, given the imperfect nature and performance of managerial man. Apparently cost-efficient companies in East (witness the record 1988 profits in the land of the risen yen) and West alike can squeeze out superfluous millions by the hundred—in IBM's case, seven hundreds of millions in annual employment costs alone. But why did the West's supposedly best-managed corporation so desperately need cuts? Because the IBM decision makers had made some fundamental errors of strategy, compounded by tightly centralized decision making; hence the latest decision (epoch-making for IBM, but routine for less inbred groups) to break up the mammoth into half a dozen still huge subcorporations.

As IBM's example should remind all managers, strategies go wrong as well as right perhaps half the time, or about the same as the percentage of unsuccessful acquisitions. The management of mergers turns out to be no different from any other corporate task: the ideal is the lowest possible cost of entry, the best possible financial return (in terms of time and ratios), and the optimum buildup of long-term market strength. The further the decision maker departs from the ideal, the harder the task must be. So if Jensen is right, and stock market values are efficient, all mergers at a premium (which means all mergers) have the odds weighted against success.

Nor is it truly a question of assets passing from the strong to the weak: they pass to the rich (or the richly banked) from the less rich, which may not be the same thing at all—only look at the decimation of many once-great businesses at the hands of their purchasers. Unless decision makers can imitate Icahn's ruthless business sense, while simultaneously copying the strategic, organic creativity that originally made IBM great, half their acquisitions and strategies alike will continue to impoverish their shareholders. And the only ones who will undoubtedly gain will be Jensen's golden parachutists.

To summarize some of the main points I've made about the expansionists:

1. One man's negative decision to rest on his laurels is another man's positive opportunity to grab them.

2. To seize big opportunities, think big—and be prepared.

3. Encourage subversives who think the unthinkable and pursue the impossible—and you may do the undoable.

4. Change the system; compel people to act differently, and they begin to think differently.

5. Make decisions that have a greater future built into them.

6. Combine controlled Arrogance with Responsiveness and Clarity and you have ARC—a light to illumine the future.

7. Concentrate strong, controlled, swift decision making on maximizing your added value.

8. Decide that only the best—and not even that—is good enough, and many other decisions will fall perfectly into place.

9. Long-term worth must rest ultimately on long-term organic improvement in all sectors of the organization.

10. The strategic benefits of mergers are worthless unless they result in a traditional payoff on financial criteria—sooner rather than later.

V

THE IMPROVERS

The dominant theme of management as the twentieth century nears its end should be the loss of relative power and effectiveness of the large Western corporation. In some respects, this decline is the inevitable reflection of the rise of the East. But this doesn't excuse the failure of many leading managements in the West to keep abreast of the technology of production and that of management itself. When companies such as Ford Motor have decided to update themselves, to join the ranks of the improvers, the results have been spectacular. What makes such decisions difficult is the vested interest in the past; what makes them so successful is the commitment to overthrow past and present in the interests of the future—or having a future.

The achievements of the corporate raiders such as Hanson Trust, not only in buying increasingly large companies on the cheap but in extracting far higher performance from the units they retain, are a massive indictment of the management of the previous owners. The raiders' methods don't answer vital questions about the long-term development of the acquired businesses, but they do point to the buried potential of corporate entities large and small, and to some of the ways that can radically improve their performance. What's lacking, mostly (and oddly), is the will to do so. Even more oddly, managers buying companies often don't have the same urge to improve their purchases—which may be the only way in which they can ever justify the decision to buy.

Commitment to improving the business, though, immediately raises a fundamental choice for top management. Do you pay attention to detail? Or do you confine yourself and your decisions to generating and achieving a broad vision of the future? Do you have to be a genius like Simon Marks, the inspirer of Marks & Spencer, to bridge the contradictions? The answer is that there is no inherent conflict between detail and vision, because the latter will fail without the detailed knowledge of the business, its markets, and the people who run it, which the genius manager achieves by instinct. Many Japanese examples show that the less gifted can achieve the same command by organization—of the company and themselves.

That dynamic impact of the apparently static principle of organization is demonstrated by the successful British turnarounds of great companies from dire distress, of which Britain had an unusual number during the Thatcher recession of the early 1980s. What Sir John Harvey-Jones achieved at ICI makes an instructive contrast with what Roger B. Smith didn't achieve at General Motors. That's because the Briton settled for nothing less than a change in the hearts and minds of his many submanagements, achieved by a change in the ways in which they were directed and sealed by the directors' commitment to go on changing if change they must. The decision to change has to start at the top, but it won't work unless it goes on down through the whole organization—and then starts up again.

The crucial moment for deciding to change, though, may

come when no change seems necessary, when the company is riding high, wide, and handsome. IBM has always been renowned, not least among its own top management, for its ability to change. But the corporate upheavals of the late 1980s were called forth because the giant hadn't changed enough; worse, its proclaimed and self-proclaimed virtues (including the ready acceptance of change) had become lip service. The crisis came about because the great, phenomonally strong decisions of the past became embedded in the present and ossified into weaknesses. Ironically, the new route IBM chairman John F. Akers decided to follow was one that had been available all along and always is, in every business: the route of individual autonomy, responsibility, and decision.

1. THE REFASHIONING OF FORD

If you believe (as well you may) that results are the supreme test of decisions, then the best ones made by the late Henry Ford II must include the firing of Lee Iacocca. It can't, of course, be proved that Iacocca wouldn't have performed even more brilliantly than the men who replaced him. But the results are there, all the same. In the first half of 1988, as *Business Week* pointed out, Ford's $2.9 billion of profit outstripped the figures for the two-thirds-larger General Motors and Iacocca's Chrysler—put together. By any standards, that's motoring.

True, the critical decisions weren't Ford's, but those of Donald E. Petersen, who moved into Iacocca's presidential chair in 1980. Petersen's subsequent actions seem to embody one powerful, if not all-powerful, decision—*to lead the market.* This sounds ridiculous, given that GM's market share is so much greater than Ford's: 35 percent of American car sales against Ford's 20.1 percent. But leadership is not about numbers. The true market leader (as the word *lead* suggests) is *ahead*; ahead of the next move in consumer taste, which the leader helps to create, ahead of its competitors on every dimension that counts with the customers, and ahead in the basic business equation of costs and prices. These are some of Petersen's key leadership decisions:

1. *To lead in styling.* Ford abandoned the box shape in favor of smoother lines lifted from its best-selling European cars; the attractions of the new designs, above all the Taurus, proved decisive in winning market share.

2. *To lead in cost cutting.* The company wouldn't have been making a profit at all without the $5 billion slashed from costs in what Petersen saw as a continuing program, with $5 billion more to come out over five years.

3. *To lead in global integration.* Former chairman Henry Ford's other key decisions included the ahead-of-its-time integration of his European operations, which gave Ford a long lead over GM. By centralizing development of a car or a component in "centers of expertise," located anywhere in the world, Petersen planned to make the integration worldwide, saving money and improving design excellence.

4. *To lead in productivity.* The job reductions, and the concentration on efficient production in efficient plants, resulted in a 50 percent increase in inflation-adjusted sales per employee during 1982 through 1986; that compared with an improvement of 30 percent for Chrysler, and only 15 percent for GM.

5. *To lead in teamwork.* In an industry dominated by hierarchy and top-down management, Ford, previously one of the worst offenders against common sense and modern ideas, sought to reorganize its effort around teams. In the "Team Taurus" project, not only were consumers quizzed to find "best-in-class" targets to beat or match in every aspect of the

car, but assembly workers were brought into the act. It was a combined operation in which stylists, engineers, and manufacturing management worked with, instead of against, each other. According to *Business Week*: "Executive promotions are now based on teamwork, as well as on personal performance, and bonuses are linked to companywide improvements in quality." That last word, *quality*, leads to the sixth and most fundamental leadership decision:

6. *To lead in quality.* Plant closures have been a large factor in Ford's cost cutting. But *Business Week* reported that candidates for the ax were selected on the grounds of poor quality rather than low productivity or obsolescent machinery, and that the quality drive, with the theme "Quality Is Job 1," had been made a permanent program. To prove the point, the Taurus was kept off the market for several months longer than planned to ensure that quality problems had been ironed out. But that's less impressive than another fact: workers on the line were also authorized to stop production if quality came under threat.

This was one proof that Petersen's Ford had imbibed the lessons from the quality gurus of the East, who in turn imbibed their wisdom from the gurus of the West. "Stop the assembly line rather than produce defective cars" is a basic tenet in the famous Toyota production system: at Ford, it has made a world of difference to a company that "used to rush out slipshod cars for the sake of sales." The refusal of Western managers to listen to the advice of those who could have helped improve production quality and efficiency was long one of the least inspiring wonders of the world. To tell the truth, though, what Ford learned from the father of quality, W. Edwards Deming, doesn't sound very inspiring, either: "How to measure the variations in a production process in order to pinpoint the causes of poor quality and then how to gradually reduce those variations." But those dry words, and Petersen's decision to heed what lay behind them, helped lift Ford to the top of the U.S. quality league—and of the whole auto industry pile.

2. SOME GURUS IS GOOD GURUS

Some gurus is good gurus—and none has come any better than W. Edwards Deming. The grand old man of statistical quality control is a latter-day Johnny Appleseed, who, whenever he passes, plants, instead of orchards, upsurges in quality and major improvement in productivity—and profits.

This isn't only because better quality improves sales (it does) and strengthens prices (it does), or even because better quality control means fewer rejects and thus higher usable output per man (it does). Deming has preached a further sermon all over the world; he has consequently been revered and followed in Japan since the end of the war, with results that are self-evident in every market from cars to semiconductors. The winning sermon is that deciding to achieve better quality control, and actually doing so, improves everything else.

Behind the dry science lies a passionate belief in man's ability to improve on the poor and the mediocre, and even on the good. If a company such as Ford goes only halfway toward living by the creed contained in Deming's fourteen famous points, the keys to this all-around improvement and performance, the consequence is a total transformation in its way of life. The fourteen points follow:

1. Create constancy of purpose toward improvement of product and service.

2. Adopt the new philosophy: we are in an economic age created by Japan.

3. Cease dependence on inspection to achieve quality.

4. End the practice of awarding business on the basis of price tag alone.

5. Improve constantly and forever every activity in the company, to improve quality and productivity and thus constantly decrease costs.

6. Institute training and education on the job, including management.

7. Institute supervision to help people, machines, and gadgets to do a better job.

8. Drive out fear, so that everyone may work efficiently.

9. Break down barriers between departments.

10. Eliminate slogans, exhortations, and targets for the work force asking for zero defects and new levels of productivity.

11. Eliminate work standards that prescribe numerical quotas. Substitute aids and helpful supervision.

12. Remove barriers that rob hourly workers of their right to pride of workmanship.

13. Institute a vigorous program of education and retraining.

14. Put everybody to work in teams to accomplish the transformation.

That's only 160-odd words. The reason living up to this brief credo will radically change the lives of most companies isn't that the Deming creed is especially demanding—it's that established ways, like those of Ford in the Iacocca era, are often so weak. Those who have decided to embrace Deming's ideas have achieved startling improvement. The prizes within reach are enormous. To take one example from a *Management Today* report on Britain's best factories, in 1988 the construction equipment firm JCB was achieving three times its 1979 turnover from the same factory with a reduced work force: between 1979 and 1988 it raised direct labor productivity 125 percent, improved the stock turn from 3.2 to 15.3, and got to the stage where it could deliver better-quality products in a mere eight weeks from order.

At another British company, one plant's manufacturing lead time had been cut from 105 to 32 days—with 24 as the current target. If these astounding gains are thought a mere reflection of the well-publicized eccentric national attitude to efficiency, what about the formidable IBM at Havant? In six years, turnover and productivity rose fourfold and quality improved 900 percent as the inventory turn was trebled, the manufacturing-cycle time fell by 80 percent, and the money tied up in inventory was halved. Black & Decker's efficiency is at least as renowned as IBM's. At its Spennymoor plant, output nigh quadrupled as sales per employee did even better: lead time was cut by three weeks to two, inventory turn trebled, the cost of quality was almost halved, scrap was quartered—and assembly rejects came down by about the same amount.

Very likely, these gigantic, cash-rich gains had been won without implementing all of Deming's fourteen points. But you cannot achieve such results without entering into the spirit of Deming or the other good gurus—such as Joseph M. Juran, another octogenarian, who makes clients choose their goals and put teams to work on achieving them; the teams pick up the master's methods and techniques and put them into practice as they go along. Juran worked wonders at a Xerox plant in Britain where scrap, waste, and rejects were consuming a full fifth of the output.

That plant, like those of IBM, Black & Decker, and so on, was probably thought quite efficient before the improvements: as no doubt they all are to this very day, when further potential for productive gains certainly exists. It's another TINA: There Is No Alternative, so managements must decide to live by Deming's point 5, the need for continual progress, constant improvement. American companies that are leading in every sense thus establish key performance measures and insist that managers improve on each one every year. Management by lip service can't win these shop-floor battles, or those in the marketplace: saying what you mean and meaning what you say are basic.

The words said and meant in a Japanese company will be general as well as specific. Deciding in broad principle what the company wants to do, and how, comes naturally to the national culture. Though the whole idea of having a corporate philosophy on these matters (point 2) is off-putting to many Western managers, the philosophy Deming advocates is straightforward in any language. It revolves around point 1: driving the management of the business by the force of quality. This necessitates involving people, because without their willing cooperation it is impossible to realize the philosophy or reap its rich profits.

Here abolition of inspection (point 3) has an obvious role: excellent quality is obtained only where people impose it on themselves. But a scientific fact also applies: beyond any doubt, reasonable or unreasonable, inspection is much less efficient than the statistical sampling on which Deming built his fame and the Japanese (who have notably fewer inspectors than the best-managed factories in the United States) partly founded their postwar rise to unheard-of levels of productivity. Only a minority of Western firms use these techniques; the few who adopt them automatically get a most valuable edge.

Deming is by no means the only source of these methods. A Japanese named Genichi Taguchi (a mere lad in his sixties) and the American Dorian Shainin (in his seventies) vie in the art of spotting key variations by the use of statistics. Faced with the usual high percentage of worthless products (typically 30 percent of an American plant's output, according to *Fortune*), Shainin and Taguchi find out where and why the process is creating the defects and stop them at their source. Shainin's simple approach exchanges pairs of parts between good and bad equipment until he finds which is at fault—and he is surprised if more than a dozen swaps are needed.

The simplicity, no less than the size of the rewards, makes

it amazing that more managements haven't followed Petersen's decision to win such benefits for Ford. They are decision makers who in effect don't decide, who are governed by the status quo and by emotional stances: like the businessman who regards price as a test of macho management—the kind of hard-liner who demands retrospective discounts from suppliers if their goods (to his benefit) sell faster than expected.

To such buyers, Deming's fourth point, his opposition to buying on price alone, is inane. But the practice adopted by the Japanese, or IBM for that matter, makes perfect sense. Get the right quality and delivery performance from the supplier, and price will look after itself. Get the wrong quality and unreliable delivery, and the stuff's far too expensive—at any price. The company can't operate on any other basis if it has made what should be the only possible decision: to follow Deming's closely linked points 5 (constant improvement in productivity and quality) and 1 (constancy of purpose toward the same). The overlap is probably deliberate. Deming continually uses words such as *never-ending*, stressing that his philosophy has to be learned and relearned continually.

This emphasis on learning (point 6) is especially valuable where it will be used: on the job. That's the wondrous difference between the old supervisory system, in which the stick rules and the carrot wilts, and the new (point 7), in which supervision acts as a source of good performance rather than the scourge of its opposite. The purpose is to help people work—not harder but smarter. The best supervisor always did provide a form of training and education. But in today's far more sophisticated conditions, these essentials can't be left to unplanned programs and personal qualities; there has to be an organized system that is integral to, and integrated into, everyday operations.

The stick and whip have no role for the management that has decided on driving out fear (point 8). Fear is a bad taskmaster, and a worse decision maker: insistent pressure for performance needs no flagellation. If departments resist working together, barriers won't come down without insistence on cooperative working, as in Ford's teams (point 9). The man who started the British subsidiary of General Motors on its way back to profits found his efforts to sell to the vital corporate users hindered by the factory's inability to meet promised delivery dates. He insisted, and won; without that Vauxhall could not have mounted GM's first serious challenge to Ford in the local market.

Point 10, dispensing with slogans and like exhortations, goes against both the American and Japanese grains. But Deming feels that slogans are counterproductive, as are numerical quotas (point 11), because they divert attention from the fundamental purpose of maximizing performance by constructive management. Named quotas set a ceiling on performance and don't help workers to maximize their contribution: it's one of the barriers that take away workers' initiative (point 12) and deprive them of pride in their work—another surefire method being to shut your ears to their suggestions. Refusal to listen to the workers is one alleged reason why GM's showplace Buick City in Michigan had a start-up so slow that its cheap capital costs were swallowed by excessive operating expenses. (Among other foul-ups, the robots deposited the windshields on the front seats.)

The keys to better worker contribution can only be education, training, and retraining (point 13), plus teamwork (point 14). GM made intensive use of the concept of teams at only one plant: the bargain-basement, unrobotized joint project with Toyota at Fremont, California. Using Japanese management ideas, including teamwork to solve problems, the plant, says *Business Week*, "is more efficient and produces better quality cars than any plant in the GM system."

This is no more than a good guru would have predicted. Quality and productivity ultimately come down to people. So do the fourteen points, and so does the reluctance of decision makers in the West to learn their lessons. If improvement were a once-and-for-all decision, the reluctant might be readier to swallow their pride and change their ways. The commitment to a never-ending pursuit of quality and productivity is a higher emotional obstacle. As the results at Ford have shown, the decision to vault that barrier can be valued in billions: the decision (or indecision) to shun the goodness of the gurus destroys value.

3. THE CASUAL CATCH OF GORDON WHITE

For the ordinary run of businessmen, purchasing a company is more agonizing than sinking their money into some personal investment. A purchased company is also an investment, of course, but the worst a stock-market buy can do is lose every cent of its value. A company can explode in its purchaser's face: money can gush out in excess of the purchase price by far; executives can walk out; customers can run out. Yet the great decision makers tackle this seemingly hazardous voyage with extreme insouciance.

Take the way Sir Gordon White decided to bid for the conglomerate SCM. This was doubly dangerous because the offer by White's company, Hanson Trust, was certain to be resisted by the SCM management. The dangers of being mistaken about SCM's attractions were thus compounded by those of entering a costly battle that might be expensively lost. Yet, according to the account given by Ivan Fallon, co-author of a book titled *Takeover*, White and the group chairman, Lord Hanson, prepared for the $750 million fray with all the care of a man brushing lint off his sleeve.

Fallon wrote in the magazine *Finance* that White had at least sent Hanson the slick and glossy SCM annual report to whet his appetite; and White had told the Rothschild investment bankers in New York to produce a study of SCM to supplement his own researches. In August 1985, White left his holiday yacht in the Mediterranean and "flew to London, ready to pick up Hanson on the way and get into battle. The SCM accounts were still on Hanson's desk to prove his interest. Rothschild's report was also awaiting White, though he later claimed not to have read it. For two of the most successful bidders of all time, the process was remarkably casual."

In fact, two days appear to have passed before White even mentioned the subject—and that was en route to New York. Hanson recollects: "Going out to the airport to catch the plane, Gordon said to me, 'I am due to have a meeting tomorrow with Robert Pirie of Rothschild, whom I have engaged to advise us on this.' " At the end of July, as White was moving into what he calls "the brewing period" of a bid, SCM shares stood at $45; the Englishman estimated that $60 would swing the deal, and that was the offer Pirie was instructed to make shortly after the two partners had touched down at Kennedy airport. It was the trigger for a ferocious legal contest.

On the SCM side, the defensive lineup included Merrill Lynch, whose gigantic fee of $27.5 million raised some Wall Street eyebrows in view of what happened (or didn't happen); Goldman Sachs; and the lawyer Martin Lipton, called by Fallon a "master of the defensive strategy," the man credited with inventing the *poison pill* (a deal or some other device by which the defense seeks to make the target company horribly indigestible). On one criterion, SCM's defenders succeeded: they forced up the price by a full third to $1 billion. Neither Rothschild nor the Hanson team had thought SCM worth that much.

A casually constructed bid that ends by overpaying sounds like a gourmet recipe for disaster. "Yet within six months," writes Fallon, "White had sold off about a third of the company to get the entire $1 billion back in cash. Hanson still has a business capable of making a profit of $140 million a year, which could be valued at something like $1.4 billion." The largest element in that amazing payoff was the $575 million paid by the British chemical giant, ICI, for SCM's Glidden Paints subsidiary. In contrast to the Hanson partners, the planners at ICI had no doubt made meticulous studies of the market and the contenders before deciding that Glidden was their mark. But why hadn't they paid a billion for the whole of SCM, captured and kept Glidden, and pocketed the profit on the rest?

It's a matter of the nature of the beast. Companies such as ICI are strategic bidders, not predators or raiders. Acquisitions, in the minds of their directors, no matter how many they make (and ICI has been prolific), are means to strategic ends, not ends in themselves. Professional bidders such as White and Hanson have a closer relationship to professional gamblers— and it's significant that many of the West's top takeover specialists, including the Hanson pair and Sir James Goldsmith, are proficient at the tables. For the old pro in both bidding and gambling, there's only one question that truly matters in the decision to bet: Is the price right?

The question is particularly pointed if the bidder is relying on a breakup for his profit. What he must know is whether the parts really are worth more than the whole. That is a much less sophisticated analysis than the calculations that demonstrated to the ICI directors that $575 million was the right price for Glidden Paints, even though Hanson and White had evidently paid far less for that part of their prize. Within such broad parameters, the bidder can get away with being "remarkably casual" and paying a third over his estimated price—especially if he is dealing his hand from the accumulated experience and acquired craft of the Hanson-White duo.

Their purchase of Imperial Group, the British tobacco-to-foods empire, produced much the same satisfactory breakup, although the $1.7 billion acquisition of a larger U.S. conglomerate, Kidde, didn't produce the same almost instant payoff as SCM. But the record of Hanson speaks for the virtues of casual ruthlessness: acquisitions alone explain its eminence of 115th position in the Fortune 500, achieved, despite all the disposals, with $3.8 billion of sales—more than Borg-Warner, bigger than Control Data, larger than Avon Products. There must be a takeover technique, deployed by the predators, that a strategically minded management doesn't use—how else to explain the poor performance of the latter's acquisitions?

According to *Business Week*, "studies generally give the mergers of the 1960s and 1970s failing marks. Some seven out of 10 acquisitions haven't worked out for one reason or another"—which, if true, is extraordinary. It suggests that the acquiring decision makers would have done better, or at least as well, by trusting to the flip of a coin. But it's also possible that their purchases would have prospered more had they learned the lessons that can be gleaned from the very men whom established corporate top managers hate and fear most: the raiders such as Hanson and White.

4. HOW TO BUY A BUSINESS

Do ace acquirers such as Lord Hanson and Sir Gordon White know something, or plenty, that the corpocrats don't? Even so doughty a critic of diversifying conglomerates as Michael E. Porter leans toward allowing that the pair's "much more effective corporate strategy" might avoid following the downward course of its failed American forerunners. Porter's favor was earned by the old one-two of acquisition: cheapness and chopping.

The double threat can be dignified by more academic language. Hanson Trust, wrote Porter in the *Harvard Business Review*, picks as target "a market leader, rich in assets but formerly poor in management." It "pays little of the present value of future cash flow out in an acquisition premium," and "reduces purchase price even further by aggressively selling off businesses that it cannot improve." Those it keeps are improved by emphasizing "low costs and tight financial controls." The restructuring (or chopping) "has cut an average of 25% of labor costs out of acquired companies, slashed fixed overheads, and tightened capital expenditures."

Hanson's critics would say that capital investment has been not so much tightened as throttled, that what determines sale or retention is less the buy's potential for improvement than the appearance of a purchaser bearing a suitably large check. But no matter; in contrast to the strategic acquirer to whom price is irrelevant, Hanson Trust regards price as the only relevance. It buys "low-tech" companies, in the main, not because of any imposing industrial strategy but because low tech tends to go hand-in-hand with high, undervalued assets on which, to use the stockbroker's expression, "a turn" can be made.

The principles of these low-tech bring-and-buy sales are low level, though none the worse for that. Far down from the Hanson millions and billions, the same principles are exemplified by a tale told by an "experienced entrepreneur" (a breed not dissimilar from the Ancient Mariner once they have you by the arm):

There was this old friend of mine who kept on suggesting that we do business together. I knew my friend was unreliable in business, and I didn't want to lose his friendship. There it rested, until one day my friend returned to the attack—but with a difference. This time, he wanted to sell. I was even less eager to buy the business, but to keep my friend quiet, I agreed to glance over a brief document outlining the prospects and the balance sheet. It turned out to be a monstrous animal. On a turnover of under

$300,000, the business had lost about $30,000; it owed money to everybody in sight, including the IRS.

The experienced entrepreneur, his worst fears confirmed, was about to turn thumbs down—when his friend suddenly died. That changed the situation. First, because the entrepreneur wanted to do something for the family. Second, because now that the unreliable friend was sadly out of the picture, the picture had changed. The entrepreneur's accountants and banker took one look at that awful balance sheet, though, and spoke with one voice: "Don't touch it." An associate got very interested at the asking price of $56,000, but asked his accountants and banker for their opinions. They also spoke with one voice—the same one: "Don't touch it."

You might have thought this would end the story. But the experienced entrepreneur couldn't get one thing out of his head: "I liked the look of the *business*. So I approached another contact, in a similar line of business, spoke to the two managers in the company—and the four of us each put up $10,000 to buy the thing, balance sheet and all. Its latest profits? $1.2 million."

In his rambling, roundabout way, the experienced entrepreneur seems to have followed four straight, direct, basic rules:

1. Don't buy businesses or start them without having or putting excellent management firmly in place. (In his own case, the sitting management wasn't strong enough to stand the strain and had to be changed.)

2. Restrict buys to businesses you can truly understand: with a new venture, you must either have or bring onto the premises somebody whose grasp of the market and all relevant know-how is all-embracing.

3. Go for something worth having—the bigger the buy, obviously, the greater the benefit if it succeeds. Why undergo

all the inevitable traumas of a new venture unless the prize is really profitable?

4. Never overpay. The lower the premium, the better the buy; most failures result from ignoring this painfully obvious point.

Any manager paying more than the rule-of-thumb dollar for a dollar of turnover (the experienced entrepreneur paid a dollar for *seven* dollars) had better have a brilliantly convincing reason for doing so. How does Hanson's purchase of SCM stack up against the ancient one's rules? For a wonderful, flying start, SCM cost a dollar for three dollars of sales. It was beyond cavil a prize worth winning, too, and the excellence (or otherwise) of the management, and Hanson Trust's meager knowledge of SCM's businesses, were made irrelevant by the approach that Porter admires. The sold-off morsels required no contribution from Hanson other than banking the check: the retained rumps were entrusted to highly incentivized managers tied to strict one-year budgets: maximizing current cash flows, rather than long-term value, is the object and the essence of the exercise.

Events had triumphantly justified Hanson's policy as far as the SCM and Imperial Group purchases—but predominantly (and inevitably) on an *asset* basis. The SCM and Imperial parts were indeed worth more than the whole, a common phenomenon in the stock market, which values companies on *earnings.* In theory, there should be no contradiction, since the value of an asset lies in its ability to generate earnings. But in practice there are exceptions. First, the asset (as was the case with both the above companies) may be undermanaged. Second, the value of the asset may have been determined not by its own worth but by the totality in which it is wrapped—again, the case with SCM and Imperial.

The third exception is similar to the second. The asset, for reasons that have nothing to do with its earnings (present or potential), is worth more to one party than to another—thus the Glidden Paints business, worth only its earnings and cash flow to Hanson Trust, seemed substantially more valuable to ICI, which could bolster its North American and its paints sides (both dearly held ambitions) at one swoop.

So you can seek to buy assets cheap, or you can buy market share (in which case, the price, possibly to your detriment, is not the prime justification), or you can buy earnings. Hanson and the experienced entrepreneur alike showed no interest in anything but the cheap purchase of assets—and for good reason. It's highly unlikely, in modern times, that present earnings will be undervalued. Therefore, the purchaser is likely to rely on future earnings, which means trusting to the predictions or forecasts whose uncertainty is one of the deepest mantraps in decision making—and the decision to buy is peculiarly pointless unless it will certainly add significant value to the buyer's purse.

In a few classic situations (where, say, the sales bought can simply be added to the buyer's, and the overheads eliminated), a purchase of earnings has this essential virtue. Otherwise, its justification rests on pious hope. There are insurance policies on the market, though. The piety can prudently be built into the deal, most notably by the earn-out alchemy with which the Saatchi magicians advanced their long march toward the creation of the world's biggest marketing and management services empire.

But the simple money principle (make more and you get more) can have some complex results. Another hyperambitious British communications outfit, VPI Group, inadvertently demonstrated the complications. It bought the Carter Organization, a mighty force on Wall Street by virtue of its skills at proxy solicitation, a perfect specialism at the hottest time in history for contested acquisitions. The deal was struck in June

1987 for a down payment of $51 million. Donald Carter, the American supremo, was granted a choice of two attractive supplementary menus: either 4.75 times his average adjusted pretax profits for the three years to end-September 1980, or three fat and juicy installments if his profits climbed to specified levels.

The total payoff could have come to $114.6 million, much of it (as is normal in these choice arrangements) in shares. The highest potential price thus looked tolerable overall, at four times pretax earnings. But having your cake (or somebody else's) and eating it is not that easy a recipe. If shares are involved, the outcome must swing on what happens to their value over the happy earn-out days and years.

If the stock soars, the strain on the acquirer is smaller—because fewer shares need be issued to satisfy the lusts of the earn-out management. If the stock slumps, so many shares must be issued that earnings per share could fall, pressurizing the equity lower still, to the point of possible calamity. The shares of VPI had nose-dived from 500 pence before the 1987 crash (only four months after the Carter deal) to 150 pence, and a year later were still mired at 280 pence. At that point the deal was refixed: the maximum payout dropped to $100.3 million, and there would be no more shares for Donald Carter.

Even that didn't cure VPI's migraine. It would need $49.3 million in hard cash over the period to purchase profits that were originally projected to total no more than $69.2 million—*before* the Internal Revenue Service took its usual healthy tax bite. Plainly the Brits' cash flow would be severely out of pocket on the transaction. So the decision maker buying earnings may well try to insure against bad judgment (about the business or its managers) by linking the deal to future profits, paying in full only if the targeted increases are met. But the good try can run into bad troubles at any time—maybe even when the golden target is actually hit.

You can understand why keen minds intent on capturing service businesses plumped for the earn-outs: the captors can't buy assets, for usually there are none, other than the wizards who take the down elevator every night and may not rise again the next morning. The earn-out is a form of fixative, the most golden of handcuffs. All the same, the idea of giving entrepreneurs the incentive to maximize future profits has a general power. That influence has made it the guiding force of the buyout and venture-capital industries—latter-day wonders, built alike on company valuation, that have seen buying and backing decisions so extravagantly successful (KKR's financing of Beatrice Foods, Ben Rosen's succoring of Compaq) as to blot out the inevitable plethora of flops.

The ways in which venture capitalists value a business in backing their would-be Compaqs are sure guides to less enterprising decision makers. What does it mean if some generous spirit offers 40 percent of a venture in return for an injection of half a million dollars? The whole cornucopia must evidently be valued by its hopeful promoters at $1.25 million. If the business hasn't earned its first cent (quite probable with a venture), how can it be worth anything at all? It can't. Prediction rides again: the investor is buying its value in a few years' time.

The venture capitalist's rule of a highly experienced thumb is that his money should fructify tenfold in five years: thus, the half-million investment cited must flourish so extravagantly in five years that 40 percent of the equity will be worth $5 million, and the entire company $12.5 million. Using another rule of that practiced thumb, a P/E ratio of ten times, that valuation implies after-tax profits of at least $1.25 million.

If that order sounds too tall, return to the true-life example of the deadbeat company that cost the experienced entrepreneur $40,000. The four partners had to earn profits as high as the purchase price (for which read valuation) in five years' time. Even on a mere 10 percent margin, that only involved lifting sales by half over the period. Put that way, the tall order comes right down to manageable size.

Sales and buys are umbilically related. The general rule for decision makers, spectacularly proved by Hanson and the experienced entrepreneur, is absurdly simple: the less paid per dollar of sales, the greater the chance of making real acquisition money. The argument for buying a new business, instead of starting one, reflects that calculation: you get an established turnover, a living cash flow, and other useful assets such as knowledge of and contacts in the chosen arena. In unpleasurable contrast, the new venture offers the pains of negative cash flow (maybe stretching several years into the future), learning a new market, major commitment of funds, and an uncertain outcome.

Most new ventures reward these pains by failing. But half of all corporate buys, though the acquirer knows what he's buying (or thinks he does), lay an equal number of bad eggs. That apparent situation, being between a rock and a hard place, is not an excuse for indecision. After all, making deals (that is, deciding to buy businesses) has helped create $7.5 billion of wealth for two American families—the Bass boys of Texas, and the Pritzkers, half a billion bucks behind them in Chicago. Far too much stands to be gained, provided that the decision maker is no less astute in his buying than the deal maker.

Like the deal maker or the venture capitalist (which in essence he is), the decision maker putting money into a venture—wholly new or an existing business—is taking a view on what the investment will be worth further into time. The venture capitalist looks for that lovely ten-times multiplication in five years not because he's greedy (though he may be) but because he knows the slips between cups and lips. One successful backer of new American businesses says that he has never known a business plan to come out accurately on either cost or time, and all experience supports him.

Paying $100,000 or $100 million for a business that, using a ten-times P/E ratio, won't be worth any more in two years' time is no way to become a Bass. The argument turns on a concept of the utmost simplicity: buying cheap and selling dear. Most of the 1,900-odd corporate divestments recounted by Porter were cases of buying dear and selling cheap; and that's equally no path to Pritzkerdom. The decision to purchase a business is always an asset purchase whose value can only hinge on the before-and-after relationship of cost to worth.

At the end of the day, the difference between the haves, a Bass, Pritzker, or Hanson, and the have-nots partly arises from natural genius; an eye for a business is like an eye for a picture. When it comes to the seven-figure or eight-figure decisions, you need an eye for an Old Master. To return to Ivan Fallon's account of Sir Gordon White's SCM coup, the far-from-white knight insisted in court that he "had not read the Rothschild report on SCM, and had barely scanned one prepared by his assistants; he was asked how, then, had he valued SCM?"

White's reply, after looking back at the lawyer "long and hard," was "Gut feeling." That's akin to the experienced entrepreneur's remark that he "liked the look of the *business*." The liking and the feeling alike spring from a deeply calculated understanding that the goods offered are worth more than the price tag. It had better be *much* more.

5. THE TYCOON AND THE TRIFLES

There's a management consultant who began his career in one of the great chain stores. Among his first jobs was a spell in one of the cafés that used to grace the shops. This particular store was in the North of England. One Saturday afternoon a small, dark man appeared in front of the future consultant and demanded "Do you know who I am?" The young man certainly did: it was the chairman, who proceeded to question him in detail about one of the café's popular lines: trifles. How many trifles had been delivered? How many were left? How many would go before closing time at six?

The inquisitive chairman said he would be back at ten to six—and left. Sharp at five-fifty, back he came. Some one hundred trifles were unsold. The little man personally took part in emptying them all out, and supervised their removal by wheelbarrow and dumping at the rear of the store. He then turned to the future consultant. "Don't keep fresh food overnight," he said, "especially not on a Saturday, when you'll be closed until Monday. Never forget that—and I won't forget you."

More than two years later the young man was working in another store hundreds of miles away in a quite different department: boys' clothing. The same short, dynamic man appeared. "You're the tall young man with the trifles, aren't you?" he asked. But this time he wanted to know about sizes—of socks, for example. How many were carried? In what colors? Then he started to check the stock on display. Where were the missing size and color combinations? In the understock? Below the counter?

The chairman put them up on display. In the stockroom? He grabbed the future consultant and led him there, demanded to know where the relevant items were, personally clambered up the ladder to get them—and carried them back to the department. When all the gaps in the display were filled, he delivered another homily. "Never forget. You can't sell merchandise that the customers can't see." It all made an indelible impression, as you might imagine—and not only the two lessons, true enough though they were.

For the chairman concerned was the legendary Simon Marks of Marks & Spencer. The energy and determination of this multimillionaire retail tycoon were a lesson in themselves.

With 250-odd large stores under his command, he could still find time to check on minute operational details—and still find the memory to recall one young recruit among his large payroll. The performance sounds as it looked to that young man: amazing and deeply impressive. But is this truly the model that other decision makers should imitate?

6. INTERFERENCE ON VISION

Right or wrong? The ideal chief executive pays no attention to operational details. He delegates all operational matters to his subordinates and spends all his own executive time on the few crucial decision areas he reserves unto himself.

Right or wrong? The ideal chief executive has his fingers on every pulse in the corporation, has the detail of its every working at his fingertips, and has his hands on every control. Although he works through subordinates, he knows what they are doing, sometimes better than they do themselves—and he ultimately makes all the decisions.

The two views seem incompatible. How can you both interfere and not interfere? How can you make intelligent, detached, long-range decisions if you're up to your neck in day-to-day detail? In fact, opinion swings like a pendulum between the opposing concepts—more like two pendulums.

As the 1980s unfolded, corporate executives in the United States were being berated for getting too remote from operations; the message was to get down from the ivory towers and practice something called "hands-on management" among the modern equivalents of the dark satanic mills. At the same time, though, Western executives were being berated for having their noses too close to the short-term grindstone: the message was to get away from all the day-to-day or quarter-to-quarter preoccupation and to cultivate *vision* (the word now beloved of one firm of management consultants once devoted to the cult of corporate planning).

Vision is what, to put it crudely, the Japanese have and the West mostly hasn't. It is certainly true that Japanese corporate leaders come much nearer to the first of the two ideals—the detached, farseeing chief executive whose eyes are always fixed firmly on the future, but whose feet are just as solidly on the ground. For a decade before their retirement, Soichiro Honda and Takeo Fujisawa had seen no operational papers in the great automotive company, or attended any operational meetings.

Given Honda's extraordinary advance as a pacesetting global car manufacturer during that period, it can't be said that the company suffered from a self-denial that most Western managers would have found psychologically insupportable. Whether or not the business needs their constant concern with operational detail, they do: it's their security blanket.

Examples of success exist at both extremes, from the compulsive meddler who makes all decisions on the run (or in flight) with a short, sharp yes or no, to the great, above-the-battle, supreme commanders of Japan, such as the late deep-thinking Konosuke Matsushita, whose decisions came only after long deliberation and discussion unclouded by mere temporary factors. Extremes, however, are not to be imitated. As always when there are diametrically opposed poles, the truly valuable course, the golden mean, lies in between—and the case of Simon Marks is an excellent illustration.

As a retail strategist, in his best years he had no superior. A series of brilliant decisions created a business that was still unique decades after his death. And these decisions were not based on off-the-cuff (or out-of-the-gut) hunches. Marks thought over and discussed every step with his longtime partner and brother-in-law, Israel Sieff. The vision was phenomenal: a nationwide chain of stores that would itself be a unique, single brand; a belief that well-treated, decently paid people, from executive suite to shop floor, would produce a better business for the customers (and the owners); a system under which the store, not the manufacturer, would specify the design and cost of the goods; an emphasis on total consistency, offering top quality at moderate price, that customers could come to take for granted.

No other store chain in the world has ever innovated on so grand a scale or found a formula that has proved so lucrative for so long or proved so adaptable—luckily for Marks & Spencer, since without its high-margin business in foods, sluggish growth in textiles would have infected the results of the entire business. Yet the deep, big thinker behind the broad vision was the very same man who could turn up at a store and give a young man an object lesson in handling fresh food—or men's socks.

This detailed interference in the stores gave birth to one of Marks's most famous visions: he once found a salesgirl filling out forms, was stimulated into inquiring into their usefulness, and ended up with a bonfire of futile paperwork and an equally pyrotechnic saving of costs. Great ideas, as Newton found under the apple tree, often arise from observing minor detail. You can't see apples, however, from an executive jet flying over the orchard. The decision maker needs, like Honda, to have his feet on the ground: that great engineer may not have seen any operational papers for ten years, but it's a safe bet that no design went into production, nor any manager into an important job, without the master's approval.

The other side of the coin is that many master plans have been invalidated because of poor performance at the point where the decision meets the outside world. One maddened customer in hundreds of thousands may not seem serious. But if the anger is justified, it points to a failure that may well have deeper causes. Trying out the corporate services and responses at random is an invaluable support to decision making. The random visits of a Marks to a store chain have precisely the same effect.

In recent times, this process has become dignified by the name of "management by walking about." The title is too vague. There is a general virtue in top management's being seen—and heard. But the more purposeful the walk, the better its results. Good walking has two purposes. First, it informs the walker about some (a little) of what is really going on. Second, it informs the organization (a lot) about what the walker really wants to happen.

Peter Drucker, long before the walkabout proposition was formed, told the story of the successor to the redoubtable General Wood of Sears, Roebuck. Truman to the great man's Roosevelt, the new chief wasn't expected to achieve much. But he made it a practice to pull one manager's file at random every day and to ring that man's boss to find out what he was doing to further his underling's career. That one device made a priceless contribution to man management by its impact on both subordinate and superior.

Finding sensitive spots in the company and probing them is vital if decisions are to be alive themselves, rooted in corporate reality rather than the dream world of an overly detached executive suite. It's a form of management by exception—of deciding where you will interfere, either regularly or at random, in ways that will best benefit the organization and your own effectiveness. It isn't an easy art to master for the executive who has risen through the carefully delineated ranks of a teeming bureaucracy and who faces the limitations of his own ability (not to mention time) to grasp the detail of an organization that straddles the globe and several dozen different businesses.

The art comes much easier to those whose operations are smaller, or more homogeneous (like those of the exceptionally concentrated Marks & Spencer—before, that is, buying Brooks Brothers and some West Coast supermarkets). But there have been Renaissance geniuses of corporate life, men whose scintillating brains could easily absorb and recall endless amounts of detail about hugely diverse businesses—I have known three myself. Yet while all three were inordinately successful by ordinary standards, none in the end left the legacy he would have wished.

One was toppled by his colleagues when his behavior became so intolerably dictatorial that even those worms turned. Another took a series of single-handed decisions so disastrous that his successors spent hideous years unwinding his mistakes. The third could never generate the rate of corporate growth he wanted, though established in some of the highest-potential businesses in the world.

The only one of the trio whose decisions were incontestably right, even in hindsight, was the toppled dictator—but he had grown up in his business, developing the instinctive understanding and knowledge (what the Germans call *Fingerspitzengefühl*) that most great founding decision makers possess—and that is a crucial part of their ability to dominate the large organizations created by their genius. Masters of detail who operate by intellect alone, not by this informed intuition as well, tend to lose the judgment that underlies all effective decision making. Their mastery of detail gets in the way of mastering the overall picture—it obstructs and interferes with "vision."

It has to be said that the second of these genius businessmen had plenty of vision: the trouble is that his vision was flawed. This type of genius so overshadows his colleagues that he sets the pace, the style, the tone, and, of course, makes all the decisions. All three of these examples, on reflection, had one lack in common: they didn't relate to people in the organization in the same direct, personal way as the no less overwhelming Simon Marks. That is the way in which he was indeed a model to imitate; for on knowing your people, right down to young trainees, there's no issue. This is basic good management, or part of it.

On getting around the business, or "walking the factory

floor," again, no issue. That's not good management: it's a basic element. On asking penetrating questions to uncover the detail of operations when on your walkabout, that's an essential part of the walking style: that not only keeps other people on their toes, it does the same for you.

This is the final answer to the clash of the two ideals. The decision maker must have the detachment and the time to look around and look ahead. But the decisions must be founded in enough thorough knowledge of the detail to be able to interfere meaningfully—to teach object lessons to those with whom you are interfering and to learn as much as you can about the realities of the organization.

For it's not only the two ideals that are incompatible. In most, perhaps all, companies, what the leadership thinks is happening and what is actually going on are often poles apart. Good decisions rest on justifiable reliance on obtaining reasonably effective performance most of the time: right down to the trifles and the socks. But that reliance won't be effective without the random checks that, time after time, will show up individual and organizational weaknesses. This type of management by exception is worth a significant investment of the decision maker's time. Apart from anything else, every now and again the trifles he throws out will prove not to be trifles at all. . . .

7. THE REINCARNATION OF ICI

No decision is harder in its implications than the decision to change—and the larger the organization, the more difficult the decision and, far more important, the implementation. Deciding to change a General Motors is one thing; changing it, quite another. Under the chairmanship of Roger B. Smith, the board decided (or thought it had) to turn the corporation inside out, from the structure of its operations and the way its vehicles were made to the nature and sophistication of its business (buying expensively into electronics hardware and services, for its own use and for sale to others).

Albert Lee, Smith's former speechwriter, in his *Business Week* article "Call Me Roger," wrote: "After spending some $45 billion to make Smith's dream come true, General Motors has higher costs, sagging profit margins, uneven quality, and high-tech factories that don't seem worth all the trouble and expense." Certainly, if too much had been spent on high tech, too little had been done by GM to change its people and the ways in which they thought and acted. The resulting humiliation—a lower profit in 1986, for the first time ever, than Ford's—strongly suggested that more, and more radical, change was still required.

Across the Atlantic, faced with an equally imperative need to change, Britain's largest industrial company, the chemical giant ICI, had shown the true way. Its chairman changed (comparatively speaking) little in the organizational structure and made no giant-size, ambitious acquisitions to diversify the corporation. But Sir John Harvey-Jones, unlike GM's Smith, regarded his mandate as one to change, not so much the organization as the way people behaved inside the whale. Before rising to the top, Harvey-Jones had made no secret of his heretical ideas. Unusually, ICI elects its chairman. Harvey-Jones took that vote as a license to kill, to destroy, the old established ways and replace them with new—and better.

As always, in matters of leadership, at first sight it's difficult to separate Harvey-Jones's actions from his personality and personal style. A bluff, seemingly jovial former naval type, he talks in blunt business terms, and sought to instill blunt business thinking into his management. For instance, in a market where Du Pont leads, it wouldn't be sensible, with that particular rival, to try to dislodge him. If ICI did, the reaction would have terrible results for prices and profits: a Harvey-

Jones would rather contentedly settle in behind and make a great deal of money.

Conversely, if ICI is number one, it should never attempt to grind Du Pont down still further, but concentrate on maintaining, rather than expanding, its market share. The realism is much the same as that shown by Chrysler's Lee Iacocca. Speaking to *Fortune*, he said that "if GM gets 33% of the market and the imports get 30%, that leaves 37% for Ford and us. That's okay. That would give Ford 22% and us 15%, which is about right. We figure we should get about two-thirds of what Ford gets." Iacocca then wondered whether GM would be content with 33 percent, and read its executives' minds. "I'll bet you that internally they believe anything under 35% will be a disaster. So everybody will go nuts over that last 5%."

Going nuts is bad business and leads to bad decisions. Realism of the Harvey-Jones/Iacocca variety may sometimes lead to lost opportunities: it isn't the way Japanese think about market shares. But the realist sets parameters within which he can make sensible decisions. It's notable that great decision makers very often talk and act in terms of blunt common sense. For instance, listen to the authentic note of Harvey-Jones:

1. Use your young people as the initial contact in recruiting the young—but leave the hiring decision to your ripest and best.

2. When it comes to executive talent, work with what you've got as far as possible—only get new management when forced.

3. Hire women: they're so excellent that they have constituted 30 percent of ICI's recent graduate intakes.

4. Never make unfriendly acquisitions, and never make them just for financial reasons; do it either for the technology or (more likely) for the market share owned by the acquired firm.

5. Suit your products to the markets—ICI hasn't sold a single product to Japan unchanged.

Suiting your decisions to yourself, though, is the first essential for a chief executive, especially one who is in a hurry. Harvey-Jones had two reasons for haste. First, his term of office had to end, by company rules, in the spring of 1987. Second, ICI's business was sliding badly. In the third quarter of 1982, the group actually went into loss. There were plenty of reasons, or excuses, that were outside ICI's control—such as the strength of sterling and the weakness in world markets.

But the loss shocked the senior management into a mood of acceptance of change. This made it possible for Harvey-Jones to exercise his self-ordained mandate. The pressures were less imperative than those Iacocca had faced at Chrysler (which was out of cash and dying fast) but more imperative than they appeared to be at GM—where the Japanese threat didn't feel (as it should have) like a knife in the giant's ribs. But the new leader at ICI exemplified a crucial truth: deciding to change is only a first step; deciding to make the change effective counts more; making it effective ("making it happen," are the words that Harvey-Jones used in the title of his account of his remarkable stewardship) is the only decision that counts.

8. MAKING CHANGE PAY

All effective change begins from proper analysis of the starting point: where the company is now. Even in a $20 billion colossus such as ICI, the analysis seldom turns on sophisticated issues. The defects on which Harvey-Jones fastened could as easily have been discovered in a $15 million company—maybe even a $1.5 million one. That ICI had lapsed into loss wasn't surprising, given that, on its chairman's analysis:

1. Nobody was looking after the interests of the company as a whole.

2. Cash wasn't being managed properly.

3. New business wasn't being generated fast enough.

4. There was creeping centralization—the bureaucracy kept on swelling.

5. People weren't profit-conscious.

The *first* decision Harvey-Jones made was to take the board away for a week to reconsider the whole basis of the company. Even when the board is effectively one person, the proprietor, it's worth doing likewise. Getting away from the heat in the kitchen, and taking time out to think over the large decisions, is the surest way to clear the mind.

Second, out of that flowed a number of new decisions: new to ICI, that is. Thus, the group decided that no layer of management would be kept unless it made a "unique contribution." It always pays to ask Is this manager or this operation really necessary? What would happen if he or she or it disappeared? The answer may be most pleasantly surprising (except for the superfluous themselves): ICI got rid of *half* its layers.

Third, Harvey-Jones and his colleagues looked at many models before deciding what kind of company they wanted ICI to be. The choice fell on "chemical service company." Businesspeople who think such definitions pretentious and meaningless are not thinking. The definition was part of the decision to change. It meant stressing selling, not producing— and that in turn involved bringing the sales-and-research people into open contact (instead of the usual open warfare).

Asking what kind of company yours is or should become is only another way of finding out how and where the business can make the most of its existing resources and thus create the maximum quantum of new resources (that is, true profit). Size has nothing to do with that necessity. What business really makes the money? And does that business make sense? More, does it make enough of the money?

Since ICI self-evidently didn't make enough, and to ensure that the future would be different from the past, Harvey-Jones insisted on getting, from each part of the business, continual improvement compared to that past—and relative to the best competition. This *fourth* decision is vital. It means that performance must be measured all the time; for what isn't measured will improve only by accident, and what isn't subjected to demands for betterment almost certainly won't improve.

Fifth, Harvey-Jones decided that to achieve the "open company" he wanted, he had to start with a board whose numbers were low enough to manage an open relationship. Instead of two deputy chairmen he would have none. With the total board halved, Harvey-Jones was left with just seven executive colleagues; he insisted that the group had to discuss everything as a group—and discuss with no holds barred.

Sixth, the new chairman insisted that other managers should fall into the same pattern, breaking the ICI mold of conformity and forming "a federation of free men coordinating themselves." The decision was to abolish all head office controls, to wipe out the old idea of "divisions," with its bureaucratic implications and realities; instead, the eight central directors looked at the group as a collection of *businesses*—and each of these many businesses had a manager placed clearly and responsibly in charge.

There's nothing wonderful or complex about these last two points; right down to those of very small size, businesses are supposed to run that way. But in many businesses far smaller than ICI, discussion is neither free nor frank. Often, it doesn't exist; people don't say what they think, often for fear of angering the all-decisive (or all-indecisive) boss, and any contribution that other people might make is swamped by one-man decision making.

The strength of a Harvey-Jones is required to employ

people who express strong and contradictory opinions and actually to encourage them to be blunt to the point of painfulness. The habit of circumlocution, a particular vice of the British, leaves it unclear to anybody, often including the speaker, what is actually being said. While possibly more comfortable than bluntness, the habit leads inevitably to less effective direction and decision.

The *seventh* ICI decision hinged on this concept of clarity—saying clearly to management what was expected from them. At ICI, the business heads were all given simple, one-sentence general objectives: the manager running the colors business, for instance, was told decisively to stay in colors, improve his performance, make a specified financial contribution to the center, and live off his retained cash flow.

Again, this decision is applicable to any business. Managers who don't know what's expected of them and, anyway, are not given the authority to achieve whatever might have been expected, will not make the right decisions—and may make none at all. Drawing up brief statements for all key managers forces them to think; and because their bosses must define the tasks, makes the bosses think even harder.

Operational autonomy needs to be flavored with an essential oil: readiness to criticize. At ICI, Harvey-Jones and his seven cohorts staged three-monthly meetings at which they self-criticized one another, again with all holds allowed. The board meetings, too, were very carefully prepared: nobody was allowed to pass an issue without comment—and everybody's opinion was requested and given in turn, in a way far more reminiscent of Japanese top-level decision making than of the traditional Western style.

Indeed, that ICI principle is in illuminating contrast with the self-congratulatory, ill-focused board meetings that are the general Western rule (or misrule). A law of life as well as management is that the more you put in the more you get back. Most board meetings only take place because they are scheduled to take place. In contrast, the great decision makers in a decisive organization always have a reason for any meeting—and insist that the reason be reflected in the results.

There's a final lesson in what Harvey-Jones had to say in 1987 about progress so far: he observed that ICI was going reasonably well but that reasonably well wasn't good enough. The essential is to achieve dissatisfaction with performance, because dissatisfaction is the engine of change. The vehicle has a brake, too: it is fear of what change will bring and involve. A crucial part of the leader's job in deciding to change, and to make change permanent, is to ensure that people are neither afraid nor resting on their laurels—to make them realize that good isn't good enough, that only the "best" will do, and that even "best" doesn't end the story.

Change is a continual embracing of the best. The decision to enforce radical change, à la ICI, à la Chrysler, must be the outcome of the worst—of bad past decisions. The heroism of abandoning bulk manufacture of polyethylene plastic and polyester fiber, both great innovations originally launched on the world by ICI, was heroic only in its own terms. These pullouts of the Harvey-Jones era trace back directly to poor past management decisions that left ICI weak in the very world markets where it should have been strongest. Continual change to meet continually changing circumstances is the essence of good management, and the only means of avoiding situations in which, to use a phrase of Harvey-Jones's successor as chairman, Denys Henderson, only a program of *re*s will work.

ICI had to *re*structure, *re*duce costs, *re*shape its businesses (by widening its markets geographically and moving from bulk goods into "effect" chemicals—doing specific jobs for specific customers), and *re*generate them with new life and profit growth. That left little untouched, because very little didn't require touching—and heavy touches, at that. If that's the diagnosis, there's only one cure: decide to change everything, especially the hearts and minds of the people. If a Harvey-Jones can begin to do that in a far-spread group the size of ICI, then any organization on any scale can: even General Motors.

9. BIG BANG AT BIG BLUE

Of all the world's great companies, none has ever seemed more secure in its pattern, or surer in its methods, than International Business Machines—nor has any great business seemed to have better reason for self-assurance. It virtually created the computer age, catching up after a late start with a bulldozing momentum that swept all competitors out of its path. After another belated entry, it threatened to bulldoze through the personal computer upheaval in the same irresistible way. But, then, IBM was famous for, and prided itself on, its ability, rare among colossal organizations, to change and to manage change to its own vast and perennially growing profit.

The 1988 "Big Changes at Big Blue" (to quote a *Business Week* headline) were not, however, an evolutionary response by a smoothly running management machine to capitalize on changes in trend. Revolution, not evolution, was abroad. Chairman John Akers had been "handed an unprecedented challenge: masterminding the turnaround of a $50 billion company that no one had expected to be in trouble. . . . Dissatisfied with what he sees as temporary fixes, he has embarked on a strategy that involves nothing less than reinventing IBM." Security, sureness, and self-assurance no longer applied: the magazine talked about "arrogance, inertia, self-delusion and plain old corporate flab"—which, if you think about it, are the other sides of the same coin.

Successful organizations, like successful men and women, are easy prey to conceit, which helps to pack every success with the seeds of its own failure. In hindsight, the turning point for IBM came in 1984, when profits peaked at well over $6 billion. The peak coincided with the high point of IBM's onslaught in

PCs, and with a highly effective PR campaign promoting IBM as the mammoth whose competitive energies had been unleashed to thrilling effect by the end of a long antitrust case. Both insiders and outsiders swallowed the publicity whole. The real world didn't.

Stagnating sales and sliding profits (which slipped to under $5 billion) were the unhidden persuaders leading Akers to decide on IBM's most sweeping restructuring for three decades. For all that time, and indeed for all its history, IBM had been governed tightly by a small group of top managers (if not just one Watson). Now power was devolving to half a dozen general managers, each with a clearly defined section of the corporation's business put into his tender, loving care—or hers. In a spectacular and symbolic departure, not just for IBM but for American big business at large, IBM decided to place a woman, Ellen M. Hancock, in charge of a communications group that generated $5.5 billion of annual revenues—a number so vast in itself that it demonstrates the enormity of IBM's overall problems.

Akers had already had one try at shaking leviathan out of its complacency, with a massive program that led many thousands of employees into early retirement and forced others out of cushioned head office jobs into the hard front line of sales and marketing. That clearly wasn't enough. Did the new shake-up promise any better? Only if Akers could convert words into deeds. According to *Business Week*, he believed that "general managers can learn to think like entrepreneurs." His message to the new leaders was "to think of themselves as chief executives. In their markets, each one has a different set of competitors and role models."

Ellen Hancock thus had to aim at companies like AT&T, Northern Telecom of Canada, and Siemens of West Germany in the difficult effort to make sense out of the Rolm private branch exchange business (one of IBM's rare acquisitions, widely criticized for its price, its timing, and for having been made at all, Rolm has now been sold). Her manifold other problems—such as getting IBM's many computer systems to communicate intelligibly with one another—illustrate what has really shaken up IBM. Its once-homogeneous world has fragmented into businesses that interconnect but now must stand on their own (and sometimes failing) feet in sectors where the competition is formidable, often more so than IBM.

That's a major culture shock for a "king of the castle" or "cock of the walk." The IBM culture, however, is still intact and central, praised by none other than Robert Waterman in his book *The Renewal Factor* for keeping "fundamental business principles" in view: Andrew Campbell and Michael Goold, authors of *Strategies and Styles*, also laud the company for adhering to the "ideals" that, rather than any specific organizing principle, lead in their judgment to the best decision making. When Akers shook out 16,200 employees, for example, he did not abandon the company's famous commitment to avoid redundancies.

Cynics may see little practical difference between being fired and learning that your job is disappearing and wouldn't it be nice to take an early pension. Apparently the program helped to maintain the company loyalty that has always fortified IBM. But loyalty is one of those sides of the corporate coin with a less acceptable, antientrepreneurial reverse: inbreeding. The IBM way of top-down management, too, was another antithesis of the entrepreneurship that Akers had to encourage.

Not that IBM has failed to achieve great and fabled entrepreneurial success in the past. The most recent triumph was the IBM PC of 1981, which took Apple's industry by the scruff of the neck, established a new standard, and soared beyond anybody's expectations, including IBM's, to lead the market onward and upward. The public relations machine wasn't slow to blazon forth the secret of the PC success. The mountain had moved. Confronted with the surge of the Apples and the rest of the orchard, IBM had entrusted the whole PC onslaught to a separate group that, operating out on a limb in Boca Raton, Florida, had vital independence from the all-powerful IBM management machine.

Looked at from the perspective of the Akers reshuffle of 1988, why didn't the 1981 triumph of the boys from Boca Raton become the precedent for a much earlier breakup of the monolith? After all, they *were* separate; the business *was* discrete; the competition *was* identified ("eat Apple"); they *did* railroad through a great entrepreneurial achievement. But the machine wouldn't accept the independence—after the PC operation waxed large (and its managers messed up the smaller PC jr launch, et al.), back it went inside the Information Systems and Communications Group.

But where the original PC took a stunning one year to reach the market, its crucial successor, the Personal System/2, expected in mid-1985, took almost two years more, by which time IBM had lost a third of its market share to clones. This can stand as a parable showing exactly why IBM so badly needed the Akers shake-up. But organizational change, even if it made IBM's new general managers into entrepreneurs, wouldn't do the trick by itself. What about the people below them? And those lower down still? One IBM escapee (typically, now the boss of a rival PC company) pointed out to *Business Week*: "You really need to bring out the wild duck in people. And that's going to be difficult to do in a culture that prizes uniformity of approach and style."

Strenuous efforts down the years have gone into making the giants of commerce behave like one big business, even while selling varied products in multitudinous world markets. Now, paradoxically, they must be made to behave like several smaller businesses, none of which have the old easy dominance over the competition. IBM, Akers told Waterman, never reorganizes except for a good business reason, but if it hasn't done so in a while, "that's a good business reason." What happened at IBM, though, has several powerful, pressing, urgent, and ineluctable explanations. And they aren't business ones.

10. SEVEN CRACKED PILLARS

The reasons that demanded the Akers reforms of 1988 lay not in IBM's business present but in its cultural past. In its brilliant history, under the two Watsons, father and son, and the expert professional managers who succeeded them, a series of eminently justified decisions paid off in a market dominance, profitability, and technological capacity that no other organization has ever matched. And therein lay the trouble. To understand it requires backtracking to the earlier 1980s.

Then, as for many years, the computer giant had the most respected management in American and world business. IBM had seemed to slow down more than somewhat in the 1970s. But then it came bouncing back with the overwhelming success of the PC: "The Colossus That Works," announced a cover story in *Time* magazine. "Big Is Bountiful at IBM." Yet just forty months later, according to *Business Week*, Akers had "set up task forces to ask tough questions." Had IBM become too bureaucratic and slow? Was it too concerned with selling what it made rather than making what customers wanted? Was its traditional view of the world computer market out of date?

Amazingly, the weaknesses implied by this inquisition were in the very areas where IBM was supposed to have it supremely right, earning its place among the superhero companies in the superseller *In Search of Excellence*. This giant was supposed to have overcome bureaucracy by delegating authority down the line. As for getting out of date in the market, the theory was that no sparrow fell out there without IBM hearing the thud—and reacting. Above all, executives would tell you at the drop of a question, IBM was "customer led." So how could it have become production-oriented? What are the lessons for other companies? If so intensively managed a company can go so wrong, all are vulnerable to the same disease.

The germs of that disease can be found in the foundations of IBM's dominance, which rested on seven pillars of wisdom and strength; all seven built by long-standing decisions, some taken as far back as the founding Tom Watson and apparently confirmed by all the years of subsequent unexampled success. Read these seven decisions, moreover, and it's impossible to fault their sense or their coherence.

Decision 1. Hire the brightest people you can find, develop them intensively, and promote exclusively from within. This gives you a tightly knit, highly motivated group of executives who know the business deeply and intimately.

Decision 2. Build management in great depth—so that whatever happens, and wherever it happens, the company can respond in full force with able, experienced people.

Decision 3. Don't stint on the spending required to keep you in the forefront on all aspects of the business.

Decision 4. Give employees total security. So long as they want to work for you, there's a job—and this lifetime guarantee will provide the basis for powerful motivation, loyalty, and excellent labor relations.

Decision 5. Build such market dominance that the market invariably waits on your next move. When that comes, your control over customers is so powerful that the opposition, like Apple in personal computers, is holed amidships even after an undisturbed two-year run in the marketplace.

Decision 6. Lay extraordinary emphasis on the sales side, and pride yourself on "closeness" to the customer. This not only produces amazing market shares, but makes much of the selling semiautomatic—customers feel unsafe buying any product other than yours.

Decision 7. Cover the waterfront. Your market is your domain, and you ensure that customers need go nowhere else for their requirements. It's one-stop shopping, and you're the only stop.

These seven pillars of IBM's wisdom, however, all have consequences and reverse sides, just as all the great decision makers recorded in the Introduction to this book have gross failures to offset the shining successes. They included one of IBM's chairmen, John R. Opel, whose decision to attack the personal computer market triumphed, but was created in such a manner, possibly because of the very low sales expectations, as to engender attack by smaller companies. That onslaught proceeded to inflict more damage on IBM than the opposition of all its mainframe competitors put together.

But the erosion of IBM's market share, nibbled away by minnows, had been going on for a long time before the PC clones had thought of cloning. Over the 1970s, the whale's world market share had shrunk from 60 percent to 40 percent—if the market were defined (as it should have been) as the entire field of electronic data processing. But IBM failed to build its strategic decisions around what should have been a disturbing loss of share. Even when it did attack in personal computers, it wasn't with any idea of creating a major second front: the company was taken aback by a strength of demand that forced total reappraisal of its long-term strategy.

This loss of market, no less than the loss of insight into the market's changes, reflected IBM's lack of awareness that its seven strong, superb decisions involved seven other decisions—all potentially terribly wrong, and all requiring other decisions to act as antidotes to insidious dangers. To recap, those Seven Pillars are:

1. Internal promotion.
2. Management in depth.
3. Intensive investment.
4. Job security.
5. Market dominance.
6. Sales leadership.
7. Waterfront coverage.

The seven consequent and countervailing unconscious decisions stem straight from these.

1. To have an inbred bunch of people who look only inward and ignore what's going on outside—even the obvious. "There are a lot of guys at IBM headquarters who have never seen a Macintosh," one refugee said to *Business Week*, referring to Apple's highly innovative best-seller.

2. To have the many layers of management that inevitably go with depth—meaning that your decisions get slowed to the point where, said another IBM refugee, "you can't make a change in a year. It takes more like three."

3. To spend too much. IBM lavished $28 billion on investment in five years during which the computer market was heading for recession, and paid the price in sluggish profits. Spending subsequently came under heavy pressure ("So it's farewell," noted *Business Week*, "to sunny California conferences and 'must' visits to IBM's lab on the French Riviera"); but the damage had been done.

4. To be overstaffed. The cost of excess employees was running at half a billion dollars a year, or an eleventh of IBM's profits. The company had to resort to natural wastage, early retirement options, insisting that people take accrued holidays, and only hiring 1,000 graduates a year—a sixth of the level three years back. Also, the insistence on moves from HQ jobs into sales offices included farflung places people would hate enough to quit.

5. To have your people believe that they are the market, and can follow their own timetable in introducing new products without bothering too much about the competition. Digital Equipment exploded that one in IBM's face. With 85 percent of its products less than eighteen months old, against only 40 percent for IBM, DEC ripped into IBM's share of the corporate market. In PCs, competitors such as Compaq have again set the competitive pace.

6. To have a sales force that's conceited and underestimates both the customers and the competition. According to an IBM man: "We focused on the competitiveness of each individual computer and lost a little sight of the customer's needs." Being translated (into the words of a customer), that meant "trying to ram a product down your throat." Said another: "Now, they're willing to spend more time understanding our needs."

7. You decide to have a business so broad that it's impossible to concentrate on everything at once—especially when all decision making is centralized.

Of course, it's brilliantly easy to be clever in hindsight. Nobody suspected that the Seven Pillars, like the massive supports for Wren's St. Paul's Cathedral, were filled with cheap material that threatened to crack the pillars and bring down much of the structure. Even after IBM's profits, on those stagnating sales, had executed their downhill run, both insiders and expert outsiders found it hard to believe in fundamental faults. Buck Rodgers, IBM's former marketing director and author of *The IBM Way*, thought the company way was still largely OK: Robert Waterman, co-author of *In Search of Excellence*, cited IBM and Akers most, and most favorably, in his *The Renewal Factor*, basing his verdict partly on profitability, which was significantly greater than DEC's. A hasty postscript acknowledged that, after 1986's results, this uplifting difference no longer held.

DEC had taken the lead on this count, just as it had long led IBM in one of those markets, minicomputers, where IBM, locked into rigid thinking by the Seven Secret Decisions, had failed to compete very effectively. These situations, by their nature, are subject to change. Now, as noted earlier, IBM prided itself on abnormally high ability to change, a flexibility almost unique among corporations of great scale. But the Seven Pillars held IBM immutably into a stiff pattern that actually inhibited the changes that the giant patently needed.

An eighth decision must be made to make an organization magnificently mutable. Decide that no decision is ever final. IBM seemed to have passed this ultimate examination splendidly when it spirited the PC operation out of the corporate hulk and gave it that near-total autonomy. If those who praised this novelty (myself among them) had known that the PC group would be pulled back inside the whale, the plaudits would have been stillborn.

Will the 1988 decision to replicate the essence of the Boca Raton decentralization by subdividing the entire corporation fare any better? Not without that eighth decision that no decision is ever sacrosanct. That demands incorporating another eight elements into the decision apparatus—both in the mind of the decision maker and in the climate of the organization.

First, since every strength creates a potential weakness, decide in advance what the risks are. Play devil's advocate, or get another devil to criticize the present and potential defects of the operation. Discuss the threats at a special "off-campus" meeting—and act decisively on whatever the discussion throws up.

Second, decide against inbreeding, and watch out for its signs. Persistent and automatic denigration of the competition is one. Force people out into the marketplace to experience what competitors are doing at first hand. Look for opportunities to bring in new blood—and don't make new people conform to the corporate norms until they have been given the chance to suggest possible improvements from their past experience. Always ask all hands, old or new, whether there's a better way—especially where the old way has operated for all living memory.

Third, decide to keep layers of management down to a minimum, and never allow hierarchy and bureaucracy to slow the decision process. When a subject comes up for a decision, always fix a date by when that decision must be made. Don't overrun without compelling reason—and always fix a new deadline if inevitable delays occur.

Fourth, don't get carried away by boomtime results. Decide against extravagance in current and capital spending as strongly when business is magnificent as when it is miserable— and that includes staff numbers. Be careful and parsimonious in hiring (but never be mean on pay).

Fifth, decide that no part of the market will ever be taken for granted, no matter how strong the company's position, and that no fall in market share or any other vital statistic will ever be ignored—the figures may be messengers bearing bad news that nobody wants to hear.

Sixth, never boast about how close you are to the customer; let him boast about that. Decide to hear what the customers say about the relationship, and act on what they say.

Seventh, decide on the business areas where you must concentrate your efforts, and concentrate a good, responsible management around each area.

The last decision is the historic one Akers took in 1988. But any decision to change the organization, to alter its ways, convert its weaknesses into strengths, and accentuate its positive virtues, must be backed by an eighth point. After choosing the right people to manage the right businesses in their own right ways, decide to let them manage, to make their own decisions, and stick to that principle so long as the chosen justify your trust. Then, perhaps, the company will be as good as IBM was supposed to be—and could still be again.

To summarize some of the main points I've made about the improvers:

1. Leading the market is more than market share: it means leading in everything.

2. Deciding to achieve total quality can make billions: not making that decision can cost billions.

3. For the old pro in buying companies and betting alike, there is only one question that truly matters: Is the price right?

4. Don't buy companies without (a) excellent management, existing or available; (b) deep knowledge, existing or available, of the business; and (c) a big prize in prospect *and* available.

5. When it comes to detail, manage by exception; intervene at random, but vigorously.

6. When it comes to overall strategy, forget the detail— but never forget that the vision depends on the reality.

7. Deciding to change is only a first step; deciding to make the change effective counts more; making it happen is the only change that counts.

8. Unless you build continual change into the corporate way of life, you will fail to meet continually changing circumstances.

9. Every right decision carries within it the seeds of its own destruction.

10. Choose the right people to manage the right businesses in the right way. Let them manage and let them make their own decisions—so long as they justify your choice.

VI

THE
PLANNERS

Planning comes and goes with the tides of management fashion, but the basic activity of plotting the future of the organization can't stop—not if the organization is to have a future. The trouble is that planners in different companies tend to march to the same drum, not surprisingly, since they share basic assumptions about the present and future, as their predecessors did in the past. History in turn means that many big thinkers will be starting from similar positions, as well as heading for the same goals. The gyrations of Dart & Kraft, from separate food and nonfood giants, to union, to unscrambling, or those of Gould from smokestacks to high tech to smokestack takeover, are extreme proofs of a truth that applies to management as to investment: you don't make the big money by following the big crowds.

The weakness of the conventional wisdom is even more dramatically demonstrated by cases like that of the also-ran Japanese brewer, Asahi. Its management rightly concluded that its fragility and feeble performance arose not just from its own failures but from those of the whole industry. Acting on that perception produced a turnaround of the spectacular variety that is always possible for decision makers who base their planning not on extrapolating from the company's and the market's present position and preconceptions but on going outside both the company and the conventional wisdom to uncover an almost inevitable gap: the divergence of consuming interests from those of production.

That gap has been the key to the unprecedented competitive pressure exerted on IBM by almost infinitely smaller computer makers, even by start-ups. None of the latter has grown faster or further than Compaq, for the good and sufficient reason that its decision makers set their minds, plans, and decisions on achieving that exceptional growth from the very start. That meant applying the same ambitious standards and targets to every aspect of the operation—and the lesson of all companies wishing to achieve similar strength, whether or not they are competing with omnipresent giants, is that the planning must be comprehensive: the whole will fail unless all the parts are equally strong.

It's notorious, however, that the parts of large corporations are as uneven as a flood-damaged country road. But the failures of the pothole divisions don't necessarily flow from weak management or bad businesses at the subsidiary level. The fault lies at the center of the corporation whose planning revolves around pushing enterprises into categories and treating them accordingly. Starve any company of investment funds because it doesn't meet planning criteria, assign it and its managers a lowly place in the corporate priorities, and you virtually guarantee that it will live up, or down, to your low opinion. What its corporate parent did to Premier Brands flies in the face of all logic: no organization can be maximized unless optimum performance is obtained across the board, and that, as Premier's bought-out success proceeded to show, demands dynamic, not static, planning.

The organization tends to a static view of itself and its marketplace; it creates its own conventional wisdom, which may be just as unwise as the external consensus of the corporate lemmings. The anonymous West German manufacturer, cited in this Part, section 9, "The Mercedes of the Industry," which was wholly wrong on four strongly held internal views, is no exception. Nor is it exceptional that the correction to its planning assumptions had to come from outsiders. The extent of corporate inner blindness is one powerful reason for supposing that boards of directors are ineffective strategic guides. The strategy and the style are set by executive top managements that have inadequate checks and balances. The most effective counterweight, though, is the one that top executives in the West find hardest to allow: the right of lower management to be right, and to have its rightness accepted and enacted.

1. THE DIVORCE OF DART & KRAFT

Once upon a time, the conventional wisdom held that food manufacturers were vulnerable to low margins and low growth. It followed that their correct course was to diversify away from food into other goodies—preferably products where the consumer marketing skills honed in catering to the American kitchen could be brought triumphantly to bear in faster-growing markets. As for nonfood consumer goods makers, the collective conventional mind had words of wisdom for them, too: since their businesses, while growing more rapidly, were very likely cyclical, they should seek the guaranteed stability of food.

No two managements took this wisdom more deeply to heart than those of Dart & Kraft—the name the twain adopted in 1980 when the former company's Duracell batteries, Tupperware, and variegated appliances were merged with Kraft's cheese-based business in foodstuffs. It's a commonplace that only half (at most) of all mergers succeed, but it's very rare for mergers of giants to be unscrambled, especially by the same man who whipped up the eggs in the first place. But John M. Richman in 1986 decided to split up the $9.9 billion corporation that he had created only six years previously—and apparently for good reason, or reasons.

As *Business Week* tells it, the conventional wisdom had got it wrong. Food outgrew nonfood, and not only because a tightened-up Kraft management struck gold with Velveeta Mexican and other new treats, which helped push up operating profits by 10.3 percent compounded over five years. The other main factor was that crucial nonfood businesses, above all Tupperware, failed to perform. Like Avon's cosmetics, which similarly depended on woman-to-woman selling in the home, Tupperware had reached the point of diminishing returns—its margins had all but halved.

A former executive told the magazine that "Tupperware had such high market penetration and profitability" at the time of the merger "that to expect it to continue to grow was probably unrealistic." By the time of the de-merger, expectations for Tupperware were so low that Richman placed it in the ragbag of companies left behind as Kraft's foods headed off after new glory—along with the inedible Duracell batteries, included for no better reason than that their sales were the fastest-growing segment of the six-year merger that literally came unstuck.

Which of Richman's decisions was correct? The one to merge, the one to split, or both? It's true that, even over so relatively short a period as six years, circumstances can change sufficiently to turn right into wrong; it's also true that great decisions sometimes demand great changes of mind. But the governing factor in the de-merger decision wasn't simply the disappointing performance of Tupperware or any other component of the business. As Richman explained his move: "Our progress is developing on two separate tracks. Over time we feel Kraft would not be recognized for the power it is in the food industry."

Being translated, this meant that the conventional wisdom, which six years before had held food companies in disregard, now strongly favored what *Business Week* called "back-to-basic food stocks": none more so than Philip Morris, which, in late 1988, bid $11.5 billion, then a world nonoil record, for Richman's baby. As for nonfood consumer products, that same conventional wisdom now distrusted their cyclicality much more than it fancied their growth. Back in 1980, by the same token, the conventionally wise didn't fancy the growth prospects, or anything else, involved in the traditional, boring American industries such as making batteries, which were far outshone, in the eyes of the wise, by the promise and performance of electronics.

Nobody took this view more to heart than William T. Ylvisaker, as noted in the Introduction. His company, Gould Inc., had been selling $100 million of batteries when he took charge. By the time his traditional lines, and their profit performance, grew boring to him and Wall Street, sales had multiplied twenty times in a decade. He decided to shed everything save the high-technology electronics businesses and to add to them by vigorous acquisition until Gould was totally gee-whiz. By 1983, three-quarters of its $1.7 billion in sales, and virtually all its earnings, were electronic.

But by then, too, the conventional wisdom was becoming disenchanted with high technology, even more so when the semiconductor business staged one of its periodic declines shortly after a large Gould acquisition. Failure to price a naval defense contract properly only emphasized the defects of Ylvisaker's original decision: its error was rubbed in by huge profits earned in the very smokestack industries Gould had deserted— and that the conventional wisdom now applauded.

Nippon Mining, a Japanese company with a nonferrous

metals business full of smokestacks, bought what was left of Gould for $1.1 billion in 1988. Ylvisaker, who had departed two years previously, was no longer there. He had bet his company and his career on the conventional wisdom and lost. Is the conventional wisdom ever wise?

2. GOING AGAINST THE GRAIN

Many of the most brilliant decisions in history, and not just business history, have been made by geniuses who went against the grain of accepted opinion, of that same conventional wisdom. In the Battle of the Bulge, two unconventional strokes canceled each other out—von Rundstedt's winter thrust against all the traditions of German armies was trumped by Patton's decision that his enemy had done precisely that. That great German gamble ultimately failed because it relied on an opposition that would not expect, and thus would not react to, the unexpected.

The history of stock markets, however, gives the clearest guide to the value of the unconventional wisdom. Most of the truly great investors have belonged to the school that has come to be known as "contrarian." It isn't as simple as saying that if everybody else is buying gold you sell, and vice versa. The true contrarian isn't interested in what others are doing at all. He may well be a Grahamite—one of the followers of Ben Graham, who sensibly seek "values" for the money they invest (see the discussion of this in "Hunting the Anomaly," in Part III).

A "value" could be discovered on a rising or falling market; the contrarian is only interested in whether the current market price significantly undervalues the asset. But, of course, undervaluation is far more likely to arise when nobody is buying the stock, commodity, or some other gewgaw than when everybody is pouring in loot. By definition, the contrarian tends to be in a minority. But why on this earth should the maverick, the rebel in the crowd, ever be right and the mass ever wrong?

In stock markets, the answer is easy. Any generally held view—as in the first half of 1987—to the effect that Wall Street is moving inexorably into the blue sky beyond becomes a self-fulfilling prophecy. Share prices rise because they are rising. Worse, vested interests develop in the boom: the major institutional investors, who are massively invested in the risen shares, have as much interest in sustaining the bull market, in words and deeds, as the small private investor. The pundits are no different: like the big investors, they look over their shoulders to see what the other fellows are doing.

For example, suppose some busybody had wished to know how fast the American economy would grow between the fourth quarter of 1986 and the closing three months of the new year. From the forecasts of thirty-nine business economists assembled by *Business Week,* forecasters whose employers range from Prudential Insurance to Reynolds Metals, you could take your pick between a GNP rise of 5 percent or a decline of 1 percent and that's the difference between boom and serious recession. Now turn to the professional pundits whose tool is the *model:* the sets of complex equations (2,500 are used in the Wharton Annual and Industry version) that mimic the real relationships in the real economy. Number-crunching computers run the models, but does their sophistication yield any better results?

On that same crucial point, the year's growth in the U.S. economy, eleven econometric services showed a much smaller variation than the thirty-nine business economists: between 2.1 and 3.9 percent (although a divergence of 86 percent is scarcely negligible). A cynic would explain the closer identity of the commercial services not by their greater sophistication but by general hedging of bets. Forecasters will tweak a computer number that doesn't fit with their uncomputerized expectations, and if they tweak in the direction of the consensus, nobody will be a bit surprised.

But managers can't claim any greater wisdom. The same magazine in 1985 reviewed thirty-three corporate strategies that it had described in 1979 or 1980; only half a decade later, nineteen "failed, ran into trouble, or were abandoned." Worse still, the list of fourteen strategies that could then "be deemed successful" included a couple, American Motors and Gould, that have since come notoriously unstuck.

For managers as for economists, it's far less dangerous professionally to be in step with almost everybody else than to be out on a limb that may, at any moment, be sawn off. It takes a bold fellow such as Sir James Goldsmith to take one intuitive sniff at a roaring bull market, dislike the smell, and dump over half a billion dollars of holdings—thus avoiding maybe $200 million of Black Monday losses. Only after October 19 did the great majority of alleged experts draw attention to the myriad of signs from which those lacking Goldsmith's intuition could have decided, with perfect rationality, that a Wall Street bubble had formed and was about to burst.

The bad (for which read average) investor is psychologically unable to think—or at least to act—in contrarian style. When stocks or a whole stock market are bizarre bargains—the London market fell below 150 on the *Financial Times* index in 1973, at which point dividends were practically being given away—the average investor stays clear for fear of even grosser disaster. The average decision maker is no different: he fears making a decision that contradicts the general view because he fears that the mob knows more than he does; by the same wrong-headed token, he climbs on bandwagons because he fears being left behind.

In the supposedly exalted realms of international finance the Gadarene phenomenon has seen swinelike rushes to lend billions to Third World countries with no visible means of paying the interest, let alone the debt, or, more recently, to risk vast sums to finance highly speculative takeovers at grossly exorbitant prices. In national banking, the rush over the precipice has been no less unanimous. It took a seemingly suicidal Texas banker to resist the clamor for energy and real estate loans. After all, his local competition was rapidly building its business in these sectors, whose security was underwritten— according to the conventional wisdom—by the scarcity and soaring cost of oil.

One Texas bank, MCorp, the second largest in the state, while not suicidal, was thought at least circumspect: a mere third of its loan portfolio was in real estate—a piddling (for a Texan) $4 billion or so. By mid-1988, true, a quarter of these loans were foreclosed or *nonperforming* (a euphemism for dead as a doornail), but that again was modest for Texas. The modesty didn't outlast a visit by bank examiners in July 1988. Their critical view of MCorp's real estate debt cut the bank's equity to under 2 percent of assets, spelling finis for "the most conservative bank in Texas." As the *Financial Times* summed up the all but unbelievable truth: "Every major bank and savings institution in Texas has now effectively failed."

The conventional wisdom may, of course, actually be right. But there's inherently less value in riding with the mob than running against it. When ninety-nine managers out of a hundred believe that personal computers will yield huge growth rates and vast profits forevermore, the following results must follow:

1. The number of competitors will increase beyond the point of comfort.

2. In consequence, the individual competitor's volumes, margins, and growth rates will tend to be lower than anticipated.

3. A small hiccup in the market's overall growth will

herald major intestinal problems from which some competitors will die, and all will suffer.

The clever contrarian tackling a bull market looks for a loophole—a way in other than the main gate. The Japanese customarily investigate distribution methods very closely when invading a market. If the established companies are selling directly to independent retail outlets, the Japanese will turn to wholesalers or owned outlets—and vice versa. When they tackled the personal computer market in Britain, however, they went along with the prevailing wisdom—selling through existing retailers and with home computers very little different from the largely American competition. They failed.

A local competitor, Alan Sugar, cut his teeth on home computers sold through the same outlets that handled his main product line, stereos. If Amstrad had stuck to this market, it would have stuck. Sugar took an imaginative, contrarian leap. Since word processing accounted for the overwhelming bulk of all PC usage, why not make a dedicated word processor? And, instead of undercutting the competition by a few pounds, why not bring the product in at under half PC levels at $570, far less than the price of an IBM PC and also below that of an IBM electric typewriter?

Sugar got his machines made cheaply abroad, using obsolete technology whose passing had left Far Eastern suppliers desperate to unload outdated components cheaply. The contrarian then became the first computer marketer to attack consumers directly with his advertising. The launch was a disaster—the manual didn't make sense, some purchasers were spending ten days on what the manual called "your first twenty minutes with your Amstrad," the print quality was poor, the floppy discs couldn't be bought—but the product was a triumph. Amstrad was soon selling 50,000 a month of an obsolescent machine that became the market base for a serious, sophisticated onslaught on higher-up reaches of the PC market.

The conventional wisdom holds that a market is defined by its current boundaries and its future extrapolated growth. This makes absolutely no allowance for "the Amstrad effect," in which market size is radically uplifted by the impact of mass-marketed, low-priced entrants in a specialized, high-priced sector. This would be the highest-risk ploy for a manufacturer: but Amstrad was a "hollow corporation," engaged in design and marketing only, which had been its wont ever since Sugar began his odyssey from antenna salesman, via packaged stereo (really repackaged radiograms), to his status as PC lion of Europe.

The totally unconventional decisions Sugar took all along that course (which made him a demibillionaire in sterling) stem from a rough, tough personality that had no time for listening to those who told him what couldn't be done—for this kind of chorus: "I do not find it easy to see. . . . I find it hard to understand. . . . I cannot see how. . . . It is impossible. . . . It is difficult to see."

These five wimpish nonstatements came from no less than eighteen similar warbles quoted by Richard Dawkins in his brilliant book *The Blind Watchmaker*; found in a single chapter of a distinguished theologian's book, the chorus is stigmatized by Dawkins as "The Argument from Personal Incredulity." The incredulous cleric was refusing to believe in natural selection, but the quotes might as well have referred to the possibility of selling computers like cornflakes. Whenever the true contrarian hears people talking out of prejudice rather than persuasion by fact, he reaches for his checkbook.

Great decision makers instinctively subject the conventional wisdom to rigorous testing. Why does "everybody" believe that this view of the market is true? Write down all the reasons, good or bad—and then become devil's advocate. Why might "everybody" be wrong? First, challenge *their* reasons; second, write down any of your reasons, in your role of diabolic advocacy, for believing the opposite. Next, what will the consequences be if you go against the conventional wisdom and (1) it proves right or (2) it proves wrong?

Almost certainly, the risk/reward ratio will be strongly in favor of (2): that is, you stand to make far more profit from an independent swim against the stream (Sugar's profit virtually doubled every year from 1980 to the $173.2 million net of 1987) than you risk from not joining the shoals of fish going in the opposite direction—provided that your analysis has been thoroughgoing and conclusive. It will often show that the conventionally wise have been neither. Take the accepted view that world financial markets were going to be dominated by massive conglomerates formed by colossal mergers—groups like Phibro-Salomon. In practice, hit by massive overstaffing, narrowing margins, and then the Black Monday crash, the whales became vulnerable, and Salomon was forced into heavy retrenchment even before that awful October day.

That was bad news for one investor, who had paid heavily for his company's 12 percent stake in Salomon and saw its value halve in weeks. His name? Warren Buffett, the intellectual heir of Ben Graham, and the man who became a billionaire by bucking the crowd. Even contrarians can get their decisions wrong, especially when "everybody" agrees that they are right.

3. THE DRY BEER OF ASAHI

Being an also-ran can become a way of life. It's seldom a very profitable one. If Heller's Law of Markets holds (and it generally does), only the two leading companies and one specialist earn acceptable returns from any market; the few exceptions (such as personal computer companies in the mid-1980s) are so few that they merely prove the rule—and the exceptional conditions seldom last, anyway. This might seem to make the sad lot of the also-ran permanent: it has neither the market share nor the money with which to finance its elevation.

The decisions made by a brewer named Hiroharo Higuchi, however, demonstrate that the only necessary permanence of the permanent also-ran is the stuck mentality of the management. An also-ran has certain strengths, both negative and positive. The latter include long knowledge of and acceptance by the market—the business isn't rising from the seafloor. Higuchi's brewery, Asahi, had grown vigorously up to the death of its postwar founder in keen competition against the two leaders, Kirin and Sapporo. Death was followed by decay: when Higuchi took hold in 1986, market share was down below 10 percent. But that was at least a positive base.

On the negative side, any company that has suffered market erosion of that gravity must be guilty of profound and blatant error. Not only is the also-ran full of sin, but there's a more intriguing probability: that its superior opposition also has vulnerable points—especially since also-rans tend to follow their leaders, only ineptly and with less muscle power, hence their inferior results. Higuchi decided that this weakness lay in an endemic fault of brewers the whole world over. As an Asahi manager told the *Financial Times,* his company and its conquering competitors believed alike that "customers would drink whatever the brewer said was good for them."

Finding out what the customers want has a certain basic simplicity. You ask them. Market research among 5,000 store customers established that they liked, but didn't get, their beer strong in flavor, high in alcohol, and low in aftertaste. Asahi had found the platform for a product new to the Japanese market, a beer with distinctive qualities that, if the researchers were right, would win high consumer preference. But Higuchi's professionalism included the knowledge that good decisions cannot soar from weak launch pads. Before trying the new, he revamped the old.

The existing beer was relaunched with new labels and free sampling (a million-can giveaway) in a hard, thorough campaign. Its thrust was to push the Asahi name and corporate identity in front of the customer and (so to speak) down his throat. Sales rose by 10 percent, setting the stage Higuchi needed for the launch of Dry Beer—which, of course, isn't dry at all. The increased alcoholic strength (5 percent against 4.5 percent) did make the cunningly named Asahi Super Dry taste marginally less sweet. It thus met the market research brief, but nothing prepared Asahi for the phenomenal surge in demand.

According to the *Financial Times*'s Stefan Wagstyl, Asahi expected its now-proven marketing technique, complete with one million given-away cans, to sell a million cases between launch in March 1987 and the end of the year. The actual sale was 13.5 million—a bonanza that the other brewers dared not ignore. Wagstyl reports that Asahi started to attack the me-too "dry" products as commercial theft before it realized that the rival brews were widening the whole sector dramatically. Despite (and partly because of) the competition, Asahi doubled its amazing 1987 sales in just six months of 1988, as its doubled market share came desperately close to the second-ranking Sapporo.

Of course, Higuchi made many decisions of detail that in hindsight look brilliant—like using advertising with a he-man image. And, as Wagstyl points out, purveyors of basically unchanging beers were missing out in a national market that, in product after product, was splitting (like many markets the whole world over) into more and more diversity of choice. But the ultimate factor behind Super Dry's supersuccess was Higuchi's decision that an also-ran could win—decide to the contrary, and there's one certain result: you can't.

4. DESIGNING THE DIFFERENCE

Heavy corporate long-range planning has lost vogue as a method of making decisions. Its present downs, like its previous ups, spring from flawed understanding of what planning is. True, decision makers would dearly love to paint an entirely correct picture of the environment and the market, assess accurately the resources the corporation can deploy in the present, and point to those that will be required in the future to meet the plan's wonderful objectives. In those perfect conditions, decisions could be torn off the corporate printout page by page—and nobody would need to agonize over their soundness.

But conditions are never perfect, assumptions about the environment and the market are often false, and corporations make ludicrous errors even in planning their own manpower and manufacturing needs. Perfect planning rightly attracts the scorn of skeptics like a leading British industrialist who demanded to know if anyone could tell him the consequences of the impending privatization of a critically large customer. Without that knowledge, how could the future of the business be "planned"?

At first sight, the surge of Asahi might seem to support the cynic. After all, a plan that aims at shifting a million cases of beer, and ends by moving thirteen and a half times as many, can't be maintained as a model of accuracy. Asahi's previous weakness must have been a saving strength: the awful fall in its sales presumably created huge unused capacity for the new beer boom. Asahi was thus spared the embarrassment of IBM when demand for its PC took off into the wildest and bluest of yonders and couldn't be met.

Many decisions are only as good as the accompanying contingency *planning*—there's that word again. It means working out a course of action in advance; it is not a prediction (which is where the industrial skeptic went wrong), but a map for traveling from A (where you are) to B (where you want to be). A man of utterly different stamp from the skeptical industrialist had grasped this essence; with his colleagues, this creative expert, one of a breed looked down on by practical men, had decided where their middling-size advertising agency wanted to be in ten years' time.

This was in a business, note, that can be cast into turmoil by one unplanned, unplannable loss of a single major advertising account. But that by no means invalidated an exercise whose very existence greatly strengthened the agency's chances of reaching its "planned" destination.

Methodically mapping the future in this sensible way seems to come more naturally to Japanese than to Western minds. The Western brain focuses readily on aims such as achieving a 15 percent annual increase in earnings per share (which sounds as hard as nails, but is both meaningless and useless), or running at a return on capital employed of some given figure (better than the earnings-per-share target, but not much).

There's no good reason, or reason at all, why planning where the corporation wants to be, in qualitative as well as quantitative terms, should come less easily in the West. After all, Higuchi's objective, presumably to overtake Sapporo and become number two in Japanese beer (if not number one), is as "hard" (in both senses of the adjective) as any financial objective. The difference is that Higuchi's target embodies a qualitative decision: to improve the market recognition and penetration of Asahi's beers so that its share will more than double.

Financial objectives, however concrete, tell you nothing about how they are going to be achieved. The horse is put firmly behind the cart. Nothing has been decided, except to make some as yet unspecified decisions. It's true that corporate plans that began with these mighty numbers went on to specify the means, including both acquisitions and organic growth, by which the targets were to be achieved. But these plans, for sure, were far less often realized than Japanese strategies in which product quality, status, and success were the be-all and end-all.

Part of the sea of troubles with Western corporate planning was the partial divorce between the planners and the management. The plans of individual businesses, true, were bound together in the corporate whole, but the ethos forming, the number crunching, and the decision making (for what it was worth) took place at the head office. This often drained the entire process of vitality, even of commonsense management and practical planning, if both words are used in their true senses.

To give one example among tens of thousands: a division of General Motors produced a plan for a new model; it hinged on selling the car at $10,000. All price decisions at GM, however, are made by a head office committee. It insisted on riding over, and overriding, all the arguments the divisional managers could offer; the price was fixed at $12,500—at which the car duly flopped. Now, it can't be proved that $10,000 would have brought success (though it would surely have brought larger sales). But it can certainly be proved, up to the hilt, that this was a rotten way to run a car company, or anything else.

No new model can be planned intelligently without the price's being built into the plan. Without that, managements are wasting their time in planning at all—and without detailed, clever, exhaustive planning, they are wasting most of their time in launching new products.

According to one survey, firms that planned their innovation, concentrating on screening ideas more effectively, cut the number of ideas considered per successful introduction to seven over a thirteen-year period. If that doesn't sound impressive, consider how many ideas were needed per success at the outset: it was *fifty-eight*. And if *that* seems excessive, study after study has shown that a figure very close to it, and possibly higher, is the norm. The key to this reduction is the same methodical analysis of good information that lies beneath all effective decision making.

Not only are fewer ideas needed for success, but more new products succeed than before. Companies that planned their innovation saw the proportion of successful new investments rise from 30 percent to 54 percent over the thirteen years. The improvement represents an 18-karat saving in time and money; but the final outcome doesn't seem any too marvelous. All that time and trouble—and the odds on success still work out at no better than evens. Surely something is wrong. Why aren't all new products like Asahi Super Dry?

Success a great deal less super would do nicely. It isn't obtained better than half the time, even in companies that are relatively good innovators, because of a very limited number of mistakes by the decision maker. He can be wrong about any of the following.

1. The potential size of the market.
2. Its readiness to accept the innovation.
3. The fit between the product characteristics and the customer demand.
4. The price at which the innovation could be launched.
5. The effectiveness of competitor retaliation.
6. The time it would take for the innovation to be accepted.

These errors aren't mutually exclusive; decision makers often get them all wrong, as IBM did when it launched the PC jr, the down-sized, lower-priced, and ill-conceived attack on a home computer market that was about to slump. But you needn't get them all right—Asahi's plan contained some spectacular errors, fortunately all on the right side: underestimates rather than overestimates. Its success hinged on number 3: the fit between the consumer preferences shown in its market research and the beer itself. In food and drink products, there can be no other hinge. In any market, an opposite, adverse reaction must mean death—making this the area where the most and best information, and the most searching and thorough analysis, are most essential.

It's also the area where also-rans are least effective. Maybe they operate in a market where the leaders have the waterfront covered and every taste and need tapped. This, however, is no more likely than the flights of science fiction. The also-ran is a me-tooer by nature. Me-too is a decision to fail. Asahi's decision to succeed was a decision to be different. It sounds more daring than imitation. Actually, it's far safer—and more sensible.

5. THE EARLY RUN OF COMPAQ

In the summer of 1987 a major European retail chain was about to place an order for electronic point-of-sale (EPOS) equipment. EPOS is the sine qua non of modern retailing, the technological magic that turns the familiar cash register from a mere till into a management tool. You would expect a company that began and lived as fabulously successful a life as National Cash Register to be in there fighting for the contract. There was a short list of seven: and it didn't include NCR.

In its heyday, while its semisane founder, John H. Patterson, was still around, NCR was the world's most conspicuous example of *bulldog management:* meaning, once you have hold of a market, never let go. In fact, Patterson's techniques were sometimes more reminiscent of pit bulls. A promising manager named Thomas J. Watson made his bones by organizing bogus used-machine retailers that knocked out would-be rivals to NCR by buying up their products.

Watson went on, after a clash with his megalomaniac employer, to run the little company that he turned into IBM. Finding NCR unable to compete in EPOS is somewhat like finding IBM out of the competition to supply a mainframe computer. The management of NCR, while diversifying into computers late in the day and without making any significant impression on IBM, had notoriously neglected the new technology.

The subsequent wholesale revamp of its Dayton, Ohio, manufacturing base was one of the most traumatic experiences, and the most costly in terms of lost jobs, in the history of America's mid-century industrial neglect. It succeeded: NCR became a great, modernized force in retail banking, for example. But in these processes NCR's world market domination in its onetime core business had been inextricably lost—and Patterson had every right to be revolving in his grave. All the successor managements had to do, after all, was follow his formula.

He kept NCR products ahead of all others, and made them in plants that were more efficient than anybody else's; he knew more about the market than any competitor, and he would introduce new products at speed to protect his position; he saw the importance of global spread, and moved to dominate European markets early on; and everything was done with a total commitment enforced by effective management of men (it was also notably brutal—one part of Patterson's formula that belongs in the discard of history).

The formula hasn't lost its power over the subsequent decades. When Rod Canion and his cohorts at Compaq decided to challenge Watson's creation with portable computers, they also decided to apply concentrated and dedicated management effort to keeping ahead of IBM technology (Compaq was the first company to use Intel's advanced 80386 microprocessor in an IBM-compatible computer, seven months ahead of IBM); to invest enormously in relation to the company's size (not only in plant but in advertising—which at one point equaled a staggering 20 percent of revenues); to inform itself fully about the market by operating exclusively through dealers (with whom Compaq would therefore not compete); to maintain a flow of product introductions that would diversify the range away from total dependence on portables; and to go international when they were barely established in the United States.

In its first year, Compaq sold $111 million of "luggable" computers; four years later sales had passed $1 billion—a record-breaking run. It had one in six of PC sales through its cosseted dealers, and 25 percent of total market revenues (against 30 percent for IBM). Canion's fundamental decision was to start with that kind of scale in mind, so that its original accounting system and management structure were still virtually intact when sales were passing $2 billion (achieved in another record time, seven years). All the above decisions were based, so Canion told *Fortune*, on tearing "down positions to reasons. And when you get to reasons you find facts and assumptions. Then you try to eliminate the assumptions and come to agreement on the facts. Almost always, when you get your team to agree on the facts, you agree on the solutions."

Compaq's fact-based decision making ("Doing what makes sense" being the motto) doesn't sound like a very magical potion: "You don't want any mistakes," says Canion, "so it justifies putting the time and resources into making the best decision possible." It follows that, where mistakes are made, too little time and/or resources may have been deployed, or that the decision makers were not so fully committed. This commitment explains why Canion's decision to get ready to run, when Compaq had only just begun to walk, paid off so handsomely. NCR's indecision, which led it to walk when it should have run, underexploited one of the world's most triumphant brands by neglecting seven decision areas its management should have known backwards: old John H. did.

6. SEVEN INS OF HAPPINESS

The *pit bull manager* subordinates all decisions to one basic tenet: he will hang on to his brand's strength and market supremacy and never let go. Both are more easily lost in the turbulent market conditions of the late century than ever before, as both NCR and IBM (with its heavy losses of share in the personal computer market) have been compelled to discover. In the crucible of modern competition, even a famous brand name, attached to one of the leading forces in a market, can lose currency. In the 1980s, managements throughout the West have suddenly faced grueling climbs back to where their brands once belonged by right—on top in every sense.

Maximizing profits in any business hinges on winning top perception in the marketplace—the pole position. Firms should in theory never lose leads built through mold-breaking innovation; yet in the 1980s many products that created their markets, and were backed up by subsequent technical wonders, have slipped down the mountain.

Leadership in the technology of the product can itself lead the business astray. As Sony's Akio Morita has remarked (see "Nine Masterpieces of Morita" in Part IV), people won't know that they want your product unless you show them why. The brand name should be an unmissable signpost—but ill-advised companies such as Konica, which for years compounded its flounderings in the photographic market by selling its film under a different name (Sakura) from its cameras, exploit fully neither the brand name nor the corporate title. That is itself a brand, another point made by Morita: money is highly liable to being wasted if the brand and the company name are not the same.

But the bravura of Rod Canion at Compaq shows how a brand requires the full decisive treatment along the entire road from design and manufacture to price and marketing strategies. Compaq wasn't Compaq once—it started life as Gateway Technology. As *Fortune* tells it, outside consultants invented the name, designed the corporate logo, and plumped for international colors to run consistently wherever the new company's trademark and literature appeared. And this intensity, remember, was devoted to an infant start-up.

There's no benefit, economy, or sense in superficial decisions: strategy and its execution must be in-depth. The emphasis goes on the *in*, because an in-depth strategy requires six more *ins*—*in*novation, *in*vestment, *in*formation, *in*troduction, *in*tensity, and *in*ternationalism. The six ins are potentiated not just by their own essential contributions but also by a seventh: *in*tegration, for the six must work to support and strengthen each other. The winning formula is the same with a Patterson at NCR or a Morita at Sony—or a Canion at Compaq, striving to emulate past masters of the Seven Ins.

It would be strange, and criminal, if Compaq lagged on *innovation*, given its technological origins (put together mostly by refugees from Texas Instruments). The relative conservatism of IBM has also given Canion an involuntary assist. When the latter attacked Compaq's preserve, the giant's portable offering came in heavier and with inferior performance. Only those equal or superior to the competition in product and service can expect (or deserve) profit leadership.

Superiority demands deciding on high *investment* as guarantee of the manufacturing backup without which victory cannot be won in the competitive maelstrom. Whatever money will elevate manufacturing plant and process to the perfect state of the art must be spent, for the best available technology is the only highway or byway to optimum quality, flexibility, and versatility. Plant, however, is not enough; one marketing supremo moving into an ICI subsidiary, for instance, was amazed to learn that, while the business had long been able to vary its production to meet specific marketing needs, these valuable powers had lain unused—through human, not mechanical, resistance.

Manufacturing and marketing are twins. Meeting the marketers' need is manufacturing's raison d'être—and that includes giving the level of service on which stockists now expect to insist: such as virtual 100 percent stock availability. This costs money, though less than was needed before the new technology transformed manufacturing systems.

But maintaining correct inventory levels also requires deciding what *information* is required, and obtaining it in abundance. Compaq can draw on its close dealer links to discover what's selling where, what's going to sell in the future, what isn't selling. Information also costs some money; but efficient marketing data provide tools that cut both ways. The company gets vital market research information and also a marketing weapon, an information service that can be offered back to the customers.

Information cuts two ways in another sense, too. A vigorous marketing effort can't be conducted sotto voce—you must make a loud noise. That need for public information and communication (finding out what the customers want and telling them what you've got) self-evidently applies to a consumer goods or services company, but today that is a widening definition. It takes in Compaq as well as Amstrad, the personal computer business with which Alan Sugar demonstrated that aggressive retailing techniques apply in high tech with as much force (and as much payoff) as in low.

The escalating stakes in modern marketing make consumer advertising and its techniques increasingly obligatory tools for making decisions work. But promotion to the trade, including public relations, is also crucial. Information is the *in* over which too many decision makers stumble. They don't like spending on market research, they detest giving money to public relations consultants, they resent every penny spent on advertising, and they think, quite wrongly, that the sales force (if it's doing its job) will give the trade all the information needed.

If any money spent on two-way information is wasted, that isn't so much the fault of the messenger bearing the news as of its ultimate supplier: the company. Either the company is using bad people or employing good ones and managing them badly. Money spent on informing the market should come back a thousandfold, and that will help tremendously with keeping up the pace of *introductions.* The only way to maintain the excitement of the brand is constantly to improve the existing range—and not only with major innovations such as Compaq's Deskpro computer and its follow-ups. Canion's commitment to changing Compaq's models every nine months was an impeccable decision. By definition, the truly great leaps forward only come around at irregular and long intervals. But without modification, improvement, and variation, the offer to the market cannot maintain its interest.

That demands the *intensity* of decision that soups up exploitation of the other ins. Canion and Compaq have demonstrated that nobody can cover the waterfront these days, not even IBM. One group that fought back by changing the strategy of a brand leader that had lost its way found the right words. The high-intensity decision is to go for "concentration of new energy, resources, and manpower into specific sectors and products where we know we can confidently outperform the competition." According to *Fortune,* Compaq's umbrella launch decision was exactly the same, and it's a philosophy that applies even more obviously abroad than at home.

In the competitive arena of today, there's no escape for

anybody from the pressures of the developing *internationalism* in most markets. Compaq opened its first London offfice, in a small service suite, when almost nobody in Britain had heard its name, still less used its products. The fortunate companies are those that can exploit their talents and resources directly in overseas markets. The reason is simple: even for an American company with the world's largest domestic market as its base, overseas sales can add handsomely to total volume. By some mysterious rule of thumb, it is painfully difficult to raise market share above 40 percent if three or more competitors are active: since the United States is roughly 40 percent of the world market in business after business, that gives a company confined to American borders a potential ceiling of 15 percent or so worldwide.

Beyond that, there's the seductive appeal of the new global markets hymned by Ted Levitt, now editor of the *Harvard Business Review.* Global products and brands aren't quite as novel as they sound. Airlines, airliners, scotch, films, recorded music, and business machines, for example, have been global products either since their beginnings or very shortly afterward; international car models are a more recent development, but Ford has been a global brand since before World War I.

Cooked global food à la Big Mac is relatively new, but global food brands, from Kellogg's Corn Flakes to Heinz baked beans, are ancient history. The trend, however, is for more existing goods and services to become homogeneous, joining those that are that way by nature, like oil and soft drinks; a brilliant example is the painting of the world with the united colors of the Benetton textile franchise. At the same time, technology keeps on creating more wonders that are also by nature the same the whole world over: such as all those Japanese stereos, facsimile machines, Walkmans, and digital watches—and such as Compaq computers.

No doubt, many more companies will decide to seek global presence and branding, if only because they are advised to—thus making the global market a self-fulfilling prophecy. But there's a decisive international imperative that applies even to a business forced, for whatever reason, to stick to home. Despite enforced domesticity, it needs to be fully alert to trends in its trade in the big markets overseas. First, because it may well face domestic competition from abroad; second, because it is likely, while inquiring purposefully overseas, to glean ideas that can translate into a big domestic harvest in ways that are denied to those suffering from the disease of pernicious *insularity.*

That disease can be as deadly a murrain as *indecision*—of which it is a variant, anyway. The *in* formula demands that overriding decision to maintain brand preeminence at all economic costs. The subdecisions—the *ins*—are all demanding, but so are modern markets. Their diversity and the enhanced readiness of customers to accept new products present an unprecedented range of opportunities, but also unlimited threats. Seizing the first and dodging the second mean approaching an existing brand—even one backed by decades of history—with all the passion that is automatically brought to the (as you might say) brand-new: together with total *integration* of the other six *in* elements.

Combined corporate operations are the only right way (as the Japanese have taught) to exploit opportunities old and new, just as integration of all factors of the business is the only path of sound decision making in complex markets. And without all Seven Ins, the business not only won't be *in:* like NCR in that EPOS competition, it'll be *out.*

7. THE PREMIER BRAND OF CADBURY

In 1986, the directors of Cadbury Schweppes, the British multi-product multinational, made a momentous decision—at least by the sober standards of earlier eras in world business. They would divest the company of a liberal collection of unwanted brands. By the hectic standards of the current era, in which divestment has become a routine strategic option, that was not extraordinary—until the bundle of brands was examined more closely.

It included Smash, an instant mashed potato that was one of the group's few and proudest claims to innovative success; Marvel, by far the best-selling dried low-fat milk (the perfect product for a diet-conscious age); and Typhoo Tea, purchased expensively as part of a conscious effort to diversify from chocolate and soft drinks into the wider world of food and beverages. The grand strategy had also taken Cadbury Schweppes into jams and pickles; it was in chocolate biscuits and drinks, too; and coffee as well as tea. But these diversifications, once so seductive to the decision makers, were now viewed as corporate drags—because the makers and shakers had new objects, and a new conventional wisdom, in sight.

The new plan was to concentrate on the "core businesses" of confectionery and soft drinks, building up strength, especially in the United States, by a new series of takeovers. The wholehearted pursuit of this decision left the other brands—despite their fame and popularity—out in the cold. Starved of investment, neglected by the senior executives, the brands duly confirmed their unfitness for continued corporate membership by dwindling margins and drooping returns on capital. Plainly, the sooner this dog was found another kennel, the better.

It wasn't a conclusion with which a manager named Paul Judge could very well disagree—because he had been the group planning supremo when the new grand strategy was formed. But Judge, a graduate of the Wharton Business School, saw added virtue in the disposal plan. It gave him the chance to lead a buyout team that would take the famous brands off Cadbury's hands and see if anything famous could be done with them. The management liked the notion, too; but Judge and company had to raise their offer to £97 million to fend off two rival bidders—and that presented one not so little problem.

The interest of £1,000 a day on the financing substantially exceeded the profits. But Judge had decided to practice the planning he had preached. The process started with goals, some of them imposed by the very circumstances of the buyout. To cover the thumping interest charges, the team had to reverse the continuous decline in margins and sales of the previous three miserable years. Judge decided to aim for the *average* return on sales for the food and beverage industry. That doesn't sound too ambitious, but it represented a trebling of the previous bottom-of-the-league performance—and there was method in Judge's modesty.

A lower than average return, he reasoned, would mean that his businesses, brought together under the banner of Premier Brands, were not run efficiently. A higher than average figure, on the other hand, might point to underinvestment, and the previous record had shown with painful clarity what happens to famous brands that are not fed enough money. To reach his goals, Judge decided to use the buyout as a *catalyst* for forcing change and the adoption of fundamental business principles.

This meant making everybody in the new old company aware of the need to change; getting a focus on the key assets, strengths, and priorities of the business; organizing it around its different markets and establishing clear personal responsibilities, with agreed goals, for all the people in what Judge calls the organization's wiring diagram; and establishing a performance culture by intensive use of internal communications, together with incentives and rewards for success. This last wasn't too much of a problem, as the employees had options at a penny a share—and Judge and company's decisions very rapidly made the shares worth many multiples of a penny.

From a loss of £2.4 million in 1985, Premier Brands turned in £11.2 million after taxes in 1987; and that was after the huge interest payments—trading profit had nearly quadrupled. Costs of nearly £19 million had been sucked out of the business; the savings resulted in a £43 million cash inflow that not only covered the £1,000 a day of interest but left enough over to finance a bundle of acquisitions in tea, cereals, preserves, and canning. All that, moreover, was achieved while spending £19 million on marketing (a sharp hike) and introducing over a dozen major new products and packs.

With its buyout borrowings duly refinanced, Premier Brands had achieved a stunning performance, which looked certain to double (at least) the price at which the multinational owner had offloaded the unwanted goods. True, Cadbury Schweppes had an option on 10 percent of the equity, but it had previously owned the whole caboodle. What's more, Judge's profit, with the buyout interest added back, amounted to a fifth of the former parent's, and was growing much faster. Since all members of the buyout team (no longer led by Judge after a 1989 boardroom disagreement) had been on the Cadbury payroll before, what had gone wrong—and right?

The answers tell a great deal about what is wrong and right with modern corporate planning and the pursuit of grand strategies. Certainly, the Cadbury Schweppes decision to concentrate on confectionery and soft drinks has worked out wonderfully for the buyout boys. Whether it has worked out quite so wonderfully for the vendor is another matter. The strategy of becoming a major manufacturer in U.S. confectionery, at least, didn't go according to plan. It just went: in 1988, Cadbury sold all its U.S. factories to Hershey.

8. ENDS BEFORE MEANS

In most companies, the truthful answer to an inquiry about planning would be another question: What planning? The question doesn't relate to the massive, meticulous, detailed plans drawn up by the number crunchers. It means organized looking ahead to see what action can and must be taken to meet business objectives. Alas, in most cases, this raises a further question: What objectives?

Sigmund Freud once observed that his fate was to discover only the obvious: that small children have sexual feelings, which every nursemaid knew, and that night dreams are akin to daydreams. There's something of the same phenomenon in the thunderclap reception of Peter Drucker's emphasis on the importance of objectives. It sometimes takes true brilliance to perceive and promulgate obvious truths. In any business, management must surely express clearly where it is going, and what it expects to achieve, and by when.

At Premier Brands, after the buyout from Cadbury Schweppes, chairman Paul Judge had his directors write down what they saw as the strengths, weaknesses, opportunities, and threats (SWOT) for the business and themselves; then he had all the other managers do similar SWOT analyses for the company and their departments. As a result, the entire management's sights were set on the same objectives and as high as realism allowed. Because of the buyout circumstances, that self-evidently meant far higher than the aim of the multinational managers previously in uneasy ultimate command.

The extent to which underperformance is caused by undershooting is difficult to quantify by its very nature. But a history like that of Parker Pen defies explanation on any other basis. For three years before its buyout by its own executives, the company had performed even more ineptly than Cadbury's undervalued top brands. In three years, the losses had totaled over $40 million—money lost by manufacturing and marketing writing instruments whose global brand image was so strong that Italian street crooks happily sold imitations under the name P.arker. The true Parker had once been a case history in how to extend American exclusivity into the world mass market.

Given its miserable latter-day performance, the $100 million buyout price seemed eminently just. By 1987, though, the company was earning $30 million in pretax profits, and the management was preparing to go public for a valuation of more than double the $100 million. That plan was only scuppered by the objections of the venture capitalists involved, who wanted some $260 million. Their decision to object was undoubtedly wise: the British company that was riding the Reebok sports shoe boom, thanks to a one-third stake, offered to buy Parker in 1988 for some $320 million. That deal, too, foundered; but the bid valued Parker, with neat symmetry, at three times the price of the company three years before.

As with Judge and Premier Brands, it was the same business with the same management in the same market. The difference lay only in the focus. Section 4, Part VI, "Designing the Difference," explored ways in which the decision maker, after forming the strong, pregnant, ambitions that hold his highest hopes, begins to close the gap between where he is now (nowhere much, in Parker's case) and where he wants to be (very rich, same case). There's plenty of theory to help on the way. But management theories are only as good as their results. Like government economic statistics, they are subject to later revision that may radically change the story.

For example, in the 1990s, and probably into the twenty-first century, companies will, no doubt, be urged to look with care and tender respect at the following.

1. The experience curve.
2. The strategic business unit.
3. Portfolio planning.

In America, whence these wonders sprang, the trio were already going slowly out of fashion just as, in Europe, they were slowly coming in. The loss of favor in the United States was partly the common fate of all fashions but also the result of the revelation of numerous snags. The experience curve theory, for example, enshrines the big (literally big) idea that the larger the market share the greater the cost advantage. The truth in that postulate is important, but it is only true as far as it goes, which may not be far enough.

Before companies rush out in pursuit of more market share, they should consider not only the case of Premier Brands (which took over several products whose huge market shares went hand in hand with tiny profits) but also the following quote from a *Fortune* writer: for those already big in the marketplace, "probably the easiest first step was to cut price in the hope of gaining share. The not infrequent result . . . was a kick-'em, pound-'em, wrestle-'em to the ground price war." And in that, of course, nobody won.

What the master strategic decision maker seeks is the lowest cost position consistent with getting the highest perception of value and thus the highest price. The first element, low cost, doesn't necessarily stem from the highest share. Companies such as Inland Steel, the Whirlpool appliance company, and Philip Morris (with both Miller beer and cigarettes) have achieved the lowest costs in their industries without enjoying high relative market shares.

Buying turnover, then, isn't the automatic answer to fulfilling strategic objectives—and never will be. Rather, the economies of scale have been diminished by developments in both manufacturing technology (making sheer volume of throughput no longer decisive) and markets (where fragmentation and segmentation also devalue the virtue of long runs). What about the next nostrum (which fits well enough with the said fragmenting and segmenting): making each part of the company look and act like a business on its own?

The quasi-academic name for this attractive theoretical

concept, the *strategic business unit,* or SBU, begs a question. Whose strategy is it, anyway? Judge and company proved themselves entirely capable of devising an effective strategy for the businesses that made up Premier Brands: under the aegis of Cadbury Schweppes, strategy was laid down by the center, which finally had no strategy for these businesses at all. The basic SBU principle is that of independence. But that works only if the unit really is unitary, capable of making its own decisions, and is allowed (better still, encouraged) to do so.

In that blissful state, without the necessity of a Parker or Premier Brands breakaway, the unit can plan itself with top management's active support and hurrahs. In a widely spread group, though, the unit won't be the only independent strike force; there may be a hundred or more other busy SBUs. But a multitude of units must become unmanageable—and unplannable, too. The deep thinkers, however, had a deep answer to that: portfolio planning, for which the well-known prescriptions include that of the McKinsey consultants.

The good doctors advised managements to look at their businesses along two main dimensions: business strength and "industry attractiveness." This leads to the choice of one of three strategies: (1) investing for growth, because the business is strong in that particular sector and the market is sufficiently attractive; (2) milking as much money from the business as possible, for as long as possible, and wherever possible—because while one dimension suits your strategic book, the other doesn't; or (3) getting out as quickly as you can (and rewardingly, if you can) because the business is relatively weak and its market relatively unattractive.

This idea of portfolio classification has had endless influence and much variation. The Boston Consulting Group rode to fame and fortune on the back of Stars, Queries, Cows, and Dogs (whose definitions are obvious), with matrix to match. The British chemical multinational ICI describes its businesses as "ongoing, strong, problem, and new" and their matrix as "The Pink Quadrant" (for no better reason than that its head planner's surname is Pink). It all sounds beautifully logical, and so it is.

The basic analysis is rational and rigorous: looking at hard facts such as market size and growth, the price trend, how cyclical the business is, how the company stacks up against the competition—all these, and much other relevance besides, answer the starting line question: Where are we now? With that indisputably resolved, the company can start plotting the golden journey to its new and grander destination. But the definitions and the matrices of themselves accomplish nothing. Presumably, Judge's bundle of brands would have flunked any such examination at Cadbury. How do the bright portfolio theories work out in bald practice?

Take Goodyear. Its market dominance, with 40 percent of the U.S. tire market, should have brought premium prices and cost advantages leading to lush returns. In 1986, it scraped 1 percent on assets and sales alike; worse even than Firestone and B. F. Goodrich on both counts, Goodyear lurched into the takeover sights of raiders such as Sir James Goldsmith. Only the most strenuous endeavor preserved its independence and raised return on assets to a respectable 9 percent (even then the wolves kept circling).

In the appliance industry, Maytag has consistently earned more on its assets than Goodyear, despite a market share as low as 5 percent; even in 1987, its return on assets was four percentage points ahead of the tire company's much-improved figures. If high growth were the key to high profits, the airline industry, which grew at 13.6 percent annually in the late 1970s, would not have averaged returns on capital (under 6 percent) so threadbare that the lines flew in formation into financial turbulence.

In theory, high market growth means that everybody can expand without stimulating price competition, with the consequence of fat earnings all around. In practice, the vital ratio is that between supply and demand. The airlines consistently brought in more capacity than the public, for all its valiant traveling, could absorb. In an industry such as U.S. oil refining, where slack growth and miserable profits stopped anybody from adding new plant, the result in the 1980s was a severe shortage of capacity and excellent returns for those who possessed it.

Yet lack of new entrants, through high barriers or any other cause, is no guarantee of high profits, either. The contrasting experiences of beer and tobacco prove the point: for different reasons, nobody has crashed the barriers of either business, but the tobacco returns have been as high as the beer ones have mostly been low (a fact that Philip Morris rued when comparing the numbers for Marlboro and Miller Lite). Plainly, portfolio theory is no solution to the problem of extracting the best value from business assets.

Is there any viable or valuable alternative? The trend has been to move away from mechanistic measurements toward imaginative *vision*, a word to which McKinsey has pinned its latest colors. One of its consultants, Fred Gluck, writing in *The Journal of Business Strategy*, speaks highly of his firm's "7S Model," which is familiar to the millions who have read *In Search of Excellence.* You bind together structure, systems, style, staff, skills, and strategy around the core of shared values. In other words, like Paul Judge at Premier Brands, you try to run an excellent company. This translates into five eminently practical, and Premier, decisions.

1. To concentrate on the *ends*, not the means; to achieve low costs, high added value, top reputation for quality and service, and all similar worthy, worthwhile, and essential objectives, in whatever way works best for the company—so long as it does work.

2. To ignore the conventional wisdom; reading about the

management fashions, by all means, and extracting what makes sense, but never succumbing to the delusion that panaceas exist—for you or anybody else.

3. To stay flexible, knowing that no plan ever works out precisely, and that (paradoxically) about faces may sometimes be needed to keep you heading in the right direction.

4. Despite the above rule, to construct a planning approach, based on the rational pursuit of sensible, strong objectives (like that of doubling margins to the industry average, in Premier's case) that will largely eliminate deviations and reversals.

5. To shun self-fulfilling prophecies, in the knowledge that a business labeled as a dog, and neglected as one, will stay in the kennel. A study of over 1,000 businesses making industrial products discovered that the average "dog" had a positive cash flow that exceeded the negative cash needs of the typical "star" business thought to be wallowing in growth potential. As you might say, don't give a dog a bad name.

Premier Brands and Parker Pen are two among hundreds of examples of how loudly dogs can bark. Their previous owners failed to manage the businesses on their merits, or with methods that had any merit. That's the nub of successful strategic decision making: to judge and manage every business, every manager, every line, every outlet, strictly on its merits, and to seek optimum contributions from each individual component. This process of accentuating the positive and eliminating the negative doesn't mean just selling businesses you can't run properly and concentrating on those where, for the moment, you're doing better.

The words of Premier's managers to Tom Lester, writing in *Management Today*, provide sharply relevant texts. Said one about the old order: "They were administering the status quo, not managing. . . . We were looking after contributions and variances, not profit." Said another: "We were the old gang—we were never prevented from doing some of these things before." Poor motivation is as effective as sheer prevention in killing initiative. The most demanding repeat decision in all business is to maintain forward momentum to forward-looking ends by all means in your power, and never to stop.

9. THE MERCEDES OF THE INDUSTRY

One of Europe's top engineering companies hired the Boston Consulting Group to discover how the company saw the world in which the business operated, and to put that view under the critical microscope. The results came down to six simple, strong statements.

1. "We're the Mercedes of the industry."
2. "We cannot match low-cost suppliers."
3. "The upper price point can only be sustained in large machine sizes."
4. "Our market is growing because of material substitution."
5. "Our products can only be sold direct."
6. "The Japanese are only a threat in the low-price segment."

Note how strongly five of these half-dozen statements reflect the conventional wisdom. To become the Mercedes of its industry is every supplier's dream decision; it is the metaphor for attaining the dearly beloved position at the top left-hand corner of the price-quality matrix, earning the top price for the perceived top product. That exalted position makes inability to match low-cost suppliers academic. Operating from that top left-hand corner, you needn't decide to achieve the impossible: competitors lower down the matrix can take the low-margin business, while you take the high road.

You can also dodge the dreadful Japanese, if, as you also conventionally believe, they only compete effectively in the lower end of the market. Here, of course, you decide to stay clear, not only because of your higher costs, but also on the equally conventional assumption that premium prices can only be earned at the big-ticket end. And for these large, costly items, naturally, you must sell direct. This saves you from the painful decision to set up a new distribution system—which is something all managements prefer to avoid, even when they shouldn't.

But Dr. Stephen Bungay, writing in *Management 89, The Competitive Challenge*, reports what the Boston researchers actually found.

1. Yes, the client was perceived as the Mercedes of the business.

2. Yes, it really couldn't match the low costs of the low-cost suppliers.

3. No, it was untrue that the upper price point could only be sustained in large machine sizes.

4. No, the market wasn't growing only because of material substitution.

5. No, the company wasn't confined to a single method of distribution.

6. No, the Japanese weren't only a threat in the low-price segment.

Acting on Boston's discoveries, the client, in Bungay's words, achieved the following happy state of affairs: "A potential threat was headed off, and an opportunity seized; within eight months, the company had brought out a technologically advanced entry-level machine which was sold with great success through distributors." To be wrong on four strongly held beliefs out of six in a market where you are among the leaders is no mean incompetence in itself, but to face dangerous slippage in that market as a result is far worse. Who was at fault?

Every company has at its head a group of people, some insiders actively engaged in its affairs and paid generously for their engagement, others lower-paid outsiders dispensing whatever wisdom and experience they have to offer as advisers. This committee, the board of directors, is the source from which the strategic understanding and decisions of the company are supposed to flow. Yet in this case (which is far from atypical), the smartest decision made by the board was to ask consultants to discover how the company's heartland activity was viewed *by the management itself*—and whether these basic "truths" were actually true.

Now, it's no sin, rather a virtue, to seek outside scrutiny, even (maybe especially) when you are totally certain of your course. But such scrutiny is supposed to justify the appointment of outside directors. You would surely, in practice, expect the board collectively to know how the management viewed its world, and to ensure that the view is clear-eyed and correct. You wouldn't employ the outside directors, in theory, merely to endorse the conventional inside wisdom.

The conventional corporate wisdom is a self-created trap from which good decisions are quite unable to escape. This being so, whatever it takes to establish the unconventional truth must be done. Otherwise, strengths will be wasted, weaknesses will prove deadly, opportunities will be lost, threats will materialize, and decisions will mostly be bad. In theory, it doesn't matter if consultants or iconoclastic boardroom insiders produce the accurate SWOT analysis (whose purpose is precisely to establish those strengths, weaknesses, opportunities, and threats). But if it has to be consultants, because the boardroom residents, inside and outside, can't even accomplish this basic duty, what *are* they doing for their keep? What use *is* the board?

10. BOARDS OF MISMANAGEMENT

Power without responsibility, as the press barons of Britain were once famously rebuked by Premier Stanley Baldwin, has been the prerogative of the harlot down the ages. But what about responsibility without power? That has been the prerogative of boards of directors for a shorter duration than harlotry, but possibly with graver results. To put it bluntly, the board of directors, which in theory is supposed to control the top decisions of companies, in most cases does nothing of the sort. To be even blunter, it's often quite hard to determine what, in practice as opposed to theory, actually does result from those expensive deliberations—and here speaks the voice of experience.

It is that of Robert H. Waterman, Jr., who after a most distinguished career with McKinsey left big-time management consultancy to concentrate on a career as writer (flying solo with *The Renewal Factor* after his unprecedented success with *In Search of Excellence*), as training entrepreneur, as individual consultant—and as nonexecutive member of boards. Where large companies are performing badly, he said in a 1988 interview, "the blame has to be the board of directors." And he's come to an extraordinary conclusion: that "I don't think we [at McKinsey] really knew" what goes on in the boardroom as what his book calls "groupthink" takes over. Yet the McKinsey men shouldn't have been unknowing: the like-thinking isn't surprising in a group that consists of career executives and outsiders who are "picked by the CEO and usually vetted by the succession."

Meeting generally in "very pleasant surroundings," the

board functions, says Waterman, "really as a club"—and a paid one, at that. The clubbiness makes it extremely difficult for one member to propose the removal of another—for example, the chief executive. For that decision to be carried, the dissident has to obtain support from the other club members, which is far from easy. If, as Waterman points out, it's a case of "Schwab at Bank of America or Perot at General Motors" (both powerful in their own right, but still not powerful enough), "*they* get kicked out." So you either go along with the groupthink and the company suffers, or you protest to no avail, or you go, and the company still suffers.

You can hardly argue that Waterman is exaggerating when you think of the executive blessings at Allegheny International: blessings such as a $1 million company apartment occupied by the chief executive's son, $30 million of loans offered to members of management at 2 percent interest, and $100,000 of company money spent on very fine wines, including some of J. P. Morgan's. Even if these little byblows had missed the board's hooded eyes, they must have noticed the $1 million paid to the offending boss in salary—as against a mere $14.9 million in total company profits. The inexperienced innocents who allowed all these shenanigans to proceed at Allegheny included General Al Haig (the onetime secretary of state), Jean-Jacques Servan-Schreiber (the journalistic discoverer of the American challenge), Mark McCormack (the inventor of Arnold Palmer), and no less a businessman than Tony O'Reilly, the great Irish rugby player who has run H. J. Heinz with famous success.

You can easily understand how a general and a journalist could miss a few boardroom tricks; that a tough manager such as O'Reilly and a hard bargainer such as McCormack could also is surely a different matter. Yet all four ended in the same rocky boat. As *Fortune* observes: "All subsequently resigned, citing 'personal reasons.' Allegheny went bankrupt. . . ." Why didn't the shareholders sue the board? Well, they did; but the bankruptcy "put the shareholder litigation in limbo."

If the case of Allegheny isn't enough, what about Midland Bank? Any board efforts to prevent the astounding decisions that acquired the Crocker bank on the U.S. West Coast were singularly ineffective: the deal went ahead on grotesquely expensive terms that gave the purchaser not even the pretense of control over the Crocker management. Its members duly embarked on one of the greatest overlending sprees in the lurid history of American banking.

As if the near-bust of Crocker wasn't bad enough, the wisdom of the Midland directors was likewise nowhere to be seen when, having paid heavily for the excellent Greenwell stockbroking business in London, the Midland, in another series of bizarre decisions, ran the buy into the ground at the cost of over £70 million. The fact is that the fate of companies rests on the decisions of the executive management. If the board functions well, it is because the executives have decided that it will—and most executive managements don't.

Take the basic issue of chief executive pay. Graef S. Crystal, called by *Fortune* "the dean of U.S. compensation consultants," studied 170 of the largest corporations in the country and found that 83 of them had decided to pay their top decision makers compensation that exceeded "rational" pay—by anything up to 373 percent. The wrath of the rational God may be momentarily appeased by the fact that only 22 earned 50 percent or more over the odds; but the moment of appeasement will be brief, given two further pieces of information. The "rational" compensation being exceeded ranged up to $3 million, and the calculated excess included only a fraction of the stock options granted—bounty that in some cases is worth many times the "rational" rewards.

No serious observer doubts that these financial bonanzas for time-serving executives are unjustified, undeserved, and very likely harmful to effective corporate decision making. But their existence and monstrous growth is another demonstration of the impotence of boards. None of their responsibilities is clearer or less complex than that of deciding on executive pay. But actually they don't decide even that. What happens? As Waterman explains, the executive calls in compensation consultants, and it's "very rare" for the latter to return to the hands that are feeding them to say, "Look, you're earning too much money." Instead, they perpetuate the upward spiral; small wonder that CEO pay over the decade to 1987 grew at 12.2 percent, double the rate of U.S. production workers.

So boards are a club, just as Waterman states, and the members are certainly mindful of all their privileges. It is much easier to look after those than to exercise the directors' real responsibilities—not the legal ones, which are largely irrelevant, but the managerial ones. An experience of Waterman's tells why. For various reasons, he wasn't able to make all five annual meetings of one board (and what can be accomplished in five widely spaced meetings?). Feeling guilty, he offered two days' free consultancy in compensation. During those two days he "probably learnt more and got more done": eyes now opened, he offered another company a deal of five board meetings plus (doubling his fee) five days of consultancy. The president loved the idea, but the other nonexecutives turned it down. Why? Because they wanted the same deal—not to improve the performance of the business, but to double their money.

Waterman sang the praises of one "amazingly good board" on which he sat: the company is privately owned. Of equal interest is another fact: when companies are conspicuously well managed, or when their bosses were paid well below the "rational" level in Crystal's study, or when they "gave the shareholders the most for their pay" (as cited in the annual *Business Week* compilation), there's a conspicuous presence of founding fathers with large shareholdings acquired not through options but through good, old-fashioned, entrepreneurial ownership. The abuses are those of the corpocrats; and one of the ways in which they protect their positions, as tenderly as any of Gorbachev's opponents in the Party *apparat*, is through the neutering of the board.

Although Waterman by no means supported co-author Tom Peters's wholesale condemnation of large companies, he agreed that they can be "crappy and bureaucratic," and admitted that the two authors, while they dwelt on quality and service in *Excellence*, "had no idea how bad they were" in American industry. He thought that big companies were "getting it back together," which had better be true. But the process would self-evidently be far faster if the fact of harder demands for executive performance could be substituted for the soft fiction of boardroom control—and that applies throughout the West.

The fact is that if boards are viewed as decision-making machines their wheels grind extremely inefficiently—which must be just as true of the inner executive group, whose decisions the board as a whole (for all the reasons given by Waterman) tends to endorse. These decisions, moreover, are generally made within the context of an umbrella decision, perhaps unconscious, and often with unconscionably bad results, about the center's role. This isn't simply a matter of the age-old battle for supremacy between the center and the periphery (which the former, naturally, always wins).

It's a matter of *style*, if you follow the argument of two London business strategy experts, Michael Goold and Andrew Campbell. Their important book, *Strategies and Styles*, reported on research into sixteen companies, mostly large multinationals, and concluded that boards plump for one of three broad, fundamental choices.

You can decide on the basis of (1) strategic planning, (2) financial control, or (3) strategic control. The first bunch have decided to "push for maximum competitive advantage in the businesses in their portfolio. They seek to build their portfolios round a small number of 'core' businesses, often with coordinated global strategies"; here the authors cite British-based groups such as BOC, the industrial gasses to health-care firm run by American Dick Giordano, but they could just as well have picked on Jack Welch's General Electric.

The second bundle have decided to "focus more on financial performance than competitive position. They expand their portfolios more through acquisition than through growing market share": Lord Hanson and Sir Gordon White built Hanson North America into the 115th largest company in the United States by this approach—and those American interests are only part of the Hanson Trust empire. Then there's a group that fits in between the two: the "strategic control" companies, which have decided to "balance competitive and financial ambitions."

This means they "support growth in strategically sound and profitable businesses, but rationalize their portfolios by closing down or divesting other businesses": among British multinationals, ICI fits this particular bill, but so do the majority of today's American leaders. The definitions are fairly neat, maybe too neat, too pat; but they lead to another, blunter distinction between companies that plan centrally and companies that don't—the highly planned oil mammoth BP, for example, as opposed to the gleefully unplanned Hanson.

The opposites are less marked than might appear. No planning is a form of planning (a bad one); no strategy is a strategy (of sorts). In other words, all managements have explicit or implicit objectives, all have styles and methods of operation, and the outcome of success or failure in decisions and their execution depends on how appropriate the styles and methods are to the objectives and how well the latter fit the prevailing circumstances. The latter point embraces one of the four "ideals" to which the authors were led by their fascinating investigation: "matching style to business circumstances." The others are "understanding the businesses, open communication and mutual respect, and energy and common purposes." As the authors say, these ideals "concern attitudes, atmosphere, and people rather than the design of formal systems and processes."

It sounds like a *soft* conclusion (their adjective) to arise from such hard-nosed investigation. It amounts to an endorsement of the company, which is a good place in which to work, the organization with which people can readily identify, which has no rigid ideas of how businesses should be run, where motivation is internal as well as external, which is collegial and supportive. But do these virtues truly "express the common denominators of successful decision making"? The authors cite "companies such as IBM and Matsushita" as ones that "appear to have achieved these ideals." Unfortunately, the poor decision making of recent years has led IBM into lagging financial performance and anxious problems across many of its markets.

If IBM's belated reorganization into discrete operating subgroups actually works, the result must be a marked change in the relationship between the center and the periphery. The *Strategies and Styles* authors describe "five fundamental tensions" between the two:

1. Clear responsibilities versus multiple perspectives.
2. Detailed planning versus entrepreneurial decisions.
3. Strong leadership versus business autonomy.
4. Long-term strategic controls versus short-term financial objectives.
5. Tight controls versus the flexible pursuit of long-term objectives."

As they say: "Understanding these tensions, and the trade-offs they imply, is crucial to understanding the balance of advantage and disadvantage in each style." The chief executive who does not seek that understanding, and not just in multinational, diversified businesses, is failing to live up to his responsibilities. But in the tug-of-war between top management and the business managers, who writes the rules, has the heavier team, and is pulling downhill? There are no prizes for the answer, and often no prizes for the company as a result. The decision maker who puts substance ahead of style will have to rewrite the rules.

To summarize some of the main points I've made about the planners:

1. Don't just follow the conventional *external* wisdom: develop your own insights about the outside world.

2. You stand to make far more profit from swimming independently against the stream than you risk from not joining the school of fish.

3. Finding out what the customer wants, the foundation of market planning, has a certain basic simplicity: you ask.

4. The also-ran is a me-tooer by definition: the decision to be different is a decision to succeed.

5. Pulling the corporate punches is often worse than not entering the ring at all.

6. An *in-*depth strategy requires *in*novation, *in*vestment, *in*formation, product *in*troduction, *in*tensity, *in*ternationalism—all with *in*tegration.

7. Give a business a bad name and you'll guarantee bad results.

8. Judge and manage every business, manager, line, and outlet strictly on its merits and seek optimum results, without prejudice, from each.

9. Don't succumb to the *internal* conventional wisdom, either: always challenge the company's view of itself and its world.

10. There is no perfect management style—but no style can be expected to win if the subordinate managers always lose.

VII

THE
SALVATIONISTS

Only managers who have never been through the agonies of rescuing a company from the depths will minimize the achievement—and only those who have done so, and emerged successfully on the other side, know the sense of triumph that results. *Triumph* is the right word, because a salvationist such as Sir John Egan, the supermanager who saved Jaguar Cars, rightly earns the cheers of the crowd. But Roman generals during their triumphs were always reminded of their mortality, and business success, like human life, has its span. The real test is to emerge from salvation into a winning strategy that will extend that span into an indefinite future.

But salvation raises other issues, above all why it became necessary in the first place. The famous collapse of the Swiss watch industry before the Japanese electronic onslaught was a self-inflicted wound; the partial recovery led by Swatch showed that the Swiss had always possessed the resources of technology, marketing, and initiative required to defend their position. Just as rescue hinges largely on motivation, so does decline.

Facing the ultimate corporate threat, companies are forced to eliminate their weaknesses, seize their main opportunity, and exploit their strengths to the full. The real value of recoveries and comebacks is to uncover the sins that lead to lapse and relapse, and unmotivated managements are the biggest sinners of them all.

Not only does crisis force managements to do what should never have been left undone, it makes them mobilize human resources that should never have been left untapped. The success of a reluctant hotelier, cited in section 5 of this Part, in saving a business of which he knew nothing resulted entirely from tapping the skills and knowledge of the staff and suppliers. Their underuse is typical of all companies at all times. Subordinates who aren't trusted to use their intelligence and initiative won't do so; their superiors then complain about their stupidity and inertia. The amateur hotelier, however, is a professional at negotiation, and his approach was founded on the psychological needs whose satisfaction is the key to successful bargaining—and to a successful company.

It isn't just the needs of the managed that are crucial. The needs of the managing have a profound influence on the propensity to crisis. An unimportant bank in London was allowed to run riot, almost bringing down a fine old English parent company and placing the historic Bank of England in excruciating discomfort, because neither the parent board nor the bank derived much satisfaction from control. But great decisions depend on their makers' certainty that what they decide will be efficiently executed—that is, controlled, and not undermined by the moles that can threaten any organization. Crises of uncontrol arise from precrisis lack of the quality that is essential to all crisis management—proper, intense focus on the vital issues; and in crisis-averting management, everything is vital.

For instance, if the chief executive officer of a major car

company becomes inattentive to new-product development, sales must start to slip, and cutting prices, rather than relying on true market appeal, will be the only fallback. The fact that this happened at Lee Iacocca's Chrysler Corporation, no less than the setback to Jaguar's profits in 1988, is another powerful reminder that conquering heroes have to go on earning their laurels. But a deeper issue lies in the deceptive nature of heroic management. Hero worship is a fate to which great turn-arounds tend to lead. It can easily prove fatal in an age when the future of corporations will hinge not on triumphant generals but on the truly professional quality of management, running deep into every aspect of the corporation. Only that will guarantee that neither salvationists nor superheroes are ever required.

1. THE REGENERATION OF JAGUAR

The regeneration of Jaguar Cars has become a classic, not just in the automobile industry but in management generally, because of the irresistible before-and-after contrast: from burned-out case to risen star. When John Egan, later knighted for his efforts, took over, Jaguar's only assets were its existing car design (but that was deeply flawed in several respects) and its name (but that was depreciating rapidly because of quality problems that had passed into folklore). Output had diminished to an expensive trickle, and work force morale had sunk to the lowest sustainable level.

Egan's own words tell what he found, what he decided—and what he did. Sales had halved to 14,000 in just two years, until the business was losing over $6 million a month: Egan blamed that on the fact that "probably everything" had gone wrong.

> The company had been run for some years on functional lines as part of a much larger organization. . . . People had

concentrated on all kinds of corporate objectives and not on manufacturing a good product as the principal objective. So quality was one very big problem; the whole production process was very ill-organized and disjointed; there was very bad timing, very large inventories, very low productivity. The cars weren't selling; the dealers weren't very interested in the product; nor were they doing much of a job to satisfy the customers with the products they had.

In that awful fix, Egan made one momentous decision: "The first thing we did was to concentrate on quality and getting it right first time." As he noted, there's "a productivity multiplier" on quality:

If you start getting things right first time, the whole production process flows through much easier. We also put right the inventory-control aspects of the job and actually got a lot better planning into our production processes. This was a good solid platform for going for productivity improvements. It really meant organizing work better, giving better leadership, and people working harder.

To help that along, Egan brought in a production bonus, which eventually gave people on the shop floor something like 27 percent of their earnings. "All of these things came together to allow a management-led increase in overall productivity," stated Egan; by 1986 output of cars had trebled, and so had the number produced by each employee. The $6 million monthly loss of 1980 was turned within five years to a profit of $15 million every month. The broken-down vehicle tumbling over the edge of the cliff had become, as Egan proudly boasted, "a money machine."

The failure of investors on Wall Street and the City of London to appreciate this capacity to print money by bidding up the shares was a source of chagrin to Egan. But the financial fellows may have known something he didn't, to judge by events in the long, cold British summer of 1988. Jaguar's full-year profits halved, and the outlook for making more money in the following year (still less printing it) looked dismal. Why had the money machine misfired?

There were some convincing proximate answers:

1. The strength of the pound had reduced the value of dollar sales, with a £35 million impact on profits.

2. The U.S. luxury car market had lost buoyancy in the wake of the stock market crash.

3. European luxury car makers, including Jaguar, striving to offset the impact of a feeble dollar by raising prices, had opened an excessive gap over American and Japanese competitors—and sacrificed market share.

But these were only the symptoms of something else that had gone awry, as witnessed by Egan's reactions to his disappearing profits:

1. He launched a cost-cutting program designed to remove £50 million of costs a year over three years.

2. He decided to cut annual investment by a full third to £100 million, meaning that there could be no significant increase in output.

3. The bulk of the cost cutting would come from a near-10 percent reduction in the work force, part of a thrust to boost output per worker by 30 percent—to six cars a year instead of 4.6.

In other words, planks in Jaguar's turnaround platform were now showing signs of woodworm: its high investment, its improved productivity, its automatic generation of cash. And that wasn't all the bad news. The Consumer Satisfaction Index published by a California consultancy, J. D. Power & Associates, in 1987 placed Jaguar eighth. In 1988, Power knocked Jaguar down ten places, which put it sixteen rungs below the second-ranked Mercedes-Benz, the perennial pacemaker in luxury cars. So quality, Egan's linchpin, had also slipped. The reason had everything to do with quality of decision.

2. A BRIDGE TOO NEAR

"In England, Jaguar has made a comeback, but its product line is so narrow and its volume so low that it cannot be considered a major player anymore." The judgment is that of Lee Iacocca, the hero of a Chrysler comeback that notably qualifies him to sit in judgment on John Egan. It's not a comfortable verdict, for the case was clear long before Egan took over: in the 1980s, as in the 1970s, Jaguar competed with a limited sedan range, in only one product class, and with one low-volume sports coupe.

Geographically, the spread was no fuller. Of the 53,000 car sales predicted for 1988, 21,000 were scheduled for the United States, only 2,500 for West Germany. Take away British sales, and a relative smidgen of Jaguars were going to non-British, non-American buyers. Plainly, if Egan's strategy included achieving a safer balance of sales, it hadn't succeeded. But what had his strategic decisions been?

Egan's initial decision was to move Jaguar from the hospital ward to full health by a production-led therapy. By making the same cars more efficiently, he converted losses into profits, which in turn were plowed back into lifting output and efficiency and renewing the cars (very long in the tooth on his arrival). This met handsomely the criteria that explain the true meaning of "strategy." The business academics and management consultants have woven a web of verbiage around that single noun, *strategy*, and moved it to the fashionable forefront of decision making. Put simply, it only means thinking about what you're doing, why you're doing it, what you want to do, and how that will be done. Another definition is deciding on the route from where you are to where you want to be.

Maybe the management is blissfully happy with the company's present status and modus operandi, and content to maintain both into the beckoning future. That's also a strategy—though probably a high-risk one and based on illusory understanding of reality. That luxury certainly wasn't available at Jaguar when Egan took charge; and his course of decision and action follows closely the pattern set out in an article in the *Harvard Business Review* by Frank F. Gilmore.

The article's title is "Formulating Strategy in Smaller Companies," but smallness is irrelevant. The same questions, the same considerations, the same necessity for common sense allied with thoroughness apply whether it's a junkyard or Jaguar (which, as Iacocca noted, in the context of the world car industry, is a relative midget, at a fraction of the output of BMW, let alone General Motors). Gilmore's checklist for decision makers starts at the point just noted:

1. Where are you now?
   It goes on to ask:
2. What's wrong with your current strategy?
3. What's the real trouble, if any, with it?

The idea is to establish the nature and size of the *strategic gap*—the distance between where you want to be and where you are. This should lead to the end of the rainbow, the place where the crock of gold is buried in the form of bigger and better profits. As Egan showed, this is no academic exercise. His answer was to raise the quality of the cars to the level of consumer expectation while simultaneously expanding output to meet higher demand. That led him out from his own plants into those of the suppliers, since his own quality hung on theirs.

Gap closing also enforced heavy expenditure to make up for the venal engineering sins of the past. But Jaguar did have one supreme advantage—the existing business could plug the strategic hole by improving every aspect of its affairs. At that point, innovation, experiment, and risk weren't needed. Effective strategic analysis made the decision itself—as it often will. The strategy was, moreover, perfectly suited to taking what another article, from the *California Management Review*, calls the *commander approach.*

Here the boss determines the strategy and stays in close control over the people who are executing his strategic commands. The turnaround at Jaguar couldn't have happened without John Egan's breathing down many necks. But he also used brilliantly the *organizational approach.* This means forcing through any structural changes that will help the new strategy to succeed—for instance, setting up a new product line as a separate department, and loading its leader with enough autonomy and financial incentive to make the wonder product work.

This leads naturally to the *collaborative approach.* Egan found that "the people who worked for the company did have a lot of affection for it. They were willing to allow a lot of change to take place to enable the company to survive." On that foundation, "organizing work better, giving better leadership, and people working harder" capitalized on the change at the top. "It's really all to do with the attitude of mind of the senior management," says Egan, "as to whether they want to achieve excellence or not. Wherever there's a good management team, you'll find there's a good product as well."

Collaboration thus leads straight into another word and concept overloved by the academics: *culture.* It means changing what Field Marshal Montgomery, in the historic speech to his officers that began the buildup to El Alamein, called "the atmosphere." Egan did that at Jaguar by personal example, by reasserting management control of the business, by stamping his new quality emphasis on the company, by spending vastly more on engineering, and by placing a costly new stress on education and training.

But nothing in that program could solve the strategic problem put in so neat a nutshell by Iacocca. Egan's strategic analysis had stopped short: restoring the company to glowing present health wasn't and couldn't be the final solution; it was an essential precondition to a master strategy for a robust future that would have to:

1. Spread Jaguar's engineering costs over a much larger output.

2. Reduce its dependence on the U.S. market.

3. Generate the resources required to sustain the initial improvements into the beyond.

The strategic decision might have gone against independence. Joining Jaguar to another company, either in cars or in a cash-rich business (such as the oil group with which Volvo, after some merger trial and error, finally united), was the obvious and possibly the only viable decision in the long term. It was made less likely by a single "golden share," insisted on by the British government, that protected Jaguar's independence artificially until 1990. But for want of the decision, and for want of the resources that could have financed, say, a lower-price, smaller car, aimed at the European and Japanese markets, Jaguar ran out of acceleration—and, to some extent, out of road.

Gilmore adds some further questions that go to the heart of Egan's dilemma. Once a certain strategy seems to be the answer, ask:

1. *Is there any alternative?* (There always is.)

a. What are the alternatives for solving the strategy problem?

b. Are you limited in choice by a shortage of competence or resources?

c. Are you limiting the possible choices because of your own prejudices/preferences?

d. Which of the alternatives are acceptable?

2. *Have you evaluated the possible alternatives?*

a. Which one gives you the *best* solution?

b. Which is the *best match* with the existing skills and resources?

c. Which will give you the *greatest* advantage over competitors?

d. Which do you and your management do best?

e. Which will *minimize* the creation of new problems?

The decision maker dare not get locked into a strategy that potentially creates new problems without setting the scene for new solutions. Jaguar's overdependence on the U.S. market made it overeager to follow the leaping price hikes led by Porsche. One of its own executives explained the predictable consequences to the *Financial Times:*

> Not too long ago, you could get a good American luxury car for around $26,000 against, say, $30,000 for an equivalent Jaguar or BMW. Now, the U.S. luxury car is still around $27,000 but you're talking about more than $50,000 for a 7-Series BMW, with a base-model Jaguar at around $43,500 (£25,000). It's the opening up of this price gap which is probably the biggest single factor in the Europeans' problems.

The biggest single factor in Jaguar's problems, though, wasn't this local difficulty, as some of Gilmore's subsidiary questions make clear:

1. Can you see any threats that could damage the business unless you change what you're doing now?
2. Can you see any opportunities that you'll miss unless you change what you're doing?
3. *Are you sure that the present strategy is still valid?* (This is the big one.)

By the very nature of organizations and human beings, it's painfully hard to answer these questions honestly—what inquirers such as Gilmore are asking, however kindly, goes to the heart not just of the corporation but of the self-esteem of the decision maker.

Take these questions:

1. *What's the real trouble, if any, with the current strategy?*
a. Do you need greater competence and/or resources than the company currently has?
b. What is the firm really good at? Does the strategy fully exploit that ability (what the academics call "distinctive competence")?
c. Do you have an edge over the competition? Is it big enough?
d. Your threats and opportunities—will you be able to meet the former and/or exploit the latter without changing the business?
e. Does the strategy make internal sense—does the left hand (buying, say) know what the right hand (sales, perhaps) is doing, and are they pulling in the same direction?
f. Any other problems?

The fond inquiries mostly presuppose that the decision maker could be in error, which is too rarely news that he wants to hear. He'll try to answer the questions with nos and yesses that require no further action, no more change—when maybe that next bridge is the one that must be crossed for final victory.

The new quality queries at Jaguar and the failure to achieve new productivity levels except under the pressure of new crisis stemmed alike from the fact that a stepping-stone strategic decision had become the master strategy. The greatest decision makers think big—monumentally big. Their stepping-stone decisions then lead on naturally to the next step—and the next. Egan mused to *The Guardian* that "maybe there should be a special place up there for the chairman who does everything right except for the bottom line profits." This missed the point more than somewhat. Egan had done everything right except for the *top line* strategic decision. However dark the hour, that decision has to be taken first. Otherwise the brightness will inevitably dim.

3. THE SULTAN OF SWATCH

One wrong decision has passed into repeated legend as the classic example of how conservatism can destroy even the most solidly established industry. The victims of the self-inflicted wound were the makers of Swiss watches, a national product as rock solid as Scotch whisky and French champagne. The Swiss dominated the world market all the way from top brands with evocative double-barreled names such as Audemars Piguet or Patek Philippe, to near the bottom. In cheaper timepieces, only American mass-producers such as Timex offered much opposition, and in the middle ranges the Swiss were even more entrenched.

Then the Japanese struck with their customary force and their preferred weapon: a technological leapfrog that undermines the market appeal and the prices of the opposition. Over the single decade of the 1970s, nearly half of Switzerland's watchmaking firms vanished in the face of the Japanese onslaught; of the survivors, most were in failing health. Nor was the catastrophe the result of superior Japanese ingenuity. Appallingly enough, the crucial innovation, the quartz movement, had been invented in Switzerland, not Osaka or Tokyo. Thanks to the work of the Centre Electronique Horlogier in Neuchâtel in 1967, the Swiss were well placed to exploit and dominate the electronic age, just as they had lorded it over the clockwork era.

Despite the evident potential of electronics technology, the tightly massed Swiss industry made a dreadful decision: to cling to the traditional mechanical movements in which so many decades and so much fixed investment had been sunk. The race went not so much to the swift as the prepared. It rapidly became clear that, for all but the very dearest watches, which are works of art and jewelry as much as timepieces, electronics ruled the world. The Swiss rump duly converted itself to electronics; by then the Japanese were so many time zones ahead that significant recovery seemed out of all question.

Few Western manufacturers have recaptured technology leadership from the Japanese; few have regained lost tracts of world markets, either. Japanese corporate strategy revolves around technological supremacy and ever-increasing market shares, both of which are expanded and defended with unshakable tenacity. But the Swiss had clung to their own supremacy with equal determination in that one area where the awful electronic decision had not proved fatal: luxury watches. Here the Japanese economic advantages counted for nothing, and the usual Eastern difficulties in achieving high Western style were an obstacle to their advance.

The Japanese again turned to technological weapons: in 1979 they produced a watch that was only 2.5 millimeters thick—a quarter of the conventional dimensions. Since skinniness is one of the main selling points of ludicrously expensive watches, the challenge presented the Swiss with another crucial decision; on this ground, they chose to fight. The first hero was André Beyner. Working at the ETA Watch Company in Grenchen, he saw that great space savings could be made by integrating the moving parts, dial, and glass into the case, instead of encasing them at the end of manufacture. With this approach, ETA got its most exclusive gold watch down to a width of under a millimeter. Nobody, in Japan or Switzerland, has done any better. But the real hero was not Beyner; it was his managing director, Ernst Thomke.

Thomke's decision of genius was based on a contrarian question: Could Beyner's new upper-crust approach be used lower down in the mass market? The target was to create a watch with electronic accuracy and reliability, but with the appeal of a traditional dial and hands, and the kind of price (under fifty Swiss francs) that the public had come to expect from the Japanese. The cost of production could not rise above a fifth of the proposed retail price—and that would demand still more innovation, in process and product alike. The casting had to be microprecise; the number of components was slashed from ninety-one to fifty-one; and ultrasound welding was also needed to achieve the production economies on which Thomke insisted. Convinced that all was in order, according to an excellent account in *Reader's Digest,* he decided to go ahead in July 1980.

But Thomke also demanded innovations in design and marketing, which dovetailed beautifully. The way in which his designers combined the integrated casing with the strap opened the gate to an entirely new attack on the market. The new, all-in-one format created an ideal fashion accessory, a precise, shockproof, and waterproof watch that could be displayed on counter racks in a kaleidoscope of colors and designs, changed frequently every year. An inspired marketing director christened the whole marketing mix with the brilliantly obvious name of Swatch—short for "Swiss watch."

Thus armed to the teeth, Thomke followed the classic Japanese marketing principle: if you form large ambitions, make large preparations to match. Once the crucial United States market had been successfully tested, he ordered massive production from a totally automated, secret plant. In March 1983 the first Swatch watch went on the market. Some fifty months later, 30 million Swatches had been made and annual production had passed 12 million units. The industry that had made one of the worst decisions of all time had tried again— and got it right.

4. VIRTUES OF ADVERSITY

Adversity like that faced by the Swiss watchmakers has the virtue of starkly limiting the alternatives. A company that decides to expand by acquisition has the wide world of commerce before it, subject only to availability and price. The plethora of choices is one explanation of the many poor selections. The best decisions follow when the purpose is most clearly defined. At least the decision maker then knows exactly what he is trying to achieve and why.

The Swiss were trying to achieve survival—an aim so transcendant that the Why? needn't be asked. The only important question was How? and the only answer (which their Japanese rivals have always chosen as the most rewarding approach) is to probe for the weakness of the opposition and then to kick its Achilles' heel with steel-tipped boots. In this instance, the weakness (to which Japanese business is strangely prone) was lack of modern fashion sense. The electronic timepieces were being sold as wrist machinery; that gave Swatch its opportunity.

The clarity introduced by adversity contributed, in another context, to one of the best demonstrations of decision making in my personal observation. The product had what should have been a decisive advantage. But the launch decision was prompted by two irrelevant factors—a presumed boom in the marketplace and the desire to thwart the feared entry of a competitor (any competitor) in a market the management regarded as *Cosa Nostra*.

Disaster followed. The presumed boom evaporated, and killing costs, with little revenue to offset them, were incurred. As in the case of Swatch, the alternatives (with sale ruled out by the losses) were stark:

1. Carry on in the hope that the needed revenues would eventually materialize.

2. Close the venture forthwith and take the losses like a man.

3. Change the product so that it could be shifted into an adjacent segment of the market involving lesser ambitions and lower costs.

A brief discussion established that the first course was prohibitively costly—and nobody had any burning faith, if any at all, that the corner could be turned. The second course was cheaper (though still expensive), but meant abandoning any asset value that had been created in what still seemed like a bright idea. Only the third course could preserve the asset and contain the losses within reasonable bounds. The management accountant produced figures that showed a break-even in the second year and a solid profit in the third—and on that basis the scaled-down project was launched.

The venture not only met the above projections almost exactly, it then soared beyond them to become the rich leader in its new sector and a jewel in the company's crown. But without that falsest of starts, the issues might never have been clarified so vividly, and the decision to enter the right niche might never have been taken. In a nutshell, adversity dispels the woolliness that clogs too many decisions. More, it provides the impetus and sense of direction that give good decisions their force.

The disaster had also provided the additional information on which the makers could firmly base their decision that the original concept was not viable, while the scaled-down project was—if the chaotic extravagance attending the original launch could be avoided. Nothing in that analysis had to be bought by experience, however. The faults corrected decisively after disaster are nearly always failings that should have been entirely obvious beforehand: in an impending bankruptcy, anybody can spot the surplus employees, the underused machines, the uncollected debts, the aimless overspending. Sloppiness is the disease of organized activity. But, since everybody knows that new ventures are especially hazardous, what can possibly explain their sloppy preparation and execution?

The answer lies in the anticipation of success. Nobody sane decides to launch a new venture in expectation of failure. Inevitably, the chickens have to be counted before they are hatched—and all the traditional weaknesses of prehatch chicken counting come into play. Money is spent that hasn't been earned. Far fewer eggs are laid than expected, and fewer of them hatch. While revenues are thus overestimated, costs are underestimated—and the mounting losses are compounded by a powerful tendency to throw unbudgeted money at the problems.

Companies that launch many new products have a notably superior record to those launching only a few. The more products you introduce, the better you get at the game; the cost of introductions falls by 30 percent every time the number of products introduced doubles. So it isn't just a question of coming up with better ideas: each repetition adds to the cumulative knowledge of how launches should be handled, and, even more important, this knowledge gets built into the system.

Multilaunch companies have to develop routine procedures for planning and managing their ventures, processes that run in parallel with the other business systems and are as closely controlled. It's where ventures are one-shot deals that budgets get busted, controls are lifted, and bad decisions are based on worse information.

But the success syndrome doesn't exert its evil influence only before and during new ventures. It removes the spur of adversity. The Swatch revolution was a shock to the Japanese watchmakers, who rapidly assimilated the new Swiss lessons and entered the fashion battle themselves. But they and the Swiss alike were stumped by the next move. The economics of their industry had been undermined by the falling cost of the electronic mechanisms and the emergence of unbeatably low-cost producers in Hong Kong. Swatch had shown one way in which value could be added to the basic timekeeping function. But for ten years nobody had thought of anything new.

With output rising by a full fifth in 1986, nobody had to. But the next year, the rise shrank to 3 percent; as the Japanese saw the value of their own sales slump by 19 percent, they shifted their output to the cheaper factories elsewhere. That only accentuated the problem—which wouldn't surprise C. C. Markides and N. Berg. Writing in the *Harvard Business Review* under the uncompromising title "Manufacturing Offshore Is Bad Business," they attack decisions such as AT&T's move of all residential telephone manufacture from Louisiana to Singapore.

The two Harvard Business School writers point to hidden costs that mean that apparent "savings can cost a lot"; the illogic of shifting to save labor costs that are only 15 percent of total expenses; the "hollowing" of the corporation that results from the separation of manufacturing from design and marketing, with harmful effects on all three; the evanescent nature of any advantages that may be won; the possibility of being trapped under the thumb of a foreign government; and the risks of losing friends back home.

The seriousness of these objections is evidence of the lemminglike tendency of managements to dive over the same cliff in unison. Between 1966 and 1986, offshore imports into America multiplied thirty-eight times to $36.5 billion, an official figure that the authors think a gross underestimate. But their ultimate objection is the most serious of all—faced with adversity, companies have not used its spur to regenerate themselves, in Swatch manner, but have opted, or chickened, out.

As the article says, offshore manufacturing isn't a long-term strategic decision at all: "At best, it is merely a short-term tactical move that buys time for companies to restore their competitive health at home." The article quotes the Japanese as a sharp contrast in the period 1985 through 1987, when the yen appreciated by 60 percent against the dollar; 73 percent of firms queried in one survey "reported that they will not resort to more outside contracting," while nearly three-quarters were moving production back inside their own plants.

Their recipe for the adverse impact of the yen—"upgrading their products, incorporating greater value added, and minimizing costs"—would not have been easy to apply in the watch industry. But the results of offshore manufacture haven't been happy, either. Coming now from many sources, most of the half-billion watches made in the world each year are of indistinguishable accuracy and reliability; and in the commodity market thus created, the Japanese firms such as Citizen (alone accounting for half of Japan's output) are prisoners of their own production-led triumphs.

Consider again the astonishing predominance of Citizen. It represents 15 percent of world output, which is roughly the same as the total production of Switzerland. Yet one tiny Swiss luxury brand, Rolex, exceeds Citizen's fame as Clint Eastwood does Slim Pickens's. Citizen is a make, not a brand. All the investment in technology and production has in the end led into a cul-de-sac, the very weakness that Swatch exposed, because of poorly focused and financed spending on building desirability into the Citizen name.

Its failure is merely more conspicuous because of its greater size. But other makes, such as Seiko and Casio, have suffered from the same defect. What the Swiss were forced into by adversity, the Japanese were steered away from by success. The defect is one of poor decision making, of regarding each decision as a single stage and not fully realizing that any decision, however minor or momentous, is part of the long chain of decisions that is set in consequential motion. As in physics, where every action breeds an equal and opposite reaction, so in management.

Swatch exploited the big switch from digital watches back to analog faces more cleverly than its competitors because astute marketing was the only route left open by past failure. The decision makers didn't formulate a strategy for the next stage, when Swatch would no longer be unique—and in 1987 Swiss watch output resumed the Swatch-stopped decline. In Switzerland as in Japan, the power of decision seemed to have been paralyzed by developments beyond any individual company's control.

But "beyond control" is beyond sense, no truer now than it was before Swatch broke out of the rut. There are lost causes in business as anywhere else. But, as shown by the cases of AT&T and the other U.S. manufacturers who fled offshore, mostly they appear lost only because the right decisions have not been made—because watchmakers will only decide to become marketers of jewelry, sellers of distinctive branded goods, or wizards of new technological gimmickry when their backs are pinned against the wall. The rational alternative decision always exists; as Swatch brilliantly demonstrated, the requirement, in or out of adversity, is only the will to find and take that decision.

5. THE HAPPY HOTELIER

Many decisions have to be made not with careful deliberation but in great haste, on the spur of a peculiarly nasty moment. These rushed, forced decisions aren't necessarily the worst— like work (from newspaper articles to grand operas) composed in haste against an impending, alarming deadline, hasty decisions can sometimes be the best.

Take the case of a man who had been persuaded by a hotelier friend to invest in a project. The hotel wasn't going at all well when suddenly the associate suffered a heart attack that was clearly going to keep him out of action for some time. The place was losing $15,000 a week—and there was nobody to whom the investor could turn, except himself. How was he to escape from the threatened and imminent financial disaster?

The victim tried looking at a business school study on running a hotel, but that was of little use. Then he had an inspiration. Nobody else knew that he couldn't run a hotel. In fact, those connected with the establishment would assume the opposite—why would anybody totally ignorant of hotels take on a money-losing property? So why not pose as an *expert*?

Off he went to the hotel, and told the manager to send along, at fifteen-minute intervals, every employee in a supervisory job and every supplier of food and other goods and services. As each of them came in, one by one, the investor "scowled and told him that I could no longer do business with him" if he was a supplier; if an employee, he was told he could no longer work for the hotel.

He then asked the shocked victim, "How can I continue

with anyone who is incompetent? You seem like a nice fellow, but I cannot tolerate the ridiculous things that have been going on." Then the self-justifications would begin. The investor cut them short. "Only if you can tell me that you're at least aware of how things should be done, and if you can prove to me that you know what you're doing wrong—then perhaps we can still do business."

After this bombshell,

> each and every person I interviewed during the next few days poured forth a flood of suggestions, new approaches, and new methods for improving the management of the hotel. Without evaluating a single suggestion, I put the whole lot into operation. Within one month the loss had been cut by over 90 percent. The next month showed a profit of $2,000. By the time my associate left the hospital I was able to turn over to him a hotel that was firmly in the black.

This story comes from a book by Gerard I. Nierenberg titled *The Complete Negotiator*, and the author's expertise as a leading teacher of the arts and crafts of negotiation was plainly an invaluable asset in dealing, one by one, with the people on whom he was forced to depend for his solution. For he himself was the investor in the story.

Nierenberg's preferred stance in negotiation revolves around "needs." In this case his own need, though not stated in his own language, was to get the hotel off his back and into the black. The need of the suppliers and staff, after his onslaught, was to preserve (1) their contracts and (2) their jobs. The two needs dovetailed beautifully—but only because, in a crisis, Nierenberg had correctly mobilized the vital elements of making critical decisions.

6. IT HAS TO BE YOU

Negotiation appears to be decision making in its purest form. Very few offers belong to the Godfather variety that can't safely be refused. You can refuse to negotiate at all. If you do start talking, each point in the negotiation generally needs simply the decision maker's yes/no switch. Each counterproposal embodies another decision, too, with the whole series leading up the staircase of decisions to the ultimate, decisive yes or no. Yet most negotiations are fuzzy, indecisive affairs in which procrastination and uncertainty rule right up to the often abortive end.

There's one businessman whose richly lucrative career has twice turned on successful negotiations. In one case, he won forty times the amount that other, lesser men had accepted for a lease. In the other, he doubled his share in a high-paying business for virtually nothing. What decisive technique did this maestro employ? The same words apply: virtually nothing—he just sat there, unbudging, while events unfolded around him, and to his vast profit.

This wasn't the delaying technique the Roman general Quintus Fabius Maximus decided on as his master strategy for defeating Hannibal. The two-time winner was congenitally indecisive. Because he couldn't decide, he suppressed the normal human reaction in a negotiation—or in any position where you want one thing and the party of the other part wants another. The natural instinct is to wheel and deal, offer and counteroffer, bluff and counterbluff, shift position and change proposition— in short, to bargain. The process only stops when you have arrived (if only momentarily) at a mutually acceptable decision.

The object, however, is the same as that of all negotiation: to get what you want. It starts in the same place that all wise decision making also starts: selecting a clear, ambitious objective. Gerard Nierenberg's account of how he negotiated his way out of his hotel hole teaches many powerful lessons apart from those of decision making in crisis and in haste. One, maybe, is not to get involved, even as an investor, in businesses about which you know nothing. But when the time bomb planted by that mistake went off, detonated by his partner's heart attack, Nierenberg obeyed several wonderfully right rules of crisis decision.

1. In a crisis, always sit down and *think* hard about your decision, and for as long as needed (or allowed) about ways in which *you* can resolve it.

2. It has to be *you*. That applies even if somebody else has to carry the burden of action—how you brief, direct, and control the other or others will be vital to the outcome.

3. In seeking a solution, look for a simple answer that *you* can apply rather than a complex one that requires many hands.

4. Since you're unlikely to get that answer by conventional thinking, try deliberately to be unconventional, original, lateral.

5. Part of the decision is how to use yourself. In any situation where you're an unknown factor, what people know about you is what you choose to let them know—and that can be a powerful weapon on your side.

6. In a bad situation, don't hesitate to use shock as a tool. It works much better than fright. But you must do *something* to bring home the urgency of the position.

7. Work in the knowledge that even in a good situation operations can always be improved—and that those who are best placed and best equipped to improve them are the operators themselves.

8. In a crisis, quick and decisive action is generally much more effective than deliberate and delayed response.

9. Second-guessing the opinions of those in the front line is never done by good generals. If the actions taken by subordinates are wrong, you'll know soon enough.

What Nierenberg used, because he knew nothing about the business he suddenly had to run, was a combination of psychology and bottom-up business theory. The psychology rested on the fact that, given a choice between losing their jobs and pulling their weight, people will nearly always take the second option. Nierenberg's own interpretation of how his "negotiation" with suppliers and employees worked doesn't, however, completely square with this statement. In his own words: "To put it simply, I let the other people work for their need to know and understand."

In Nierenberg's approach, "Needs and their satisfaction are the common denominator in negotiation. If people had no unsatisfied needs, they would never negotiate. Negotiation presupposes that *both* negotiators and their opposers want something; otherwise they would turn a deaf ear to each other's demands and there would be no bargaining." He goes on to say that "when closely analyzed, the techniques of negotiation under each need are seen to repeat certain forms." He divides them into six varieties:

1. Negotiator works for the opposer's needs.
2. Negotiator lets the opposer work for his needs.
3. Negotiator works for the opposer's needs and his own needs.
4. Negotiator works against his own needs.
5. Negotiator works against the opposer's needs.
6. Negotiator works against both the opposer's needs and his own needs.

You don't have to be the father of negotiating training to see that the first is infinitely more likely to result in success than the last, which is fairly certain to result in abject failure. There's another set of categories to bear in mind: "need bundles." The main thing to remember about these is that *the more forceful the need, the more forceful the negotiation gambit.* Consequently, the first bundle is physiological need: that is, if a man is starving he will agree to almost anything to get food. The rest are:

2. Safety and security.
3. Love and belonging.
4. Esteem.
5. Self-actualization.
6. To know and understand.
7. Aesthetic.

The last is the only one that is not self-explanatory—it refers to the human desire for balance, symmetry, order; thus, you can go through the items under negotiation, listing all the points on which you've agreed and ignoring the ones still in dispute. "This work of bringing order out of chaos feeds the opposer's sense of aesthetics and often facilitates a solution," says Nierenberg.

That sentence has a positively Japanese flavor—and the Japanese, among their many decision-making skills, are excellent, hard-bargaining negotiators. It was, after all, Masaru Ibuka of Sony who bought the invaluable rights to use the transistor from Western Electric for a down payment of $25,000. In negotiation, as in decision making in general, one man's weakness is another man's strength—though, as Mark McCormack very wisely remarks in *What They Don't Teach You at the Harvard Business School,* negotiating from strength doesn't necessarily produce strong results.

One of Britain's strongest and richest negotiators had set his heart on a highly prized multiple-store chain. At the final meeting, gold pen poised over the contract, the maestro took a sudden decision to suggest reducing the price by a few pence as a gesture of goodwill. The party of the second part rose, summoned his troops, and left the room never to return. His decision may have been wrong, too; as McCormack also observes: "Whoever controls the emotional content is almost always going to walk away with the bigger winnings."

In the store chain case, the party of the second part had lost that control, which is critical to all effective decision. This principle is intrinsic to the Nierenberg technique, which consists of making an accurate fundamental assessment of the psychodynamics of a situation and then choosing the best route to the maximum advantage thereof. A perfect, if painful, example is when you decide to get rid of a senior executive by the easiest and least costly route—getting him to resign. You consider cutting his pay, but that may not succeed: it works *against* his more basic need to support himself and his family.

So you deprive the man of his decision-making power and simply ignore him. Many such cases exist to prove Nierenberg absolutely right. The victims "will usually rationalize that taking risks on their more basic needs by quitting and looking for a new job is a lesser evil than being deprived of their need for self-actualization." You have thus been working very successfully *against* the opposer's self-actualization needs.

The negotiator, in other words, seeks to maximize his power, his control over a situation. The decision maker has no less a "need," to use Nierenberg's favorite term. In deciding under time and personal pressure how to handle his hotel crisis, however ably he played on the need of suppliers and supervisors "to know and understand," their basic needs for food, board, and security also came heavily into play. They were made deeply unsure about their financial futures.

That's a powerful combination of weapons, but very difficult to deploy, except in a money-losing crisis. When a company is running well, or at least adequately, the decision maker has equal need to stimulate people into the better performance that will make his decisions work—but without frightening them. This is where bottom-up management comes into its own. You can always try top-down management, in which instructions come from the top, and the managers' main task, having decided what to do, is to make people salute and obey their instructions. But that, by definition, is only as effective as the top management itself.

Time and again, senior management underrates the capability of subordinates. If they really are incapable of making decisions, taking initiatives, or contributing good ideas, why employ them at all? The business needs the best people with the best ideas and abilities that make for the best decisions and their execution. The same goes for suppliers. If they are only good for supplying what the customer has ordered (more or less) at a competitive price (more or less), shouldn't the company be looking for a supplier with more and more to contribute?

What Nierenberg obtained out of ignorance and desperate need is available to any management: the cooperation of people. The greater Japanese talent in this essential respect has long been a source of envious wonder, blamed wrongly on cultural obsequiousness. But another true-life story of negotiation gives the real explanation: it's creative intelligence.

An American chemical company had concluded an agreement with a Japanese firm: the pact, because of circumstances beyond anybody's control, was crucifying the American's company. Without much hope, he flew to negotiate with the Japanese party. To his amazement, his Japanese counterpart asked him to rewrite the agreement however he wanted—and explained that their original decision to join forces was a decision to build a long-lasting, expanding relationship. That major objective certainly wouldn't materialize if, in pursuit of a minor aim, their partner was badly damaged at the start. The Japanese (as with their domestic suppliers) prefer to negotiate marriage contracts; the Western philosophy is more like staging a one-night stand, in which the preliminaries may be more satisfying than the final result.

As the Nierenberg case shows, the successful decision maker uses the foreplay to achieve the result he desires. It's a tragedy that, in the West, it often takes crisis and confusion to achieve the clear and satisfying decisions that could have been made unnecessary beforehand by reason and cooperation. In a crisis, fear can be turned into a weapon on your side. Before the crisis, what Nierenberg calls "freedom from fear" is equally powerful. The great decision maker uses it to avert the need to make offers that other people can't refuse.

7. THE BANK THAT BROKE

Samuel Johnson's quip that nothing concentrates the mind so wonderfully as the imminent threat of hanging seems to have applied too many times to one of the most venerable institutions in the West: the Bank of England. Often only crisis seems to have focused its collective mind on flagrant offenses against prudence. No postwar decades have been free of monetary crises, especially for a bank committed to the defense of sterling, which was endemically weak all the way from 1945 to 1979 and sporadically weak thereafter. Not content with these emergencies, the bank contrived to manufacture its own.

The crisis that gave the bank nightmares in 1984 should never have happened—certainly not after the bank's shattering experiences with the "secondary bank" scandals of the 1970s. That mess was manufactured by something called "Competition and Credit Control." Deciding to do its bit for the Tory enterprise of the Heath government, the bank unleashed the most unbridled, uncontrolled expansion of credit the City of London had ever witnessed. There was, however, scant effect on the competition half of the scenario.

This was because the competitors, the secondary banks, were just that: secondary. These tiny outfits with limited resources were unable to mount a serious challenge to the primary banks, but were perfectly capable of financing an overblown bubble in real estate. When the London office bubble burst, the secondaries exploded, too, and the primaries might well have followed, except for the saving operation launched by the bank: known as the "lifeboat," and costing several billions, the rescue averted a financial crisis that could have had the gravest global repercussions.

In the wake of this near catastrophe, the view formed, not surprisingly, that the bank's control apparatus needed tightening. Not long before, the bank had been attempting to control Britain's bankers without even a separate office for the task. At last it was decided to summon a fully fledged supervision department into being, complete with analysts to scrutinize the statistical returns, and managers to act on the analyses. Now, surely, the banks were under control . . . but no. An "appalling and bizarre record of incompetence and mismanagement" was about to result in the biggest collapse in British banking history.

The words came from Nigel Lawson, the Chancellor of the Exchequer, to whom the august governor of the Bank of England in theory reports. What happened to produce this 1984 crisis was simple, though difficult to comprehend. The bank, Johnson Matthey Bankers, or JMB, was the subsidiary of a fine old manufacturing firm that handled precious metals such as platinum and gold. The metal men had been delighted by the bounding growth and profits of this very secondary bank. Despite the new controls, though, JMB had won its rise in ways foreign to normal banking prudence—or to prudence of any kind.

Sums equivalent to 76 percent of its capital had been lent to a Pakistani shipowner named Mahmoud Sipra, known as "the cobra" (and that was to his friends). Another 39 percent had been advanced to a group of companies controlled by Rajendra Sethia, a man whose ambition to become the richest Indian expired in a £170 million bankruptcy, a British record, in commodity trading. Add 76 percent to 39 percent and you get 115 percent of a bank's reserves: JMB was done for.

But the skeleton bones in the JMB cupboard added up to a far larger corpse. According to *Portrait of an Old Lady* author Stephen Fay, "the total loans by JMB came to £450 million; bad and doubtful loans seemed to amount to £250 million; but the bank's capital reserves were no more than about £120 million." Without the Bank of England's lax supervision, these dreadful sums could not have piled up, and now it had an equally ghastly decision to make: whether or not to let the offending JMB sink.

Three powerful arguments made the obvious let-it-go decision seem impossible. First, the Johnson Matthey parent might drown as well, taking down 6,000 jobs as it sank. Second, the London gold market, in which the firm was a major player, might collapse, too. Third, the whole London banking system might follow the gold market down—and out. Faced with the stark choice between letting go and launching another lifeboat, Sir Christopher McMahon, the governor's second-in-command, decided to buy the offending, bankrupt bank for one pound. To quote Fay again: "McMahon returned home feeling sick and a bit frightened. 'I foresaw all the horrors. It was easily the worst night of my life.' "

The sickness, fright, and horrors didn't flow from making the right decision in a deadly crisis. Their origin lay in having allowed such a crisis to develop. If you find yourself forced to make the most unpleasant kind of correct decisions, a number of wrong decisions must have been taken beforehand. What are they?

8. COPING WITH CRISIS

Crises develop through two channels: the predictable and the unpredictable. They in turn each have two subsets: the preventable and the inevitable. The great crash of 1987, the worst for fifty-eight years, was an example of the predictable inevitable. Its predictability is witnessed by the fact that it was indeed widely predicted. True, hardly anybody got the timing right, apart from Sir James Goldsmith and Elaine Garzarelli, the demon "quant" with her computerized, quantified analyses, who said sell a week before the evil day. True, the predictions ranged from the vaguely general ("What goes up must come down") to the apocalyptic (prophets of doom, so long as they continue to repeat themselves, are bound to be right one foul day).

But the crash was predictable for a more cogent reason. To predict, and therefore expect, the opposite—a market rising in perpetuity—was absurd. Ergo, to predict and expect a fall was sensible. Yet the predictable could not be prevented. A financial bubble has to burst: in no other way can it be removed. The stock market authorities around the world could have (and certainly should have) taken more thought for the defenses that might have to be mobilized. But like the defenders of the Gulf Coast against tornadoes and hurricanes, central bankers can only mitigate, not interdict the catastrophe.

But was the collapse of JMB, the bank that lent 115 percent of its reserves to just two borrowers of doubtful covenant, an inevitable event, like a hurricane or the 533-point collapse of the Dow Jones on October 19, 1988? It was certainly predictable. In risk-laden areas, controls and supervision exist precisely because of the high possibility (that is, predictability) that without them the rules and norms will be transgressed, maybe grossly. If that wasn't so, the controls, like the state in Marx's imagination, could safely be left to wither away.

The decision whether or not risk exists is seldom tricky:

it's the basis of the well-developed white magic of risk management, which sets out to identify those areas where prevention is cheaper than the cure of insurance. But anybody in banking who doesn't know that banks go bust, or who thinks that bankers never make imprudent loans, is like the World War I subaltern whose hobby (very briefly) was putting out fires in ammunition dumps.

It was inevitable that some bank, sometime, would submit the Bank of England to another ordeal by fire. The City of London, after all, is a microworld where, in the run-up to the 1987 crash, a great bank's broking subsidiary could let a twenty-six-year-old clerk earning under $15,000 a year pile up a macro, million-pound debt for stock market speculation without even checking his creditworthiness. It can't be said that the bankers of JMB were any better; for that matter, the regulators of the Bank of England seemed equally determined to emulate that dear departed subaltern.

One of JMB's happy borrowers, to the extent of £22 million, was a Ugandan refugee named Abdul Shamji, whose philosophy was that "you don't have to have a bank balance to be rich. You just have to persuade the banks to lend you money." Despite recent history, such as the unpaid bills of a closed Scottish factory and the £3 million paid by one Nigerian state for construction work that was never done, the philosopher had no more trouble with JMB than the doughty borrowers, Sethia and Sipra, who were responsible for that amazing 115 percent.

Nor did JMB, in turn, have much trouble with the Bank of England. The difficulty with control systems is seldom that they don't respond to problems, or fail to report them; rather, the systems work but the people don't—the red light goes on but its watchers don't react. According to Stephen Fay,

the manager whose portfolio included JMB had identified problems of weak liquidity and excessive lending . . . after personal visits to the bank the previous winter . . . the flaws they revealed in the management suggested JMB justified permanent and close scrutiny. In the vital months from March to August 1984, it did not get it.

If the regulators had done no more than alert the bank's innocent and ignorant parents to the potential problem, that might have been enough. Instead, they allowed Johnson Matthey and everybody else, including themselves, to power through the red light. The decision maker must clearly consider with great care why people might fail to obey a signal that danger lies ahead.

First, they might not see the warning. Second, they might ignore it deliberately. Third, they might ignore it for no apparent reason. The latter may sound most unlikely, even impossible. But the records of fatal train accidents include otherwise inexplicable cases in which sober, well-rested, mentally stable, physically fit drivers have driven full speed through not one warning but several, even on stretches of line where they knew every bend and regulation. Some kind of psychological blackout appears to be the explanation. Without question it occurs far more frequently in business management, war, and government than it does on the railways or in the air.

Using these train disasters as an analogy, however, provides a clue to crisis prevention. The only way to stop the express driven by a temporarily freaked-out jockey is to have an override: somebody else must have all the information available to the driver, plus the ability to slow down and stop the thundering train. That's much easier to arrange in an organization than on a rail system or an airplane. The trouble with controls and regulation, though, is that they are relatively low-level functions, cursed by the fact that most of the time they achieve no useful purpose. Those regulated, like trains, mostly stay on the straight and narrow. So regulation becomes routine, oblivious of the fact that the exception to the rule can break the back of the entire system.

A deeper implication is that, while people are shattered by crisis, managing it, emerging from darkness into sunlight, is deeply satisfying—far more so than running a calm voyage, much more so than setting up a system of checks and balances, still more so than operating that system. What and where would Lee Iacocca have ended up after his firing by Henry Ford if Chrysler hadn't stumbled into one of America's worst corporate crises? Crises give heroes the opportunity for heroism, the power to make solitary decisions, the necessity to make them quickly, the ability to enact them forcefully, without opposition and foot-dragging.

Thus, the worst night of Kit McMahon's life at the Bank of England, when he had to take full responsibility for saving the wreck of Johnson Matthey, was the prelude to appointment as chairman of the Midland Bank (where he was awaited, as bad luck would have it, by a string of crises from bad Third World debts to catastrophic overlending at Crocker National in California). At Johnson Matthey itself, the crisis gave Eugene Anderson, a calm, seasoned pro recruited from Celanese in America, the chance to make his reputation and fortune with a series of reasoned, efficient decisions that eliminated Johnson Matthey's horrifying debts and turned it into a well-managed and lucrative company.

In crisis, in other words, the decision maker gets the powers that, if they had been exercised by the right person at the right time, would have prevented the disaster in the first place. The conditions of effective decision making in crisis are thus those of making effective decisions at any time.

1. The final responsibility rests, clearly and unequivocally, with one man or woman.

2. That supreme commander has been selected as the best

person for the job, regardless of age, sex, social status, or any other irrelevance.

3. There is no alternative to success—the decisions have to be right and they have to work.

4. Nothing is sacred: decisions cannot be blocked by custom and usage.

5. Nobody is sacred, either: decisions cannot be blocked by personality obstacles, and people who are not wanted, for whatever reason, don't stay.

6. Time is of the essence: decisions must be made against ineluctable deadlines and translated into effective action on an equally disciplined schedule.

7. Everybody is in the same sinking boat, and extraordinary contributions from everybody, from abnormal effort to exceptional ideas, are the norm.

8. Progress is measurable, eagerly monitored, and widely communicated—people can see the results of the decisions and the evidence that they are working.

JMB would never have been allowed to operate on so loose a rein had it been unprofitable: the apparent cascade of growth and profits made its innocent owners lax. Their decision to diversify into banking was probably unwise in any case, but doing so without taking care to understand the brave new bank's business was worse than unwary.

Nobody can make effective decisions without effective understanding, reporting, and control of their results. To revert to the analogy of the speeding train, the decision maker must at least select the points where, if the controls (the speed limits, in this case) are disobeyed, the information passes at once up the line to the top, and in such a form that nobody along that line can or will dare ignore the message. That news must also trigger an instant response in which not only the first tier of control, but at least one more, is activated.

All this must take place within tight time limits. Again and again, in tragedies like the collapse of JMB, the disaster is compounded by delay: the runaway isn't stopped before it hits the train standing at the next station.

Finally, discipline must be tight. Failure to follow the control procedures has to be a hanging offense, and it helps to make the controller-in-chief as important as that title sounds. Giving decision makers confidence in the results of their decisions is not a lowly task.

But good control is, or should be, good housekeeping. It can't of itself achieve good decisions or avert any crises save those of incompetence, carelessness, criminal greed, and over-ambition (which account for the lion's share of crises, all the same). The ultimate defense is to recognize that, while crisis management is special, all management is critical. The best decisions spring from systems that continually regenerate themselves—just as companies that are in crisis must be regenerated to survive. That's the way to concentrate the mind: not by the fear of execution but by the anticipation of realized ambition.

9. THE TALE OF TWO IACOCCAS

In August 1988, *Fortune* devoted its cover to a smiling Lee Iacocca. It called the Chrysler chairman "the Lion in Winter," and the roaring reported was optimistic. "There's nothing wrong with our market share," said the lion, "though we should be making a little better profit on the terrific volume we're selling." Even that had its bright side, however; the result of being "the lowest-price guy" and giving away "the biggest rebates" was that "the customer sure likes me, because he's getting a good deal. If I take good care of him, I've got his repeat business knocked. If that isn't building for the future, I don't know what is."

That leonine interview contrasted oddly with an article published five months previously in the same magazine. Its burden was that maybe Iacocca *didn't* know what building for the future is—at least in the core business of passenger cars. The customers apparently liked Iacocca less than he later thought, because, wrote Alex Taylor III, they were "finding that the newness of Chrysler's cars is only skin-deep." Although the company had "labored" to launch eight new cars since 1985, each was "built on an aging chassis developed for the K car in the late 1970s, and most use an old four-cylinder engine, too," with a badly needed V-6 not due until the start of 1990.

That was certainly enough to explain why Chrysler's market share declined by 16 percent in 1987. There is also justice in Taylor's view that the profits, which should have been "a little better" (a mere $1.3 billion of net income on $26.7 billion of sales), would have been a lot worse, perhaps invisible, but for two factors that had nothing to do with Iacocca's management: the 87 percent rise in the yen from September 1985, which forced up the prices of Japanese cars; and the management mishmash at General Motors, whose 1987 models found even less favor with the customers than Chrysler's. The reason Chrysler got stuck, in the worst British fashion, with an outdated model line equipped with obsolescent engines, also rang resonantly to British ears: it had failed to invest sufficiently in new products.

The only excuse for Chrysler's failure to invest more of its readily available billions (of which nearly three and a half went on buying back its own shares and on two large acquisitions) is an awful one: because of the savage cutbacks that saved the company, it no longer had the engineering and development capacity to spend the billion or so that was required. A vice chairman told *Fortune:* "If we could have spent more money well, we would have." As for the missing models, Iacocca's excuse is equally bad. His relevant quote was this: "If I made one mistake, it was delegating all the product development and not going to one single meeting."

This makes another odd couple with the later interview, in which Iacocca harked back to the between-wars "heyday" of the company under the founding Walter Chrysler: "He always paid attention to product. If you look it up, Chrysler had more firsts—station wagons, all-steel bodies, even the first electronic clocks and engine controllers." One prime advantage that Iacocca, the self-styled father of the Mustang, had over the financially oriented management of GM was his strength as a product man. All the same, the chairman's job in a corporation of such size isn't to create the new product policy but to appoint those who can—and to use his own depths of talent, intuition, and experience to make sure that they do it superbly.

Iacocca seems to have fallen short on both counts, since the man held responsible for the model disappointments, Harold Sperlich, a former Ford ally of Iacocca, aged fifty-eight, had one potential disadvantage: that very age. He was replaced by a two-man presidential team whose average age was exactly the same. At Honda, a company the Chrysler chairman rightly admires, the new-model position is considered so much a young man's job that engineers in research and development who haven't reached top status by forty are packed off elsewhere. Although Sperlich had produced the smash hit minivan (incidentally, the only "ten-strike" winner of the Iacocca years), the suspicion must be that the aging product line was the natural product of aging executives.

Whatever happened before the winter lion retired, it wasn't a happy turn in a story of heroic recovery. Is the ultimate answer, as Taylor wrote, that "corporate stardom was also a distraction"? It is true that heroes toying with presidential ambitions, public positions and pronouncements, and best-selling authorship are apt to take their eyes off the business ball.

But that isn't the nub of the matter. Rather, the issue is whether the hired hands who are elevated to heroic stature through the making of excellent decisions, excellently executed, become condemned, by the very fact of their public adulation, to worse decisions—and worse performance.

10. FEET OF HEROIC CLAY

The long gestation period of new cars and engines, and the many years for which they must stay current if their massive investment costs are to be recovered, impose an ineluctable planning burden on automotive managers. Above all executive cliques, they are obliged to anticipate future changes in the market, to schedule progressive improvements and modifications that will freshen the product line, to create a well-oiled management machine that can generate short-term triumphs from essentially long-term programs.

Given that burden, and given the tendency of Western firms—more in motors than anywhere else—to put their trust in kings and autocracy rather than collaboration, it's no surprise that the Japanese have all but monopolized the fast lane in world markets. Their long vision, passion for constantly updating product lines, ceaseless dedication to innovation in product and manufacturing process, and consensus style are tailored to the demands of the industry—as the top-down management of a hero-dominated Chrysler was not.

What happens when you don't meet the industry needs glares forth in a passage from the *Financial Times*. It stigmatized one leading auto company for "out-of-date designs, productivity and labor woes, marketing mistakes." The latter faults are not a whit surprising once you read what the chief executive told his interviewer: "Now we know that the customer is king." That's the epitome of ostrich management: heads must have been deeply buried in the sand for that lesson to have stayed unlearned. And what is the name of this un-happy ostrich? It wasn't Chrysler or some other Western firm that couldn't fly, but Nissan—the second largest manufacturer in Japan.

That's enough to make anybody gasp, especially when you learn further that Nissan's Sunderland plant, seen in Britain as a test of the national ability to come anywhere near Japanese standards, could now be labeled as "the company's only real bright spot worldwide." It's also gasp-making, though, that Toyota, the number one above Nissan, could have been deci-sively overtaken in the U.S. market by Honda.

There's no doubt that perceived product superiority (PPS) explains this latter feat. This perception enabled Honda to obtain a price premium in the West Coast market—for the crucial leverage of PPS can enable the winner in the worldwide race upmarket to command both top penetration and top prices. The danger, however, is that the paramount lead will be held only briefly; after all, that was IBM's happy position in the PC market until the dam broke.

Modern competition constantly writes sad stories of the death of kings. They bear out the fact that planned efforts to achieve the position of market leadership have to be unrelent-ing—and not just in cars. The necessity of going upmarket has been parroted for many years now. To have the lowest costs and the highest realized prices is the dream of every manager: you cannot obtain the former without heavy investment in new processes, nor the latter without new products—and moving into the premium position. That means offering the highest relative perceived quality (RPQ)—and relative perceived ser-vice (RPS), too.

RPQ and RPS are bound to become engraved on every aware manager's heart, not simply because their message is plainly true, but also because it has been vehemently espoused by a genius of publicity, Tom Peters. As he has been preaching in his progress from *In Search of Excellence* to *Thriving on Chaos,* the PIMS data base, which first taught that the higher the RPQ the higher the growth rate and the profitability, went on to demonstrate that companies with a high RPS benefited from the same gratifying effect.

Thus, instead of Go west, young man, read Go up, old manager: which in effect means, Go east. Japan's companies are the past and present masters of upgrading product and price to capitalize on and expand market penetration. But there is, of course, a catch in the upmarket philosophy: everybody needs to climb, but everybody can't occupy the summit. The effort to do so, however, is already having the inevitable concerting effect. The price differentials between top banana and bottom berry are narrowing, sometimes in an extraordinary manner.

In the British car market of 1988, for example, the top-of-the-line models from BMW and Mercedes were bracketing the price of the cheapest model from Rolls-Royce. Plainly, the ceiling on the price leader, or what the deluxe traffic will bear, is more restrictive than that of the price followers, moving relentlessly upward. But the process also works the other way around—when the followers turn the tables and lead the price *downward.* This would be less of a problem for the traditional leaders if the quality of the upstarts was not simultaneously rising dramatically.

In the personal computer market, that price dam broke because clone makers, such as Britain's Alan Sugar of Amstrad, decided to crash through the barrier with head-on competitors that undercut IBM on price. IBM has done its utmost to parade alleged product advantages like the somewhat mysterious Micro Channel; but the uphill, upmarket struggle to make these edges decisive has fared badly all around the world—and the price differential has narrowed amazingly as IBM has been forced nearer and nearer to the undercutters.

In these ways, the ante is upped in market after market; thus the pressures for superior planning and performance get still greater; thus the penalties suffered by the inferior get more painful. In short, it's not enough to take the product or services upmarket. You need upmarket management, too. Yet this has plainly not been forthcoming—according to a study by consultant Ben C. Ball, Jr., writing in the *Harvard Business Review.*

Ball sought the answer to two belligerent questions: Have companies been wasting the shareholders' funds, which, in the shape of retained earnings, they have plowed back into the business? Would shareholders have been better off had all available earnings been paid out in dividends with which the investors could have done as they pleased? According to Ball, the answers are an embarrassing yes—embarrassing, that is, for the boards of companies such as 3M, Coca-Cola, American Express, Eastman Kodak, and Sears, Roebuck.

After his "close examination of 50 of the largest mature, publicly held U.S. companies for the 1970–84 period (with adjustments to account for such variables as market fluctuation)," Ball summed up as follows: "Many companies' profits simply never found their way to shareholders, either as dividends or as higher stock value over time. For more than half these companies, a large proportion of retained earnings simply disappeared."

Ball reckoned that an investor in Coca-Cola "received only 12 percent of its net earnings." Yet Coca-Cola had been singled out by *Fortune* in the previous year as one of America's ten "most admired companies." Worse still, seven of the other nine (IBM, 3M, Dow Jones, Merck, Boeing, Rubbermaid, Procter & Gamble, Exxon, and J. P. Morgan) were in the Ball table, and all but one failed to return a dollar (in dividends plus share price appreciation) for a dollar of reported earnings. The author observes: "Ironically, two of these low-ranking companies, IBM and Coca-Cola, were rated one and two by *Fortune* in 'long-term investment value.' "

Now, you can argue with Ball's methodology: it really hinges on the movement of the P/E ratio, which bears no direct relationship to management's ability to earn rich rewards from plowback. Take IBM: during the fifteen-year period, its market rating tended to fall persistently even as its earnings rose abundantly. Over the decade to 1984 (when Ball's studies cut off), IBM's earnings per share rose by 13.2 percent a year compound, as the result of sales margins (14.3 percent) and a return on stockholders' equity (24.9 percent, to quote the 1984 figures) that scarcely indicate any inability to reinvest retained earnings at satisfactory yields. What happened was that IBM began the period with a P/E ratio in the forties. It proved unsustainable: each slide in the P/E negated all or part of the improvement in the computer giant's earnings.

But, of course, the excellent earnings record proved unsustainable, too: 1984 marked the turning point, when profits peaked at well over $6 billion—from which they slid sluggishly down to under $5 billion. This doesn't prove that the stock market was fantastically prescient over that ten-year period of the slumping P/E. It does prove that business idols all have the same feet of clay, that the hero status, for two reasons, prevents their decisions from achieving the result the makers presumably have in mind—to enrich the shareholders.

First, the idolization will be reflected in an excessively high stock market rating—and every halving of that rating will wipe out a doubling of earnings per share. Second, because of the forces in the real marketplace, the idol won't, in any event, be able to sustain his performance. In this sense, Iacocca is only one case among many: there was no possibility of repeating the rocketlike rise of Chrysler as the salvationist raised it from the dead. This pressure can undo even companies (witness Nissan) that are in theory not culturally subject to the Western tendency for all power to rise, like hot air, to the top.

That tendency is shown by the universal trend for chief executive officers in America to imitate the bad British habit of doubling up as chairman—much to the dismay of every management theorist around, because the double harness marries two roles that should be distinct. If the chairman is supposed to supervise the executives, but is also chief among them, a conflict of interest is created at the heart (or the top) of the company. But there is a more complex, possibly more important, objection. Vest all the ceremonial, supervisory, representational, and executive powers of the company in one person, and you not only manufacture an impossible workload but also place great upward pressures on the chairmanly ego.

Since managers with the ability to rise to such eminences rarely lack a large supply of ego to start with, the result can be a personality cult within the company that destroys the collegial, collective management that is rightly the modern ideal. Worse still, the internal cult can easily become matched by external hero worship, in which case the odds are tilted still further against rational judgment, behavior, planning—and decisions.

There's an instructive contrast provided by the decisions in one company that had an extant founding genius of truly heroic stature. He was no longer chief executive, and a successor decided to move the executive suite from the customary top floor to mid-building (so that senior management would spend the minimum time elevating up and down). There are no separate offices on the executive floor, either—not even for the chief executive. He sits in a corner at a round desk. The other executives are scattered about the enormous room, also at round desks. Why round? So that anybody who wants can sit down for a discussion at will.

It sounds like the type of solution that far-out Californian gurus might recommend to Silicon Valley freaks—but it is reality, and the company is the far-from-freakish Honda.

Honda's office radicalism, given its death-defying strides in one of the world's toughest industries, can't be taken lightly. It has high symbolism. Taking the executive suite off the top floor signals that there is no exclusive, literally higher, authority. Putting the emphasis on easy access to the rest of the company signals that involvement figures high in the corporate values. Placing top executives in an open office signifies the intention to have an open style in which rank and status have no practical importance. The round tables indicate that decisions are only to be taken after full discussion among colleagues who are always on tap. The proximity of the desks establishes that lines of communication are to be short and easily opened.

The classic Western office layout, nowhere more evident than in the fortresses of Detroit, with executives shut off behind solid wooden doors, even protected by secretaries in outer offices, and reached down long, anonymous corridors, obviously symbolizes something utterly different—and utterly inappropriate in a changing world that has little patience with or respect for the sanctity of hierarchical headquarters and heroes. In many celebrated turnarounds, changing that symbolism has proved crucial to salvation, taking the form of an assault on these hierarchical HQs: the assailants simply close down the head office leviathan and replace it with a small unit, perhaps a tenth of the size. The form begets substance, and both beget the desired climate—and, above all, the desired results.

Looking back, as much in sorrow as in anger, it's plain that earlier personal and corporate hero cults obscured the underlying defects in large American companies that led inexorably to the crises of confidence and performance of the early 1980s, and thrust the salvationists such as Iacocca into the bright lights. The cultism may itself have contributed to the decline, since it encouraged the dictatorial decisions and discouraged the development of management in depth, which are respectively inappropriate and essential to times of gathering complexity and competition.

Could the meaning of the cult of the hero manager run deeper still? Is it a symptom as well as a cause of decline? Cynics who instinctively answer yes can find convincing evidence in the United States of the late 1980s. The relative decline in the performance of large U.S. corporations has some far-from-uncanny similarities to that of big British business, not least in the way that recovery is hailed as renaissance. Thus, Caterpillar emerged from three years of losses, which was much to its credit; but salvation had left earnings per share much lower than ten years previously.

The same wasn't true of Chrysler, which in 1977, before resurrection by the most heroic of the American heroes, was experiencing appalling losses. Its industry, as observed at the start of this section, has most need for the collective planning supplied by pros who shun heroics for the hard-nosed graft essential for competitive success, yet has been a conspicuous victim of the hero cult. Even Roger B. Smith of GM, a salvationist who smeared his escutcheon with an endless succession of corporate boobs like the fiasco over H. Ross Perot's appointment to the board, which he then spent an additional $700 million to undo, continued long afterward to receive the media massaging of a conquering hero.

Over at IBM, John Akers, when his attempts to turn around the erstwhile world champion of professional management were in their infancy, was being praised almost as much as if Project IBM had already achieved salvation. Over in the rival camp of Apple, a successful salvationist, John Sculley, had made impressive gains in his campaign to establish a second PC standard, but not yet impressive enough to justify an emerging hero cult, complete with what now seems (thanks, probably, to the triumph of *Iacocca*) to be the obligatory business autobiography.

What may be forgivable for a Donald Trump, whose name is over the door (and everything else), is unforgivable for a hired hand. Time after time, which should be warning enough, these exalted employees earn their adulation by undoing what some earlier titan has done—much of it, so events prove, wrongly. Today's PR-driven cult of the hero manager is dangerous for that very reason: the hero is encouraged by the often paid cultists (inside and outside the firm) into believing that all his decisions are divine. In consequence, many are bad; and the planned, collaborative upsurge over which he once presided expires in unplanned, unprofessional, one-man mistakes. Beyond doubt, Western business is going to need plenty of heroes to the end of the century and beyond—but preferably unsung.

To summarize some of the main points I've made about the salvationists:

1. Effective strategic analysis will often make the effective decision itself.

2. Great decisions are stepping-stones, in which one big decision leads to the next—and the next.

3. Adversity is commonly the mother of success because of motivational factors that could always be applied in prosperity.

4. Lost causes in business are mostly lost because the alternative decisions have either not been considered—or not been taken.

5. In times of crisis, the steps to salvation are mostly those that would have averted crisis in the first place.

6. Time and again higher management underestimates the capability of lower management—and thus guarantees underperformance.

7. Good control won't of itself make good decisions—but good decisions are impossible without good control.

8. While crisis management is special, all of management is critical.

9. It's not enough to take the product or the service upmarket: you need upmarket management, too.

10. The cult of the hero manager is both a symptom and a cause of corporate decline.

VIII

THE
COMPETITORS

It's a sobering thought (or should be) that it took the ferocious competition of the Japanese to make Western managements set off in search of "competitive advantage." Their lack of winning edge beforehand flowed from the inadequate level of prior striving, just as the winning ways of the Japanese sprang from their internecine battles back home. None of their internal trade wars was fiercer than the Honda-Yamaha struggle for supremacy in motorbikes, in which Yamaha went too far and awakened a sleeping giant. Knowing how far to go is a key piece of equipment for the decision maker. Used properly, it can take him very far.

He won't, however, be likely to reach the perfect state of imperfect competition, in which there is no opposition worth mentioning. That was never easy without breaking the law. In modern times, monopoly has become a harder and harder game to play, because of the fragmentation of markets and the rapidity of change and challenge. Even great innovatory managements, like the SmithKline team that invented Tagamet or the EMI creators of computerized tomography (brain- and body-scanning), can fall foul of the laws of competition. The only protection lies not in protectionism but perfectionism. The companies that sustain monopolistic market shares do so, paradoxically, by acting as if they were beset by formidable competitors on every side.

That was actually true of Smith-Corona, survivor of a beaten and battered U.S. portable typewriter industry. The irony of its startling recovery was that the results surfaced in the midst of a takeover battle between two conglomerates, SCM and Hanson; neither set great store by the business. But SCM's success, achieved without much encouragement or support from its supposed owners, is another Swatch-like demonstration that the strengths of underrated businesses may be far greater than the decision makers suppose. The brilliant buyouts teach the same competitive lesson: only an independent management truly in charge of its own decisions, freed from bureaucratic constraints and charting its own destiny, can hope to compete successfully.

What's sauce for the subsidiary is sauce for the parent. Onetime unchallenged champions like Eastman Kodak have seen near-monopolies in their basic markets eroded by the same bureaucratic inertia that centralizing top managements visit on their corporate offspring. Large-scale acquisitions helped to disguise the consequent weakening of competitive power, which led directly to the huge, heaving attempts at corporate revival of the 1980s. Such upheavals have to be revolutionary to succeed. But revolutionary ends can be achieved, as the Japanese have shown, by a process of continual evolution, in which the company remains true to its ideals by taking any decision necessary to strengthen its ability to live up to that creed.

Divestment is the opposite of this process: lopping off businesses that management has decided, in the name of rationalization, no longer fit the corporate objectives or strategy. The decisions are not made from strength, but from weakness: the weakness of undermanagement. All businesses operate below their true potential. This is unavoidable, given the fallibility of human beings. But the gap between the ideal and the real is the hole in the West's fortifications through which the Japanese poured. Their competition may seem discouraging, but their example is not. Just as the underperformance of businesses under the ax is often a self-fulfilling prophecy, so competitive success, against Japan or anybody else, lies within the power of decisive management to visualize and realize nonstop ambition.

1. THE MOTORBIKE WARS OF JAPAN

The Japanese motorcycle wars of the early 1980s have passed into legend with something of the aura of the wars between Mafia families that from time to time stained the streets of New York with blood. The bloodbath in Japan began with success. Yamaha's motorbike sales had pulled tantalizingly close to Honda's: 37 percent of the domestic market against 38 percent—and you can't get much closer than that.

There was a reason for the rise, as Yamaha's president Koike shrewdly spotted, and whose words James Abegglen, a veteran Japan watcher and resident, and co-author George Stalk, Jr., reported in *Kaisha:* "At Honda, sales attention is focused on four-wheel vehicles. Most of the best people have been transferred [into cars]. Compared to them, our specialty at Yamaha is mainly motorcycle production. . . . If only we had enough capacity, we could beat Honda." Suiting the action to the words, Koike decided to match Honda new model for new model; then he went for the supreme prize. In 1981 he announced a new factory that would inside one year make Yamaha domestic leader; within two years the upstart would be "number one in the world."

This was not a threat that Koike's opponent, President Kawashima of Honda, could brush aside. His reading of the situation was as clear as Yamaha's: "Yamaha has not only stepped on the tail of a tiger, it has ground it into the earth." Honda adopted a new battle cry: "*Yamaha wo tsubusu,*" which the authors translate as "We will crush/break/smash/butcher/slaughter/or destroy Yamaha." The message got across. Whatever Yamaha produced, Honda produced more, until the Japanese islands seemed in some danger of sinking under the weight of unsold motorbikes.

In innovation, the counterattack was even more dramatic. In eighteen months, Honda introduced 81 new models, against only 34 from Yamaha. That understated the full impact of Honda's devastating response. Its 81 new models were accompanied by 32 discontinuations. Since Yamaha could only manage 3 withdrawals, it was outgunned by 113 changes to 37. "The customer," says *Kaisha,* "was seeing fresh Hondas and increasingly stale Yamahas."

After a year the story had a happy ending—for Honda. The group chairman at Yamaha observed the wreckage and said, "We plunged like a diving jet. My ignorance is to blame." Koike, the motorcycle boss who had started the wars, now perceived: "We can't match Honda's product development and sales strength. From now on I want to move cautiously and ensure Yamaha's relative position." Personally, he didn't have the chance to pursue this more sensible strategy: he was out, and the great motorbike wars were over.

2. HOW NOT TO GO TOO FAR

One of Britain's wiliest entrepreneurs, Sir Isaac Wolfson, used to advise others never to aim for a larger margin on sales than

10 percent. Achieve more than that, he would say, and you attract competition. Achieve less and you go broke. Even this sage advice may have been wily, since Wolfson personally made many margins nearer to 100 percent than 10 percent. But his analysis does pierce to the heart of a crucial area of decision: How far dare you go?

There always is a point where success will attract either imitation or retaliation. But two decisions, not one, are really involved—your decision to step beyond the bounds of prudence, and theirs to take your step as the signal to react. ICI's Sir John Harvey-Jones, as quoted in Part V, section 7, was well aware when it was unwise to challenge his biggest American competitor, Du Pont. The management of Yamaha came to that awareness the hardest of all possible ways: Honda, too, had no pleasure in the financial pain of its successful counter-attack. But should any basic principles govern these decisions?

Take Yamaha first. Its president's analysis was right: Honda had diverted its attention, and its best people, to cars—sensibly enough, given the overwhelming size of the latter market. The rise of Yamaha to within one percentage point of the leader was itself powerful evidence of that diversion and inattention. Its management should have remembered the depressed anxiety of a great Japanese commander, Admiral Yamamoto, after the crushing triumph of Pearl Harbor: "We have," he worried, "awakened a sleeping giant."

Nor was anything at all wrong in Yamaha's decision to become number one in Japan (from which number one in the world would follow almost axiomatically). The issue was how to accomplish that aim without awakening the sleeping giant. In other words, the secondary objective was fully as important as the first. While Honda slept, Yamaha could pursue its laudable ambitions undisturbed. If Honda woke, even if Yamaha won, victory was certain to be punitively dear. How could Yamaha keep its great rival quiescent?

That is the essence of defeating the Wolfson Syndrome. If a company restricts its margins (that is, its prices) to less than the traffic will bear, that may (or may not) deter potential competition, but it will certainly damage its own profitability—maybe for years. The record demonstrates conclusively that competition can only be kept from the door in a succulent market if the cost of entry is prohibitive—if, for example, the sitting tenant has developed the production technology to so high a pitch that imitation would be not only the sincerest but also the most ruinous form of flattery.

Even that is no guarantee of perfect safety. ICI and Du Pont share a hammerlock on the maximally efficient production of titanium dioxide (a vital ingredient in whitening paint, for example). Nobody can afford to break this technological monopoly. But a subsidiary of SCM kept in highly profitable business: it offered a level of service (such as delivery, even on weekends, within twenty-four hours, perhaps a vital edge for a customer whose plant depended on the product) that the Big Two didn't, couldn't, or didn't want to match.

The Japanese did better still. They subjected the process perfected by the two leaders to meticulous analysis. This proved, if proof were needed, that there was no economic possibility of competition in titanium dioxide. But the exercise also pointed the investigators in two other technological directions—one generated an economic product in packaging, while the other, opening up a huge potential market, is an antidote to the production of acid rain via factory chimneys.

Nature, it seems, abhors a monopoly. Wherever one exists, an opportunity lurks within for the outsider to snaffle. It follows that a policy aimed at preserving a monopoly is liable to be self-defeating *unless* that policy is also the strategy demanded by perfect competition. If the company devotes its every working effort to achieving the highest perceived level of quality and service on every dimension, and doing so at the lowest attainable cost, wave after wave of competition can be absorbed without seriously undermining the great leader's dominant position.

In mainframe computers, IBM achieved this dominance of perception so entirely for so long that it might as well have been a monopoly—though at one time seven ostensibly powerful competitors were trying and failing to crack IBM's marketing code. The relative (but only relative) failure in personal computers resulted from inability to sustain the same absolute lead in perception—in the late 1980s, IBM still handsomely outsold the next largest selling PC brand, but was simply beset by too many rivals.

A convincing example of perception's extreme value in preserving a quasi-monopoly comes from British chain store retailing. In one test, women were asked to distinguish between the quality of an item of underwear supplied by different store chains. With the retailer unidentified, the women couldn't make any distinction—not surprisingly, because the clothing came from the same manufacturer and was identical down to the last thread.

When the retailer was named, though, the preference became dramatic: Marks & Spencer led the rest by the length of the Mississippi. The women invented nonexistent reasons to explain why its identical underwear was "better" than that of its rivals. That perception above all tells why this one chain supplies, for example, the majority of all the panty briefs worn by British women—a quasi-monopoly quite as impressive as IBM's lead in mainframes (though far less lucrative), and founded likewise on the same principles as a good speech.

Orators are well advised to tell 'em what you're going to say, say it, and tell 'em what you've said. Quasi-monopolists are well advised to tell 'em what you're giving 'em (the best), give 'em it (the best), and tell 'em what they've been given (the best). If this formula hangs together in reality (it really is the best), you move on to the fourth dimension: make 'em pay for what they're being given. Isaac Wolfson's 10 percent becomes academic in these circumstances. The dominant supplier, the true market leader in every sense of the phrase, can afford competition—and may even benefit from its entry.

That almost certainly happened with the several onslaughts on IBM's position in mainframe competitors. The champ followed a stern policy of price leadership to a degree that generated margins far better than 10 percent. The thundering growth of the market, as much as these unnatural margins, tempted large corporate rivals. But for every machine they sold (mostly at a loss), they probably sold at least one mainframe for IBM.

"The Dry Beer of Asahi," Part VI, section 3, reported how Asahi, after selling 13.5 million cases of its new "dry" beer in nine months, against a planned million, gained from the same phenomenon when its rivals retaliated: Asahi's sales doubled again in the first half of 1988. Any effort by IBM to keep out the competition by underpricing would have been counterproductive: the loss of profit across the entire range of IBM's mainframe computer sales would have been insupportable.

There are industries in which price leadership can't be maintained—where the product is a commodity (such as gasoline or airline seats), and customers can't be persuaded that one tankful, or one flight, differs from another. Here, the only effective decision is to cut off competition at the neck as soon as possible—even at the cost of introducing your own low-price contender. If these decisions are dodged, a different decision is necessarily taken: *relative* prices are being raised, and in a market in which competitive conditions have moved decisively against the leader.

The decision to raise those relative prices, though, is easy to understand. A simple tool will tell the decision maker where a given rise or fall in relation to competitive prices is liable to decrease or increase the product's or service's profit before overhead costs. The analysis generally shows that raising relative prices will not reduce profits, save in the event of an improbably large drop in sales. True, some products are "price-inelastic"—meaning that the market won't absorb hikes at all; in practically every market, too, there's a point at which elasticity suddenly and painfully disappears.

That happened dramatically in oil, against all predictions, after the OPEC producers tried their luck, and their muscle, once too often. But mostly firms wait too long between price increases, and pull their punches if they do decide to move— fearing to lose sales, they lose profits instead. One decision maker, the boss of a bed-manufacturing business, seized this point entirely. Year after year, he and his fellow directors pushed up the prices, and year after year the profits rose, just as the simple analysis predicted. But the series of successes ended abruptly in disaster: the bedmaker had gone too far.

Though the price rises had never reduced demand enough to stop profits from advancing, the company's market share, and thus the sales volume, had fallen every year. In the end, the factory was operating so far below capacity that intolerable losses were being experienced. The company is still in business—but only after savaging its prices to win back market share. Its dilemma mirrors that faced by the market leader attacked by aggressive price cutters (such as anybody faced by the typical Japanese invader). You either lose share or lose profit. It's an unpleasant choice between a rock and a hard place, but if you dither and delay you stand to lose both.

The rapidity and certainty of Honda's response to Yamaha's attack were as important to its success as the actual strategy adopted. But decisions to retaliate can't be plucked out of the ether. Honda could only outproduce and outinnovate Yamaha because of the capacity (in all senses of the word) that was already in place; not only could Honda make 113 model changes when Yamaha could only achieve 37, but the champion went on, in the nine months to September 1984, to introduce 39 changes more: in this period those in the 50cc models (which hold the key to the Japanese market) outnumbered Yamaha by an overpowering three to one.

The capacity to respond is an unwisely ignored element in decision making. If you lack the resources to make a powerful counterthrust, the decision of whether or not to react has already been made—feebly and hopelessly. Honda would have been forced to sit by impotently and watch while Yamaha roared past with its new models and factory. But if the leader is covering in advance every possible threat to its profitable corner, there's a corollary for challengers: never press home an attack on a market leader without the certainty of superior resources. Not all giants sleep forever.

Old Sir Isaac was right in principle. The issue is one of balance—the balance between exploiting any advantage (such as Honda's relative inattention to two-wheeled vehicles, the weakness correctly identified and exploited by Yamaha) and pushing it too far. The other balancing act is between exploiting a position of overweening market strength and overdoing it. Where Wolfson was wrong, however, was in identifying the undue profit margin as the excess (a natural choice for a man who made his millions predominantly in retailing).

More likely, the overweight margin is a symptom. The true excess lies in extracting too much money from a market and putting back too little. Often, unwitting companies build a basic and basically dangerous decision into their systems. The decisive pressure becomes always to mine the maximum profit from the richest seams, especially if the product or service is maturing or mature.

As every first-level student of marketing knows, profitability tends to peak relatively early in the life cycle and then levels off or even declines as the market becomes relatively saturated. As this leveling process sets in, capital spending and other investments are cut back to offset the decline in margins—and it is this decision, not the excess profitability, that makes the leader vulnerable. Had Xerox plowed back more of its celebrated profits into projects such as smaller and cheaper copiers, the Japanese could never have cracked its quasi-monopoly so easily.

The great decision makers (such as the succession of top managers at Boeing) stick to one fundamental decision: to lead the market at all times in all important dimensions. You may still, like Boeing, suffer from uncovenanted erosion of the market—in this case, the competition of Airbus Industry, which sells excellent planes at exorbitant losses. But you will not lose your market—or your *inherent* profitability.

That last phrase bears some relation to the economist's concept of the underlying rate of national economic growth: what's going on beneath the surface of year-to-year statistical fluctuations, which is all that annual profit figures are. It's a bad decision to concentrate on the latter rather than on the long-term development of the business and its market from which long-term profitability, and long-term dominance, will flow—whatever the percentage of the margins.

3. THE INNOVATORS WHO CAME UNSTUCK

The Arthur D. Little book titled *Breakthroughs!* has a curious—and very instructive—aftermath. There were a dozen breakthroughs listed in all. Look at the list again: it included Sony's Walkman, JVC's videocassette recorder, 3M's little yellow Post-it Note Pads, the Toyota Production System, Federal Express's overnight air freight for parcels, SmithKline Beckman's Tagamet, Nike's running shoes, Raytheon's microwave ovens, and EMI's brain scanner. Note that the above can be divided into two groups: the first five innovations are still making money like private mints; the second four were overtaken by competitive aggressors, with results ranging from disappointing to dire.

SmithKline Beckman reaped unprecedented profits from Tagamet, but the vigorous competition from Glaxo's Zantac, a British antiulcer therapy that initially had the advantage of fewer daily doses, in 1986 overhauled the American firm's U.S. lead after only three years—and in 1988, SmithKline had to take some $400 million in write-offs.

EMI pioneered the brain scanner and then the body scanner, had a few halcyon quarters of soaring profits—and was then forced out of the market it had created by crippling losses that eventually led to ignominious takeover.

Nike similarly opened up the market for running shoes with spectacular success, but, despite the supposed benefits of a free-form management style, lost touch with the market and got comprehensively overtaken by the British-backed Reebok, with its greater emphasis on color and the women's market.

As Part II, section 2, reported, Raytheon, for all its pioneering with the microwave oven, was quite unable to resist the Japanese tide and was forced into striving to find other ways of making money from domestic appliances. In addition, the Japanese firm that perfected the oven's crucial magnetron had to drop out when larger companies dramatically undercut its costs and prices.

Among the five sustained successes, Federal Express, facing tougher competition in the air and from electronic transmission, especially with the remorseless rise of facsimile, had failed with the loss-making ZapMail project for electronic mail delivery. Sony, while riding high with the Walkman, 8-mm video, compact discs, and other brilliancies, had been forced to surrender in VCRs: with its Betamax format worn away to a nubbin, Sony capitulated by joining the VHS club. And Toyota had lost its lead in the U.S. market to the upstart Honda.

That clutch of setbacks shows that in modern competition it is nigh impossible to sustain 100 percent success on all fronts. But four of the breakthroughs had much rich mileage left as the 1980s drew to an end—despite the long lineage of the brain waves. JVC started organized work on the VCR in 1971; the inspiration that became the Post-it Note Pads dates back to 1974; the Walkman prototypes had been built by 1979; the beginnings of Toyota's brilliant production system lay in the mid-1950s.

The four successes form an instructive contrast to the failures. The latter all represent in acute form a common cause of the roller coaster syndrome—when what goes up proves Newton right by coming down. By exactly the same token, the Four Phenomenals present striking examples of that course in reverse—of taking, or building in, the second-stage decision that consolidates the achievements of the first scintillating breakthroughs. The second stage lacks the brilliance. But the long-term payoff may be even greater. So what is the magic bullet—or alternatively the poison pill?

4. KEEPING THE COMPETITION DOWN—OR OUT

The long-run successes of 3M, Toyota, JVC, and Sony have different roots but a common result. The first, with Post-it Note Pads, has a unique manufacturing technology, very difficult to replicate, that almost certainly makes a *competitive* entry impossible. Toyota decided to develop a production system that made it and kept it the lowest cost *competitor*. JVC, too small to wage the VCR wars alone (despite its ownership by the vast

Matsushita), decided to form an alliance with key *competitors*. That gave the VHS format an unbeatable grip—and demolished the share of Betamax, with which Sony had pioneered the market.

Sony itself, however, consistently kept its lead in personal, portable stereos by innovating continuously in every possible way, generating many product variants so as to stay ahead of the *competition*. Note the emphasis on *competitive*, *competitor*, *competition*. The second-stage decision is about how to cope with the second stage of innovation—when others either start to or try to compete for the glittering prizes. With that in mind, look again at the failures.

EMI in brain scanning couldn't cope with a wholly unfamiliar production task, didn't make the right strategic alliances, and fell behind in technological innovation. Nike saw itself as making shoes for athletes—not for people who wanted to take exercise and be smartly shod. Raytheon lost control of the technology: the Japanese not only made the breakthrough to low-price magnetrons (the core of radar and the microwave ovens), but had small ovens on the market far earlier. As for Federal Express, when its original concept ceased to be unique, it tried to develop another, which, unlike the first, rested heavily on technological and market unknowns.

What's the moral? Someday someone is going to compete with any innovator effectively *unless* the company has a crucial *internal* strength that can be preserved or an *external* arrangement that protects its position.

If the business makes an equal or better product at lower cost, how will it ever be beaten? If it controls a manufacturing process or any other operational secret that is indestructibly unique, how can competition ever be effective? If its competitors are also its allies, how can it suffer the fate of EMI?

Of the three guarantees of eternal business profit, only the second is truly difficult to acquire. For most companies, the necessity is to focus on the fact that a breakthrough of any kind is only a beginning—the palmy days, when there's no competition and an acquiescent marketplace, won't last forever. Management must start to think, even while the palmy period is at its palmiest, about how to make the business terribly tough to beat, in the near-certain knowledge that nothing will stop people from trying. The necessary game is one of the most valuable in business: KYC, which stands for Know Your Competitor, or put yourself in your competitor's shoes. The Japanese take KYC to extremes. They will do intensive SWOT analyses not only on themselves but also on the major opposition, to discover how the latter's Strengths, Weaknesses, Opportunities, and Threats look in the opponents' own eyes.

Another name for this indispensable examination is *competitive analysis* or *competitor analysis.* It has become a routine exercise for the best big firms, which are supposed to rely heavily on this tool in their efforts to defend, extend, or occupy the positions now under challenge from every side. The meager results suggest that the analysis has become too routine. Properly done, the exercise is grueling and may well throw up unwelcome consequences. Moreover, it must go hand in hand with another corporate essential: KYC2. Here the initials stand for Know Your Customer. Deep knowledge of the marketplace is very hard to beat—especially for a newcomer seeking to enter from outside. Michael E. Porter's 1950–80 figures showing the three-in-four failure rate of unrelated acquisitions cut both ways: they show there should be little to fear from total newcomers, provided that established companies have kept in touch (and kept faith) with their market.

Examine any commercial defeat and often the explanation is partly that the victims have stopped talking to their customers—or stopped listening to them, which comes to the same self-defeating thing. Listening to the customers, in turn, is of no use unless the company decides to act on what it hears: to develop the RQ, or responsiveness quotient, the measures that exist in any business to indicate how fast it reacts to customer requirements and to internal decisions.

Thomas J. Peters, co-author of *In Search of Excellence*, in his new role as scourge of big companies and champion of the enterprising smaller firm, rates responsiveness among his new, far more outward-looking corporate virtues. He cites the fashion in which Milliken, the privately owned textile company, has cut the time required to respond to an order for a new fabric from eighty days to seventy-two hours. The number of levels through which a decision must pass has a decisive (or indecisive) effect. The more levels, the slower it will be to conclusion and implementation; so Peters also comes down heavily against the many-layered, but hardly many-splendored, firm, citing the old USX (once United States Steel), with its eighteen levels of hierarchy, as one grim example.

Stripping out the unnecessary layers, like so many varicose veins, is a standard item in the company doctor's surgical kit. One consultant, called in to advise on a loss-making mammoth, told its new chairman to remove two whole layers of management—divisional chairmen and their divisional chief executives. The removal made no visible difference to the business but was one major move toward saving $75 million in costs in a single year. How long did it take the consultant to come to this conclusion? One day. It takes far less time than that to test any organization; the question is whether any position could be removed without affecting any operation or requiring any replacement. If so, the response is obvious.

The third rule of self-defense is KYS—Know YourSelf. The SWOT analysis directed at the competition must, of course, be applied simultaneously to yourself, so that the two can be compared and married. The combined analysis is the crucial decision-making tool. But there are other ways of comparing where you are with where you want to be: checklists, run through periodically, are a swift form of self-analysis. This one is especially simple and telling:

1. How does our quality (as perceived by the customer) compare with the competition?
(a) better   (b) the same   (c) worse
2. How do our costs compare with those of competitors?
(a) lower   (b) the same   (c) higher
3. How does our service compare with competitors?
(a) better   (b) the same   (c) worse
4. What is our relative value for money as perceived by customers?
(a) better   (b) the same   (c) worse
5. How is our product or service perceived in relation to the competition?
(a) different   (b) the same
6. How does added value compare with last year's?
(a) higher   (b) the same   (c) lower

The object is to have nothing but (a) answers. This is far harder to achieve than it is to answer the questions. If there is no present competition, the decision maker looks at the comparative questions in the light of potential intruders. Thus, on the first five questions, does your Achilles have any vulnerable heels for the foe to attack?

That second stage is mandatory. How are you going to convert the breakthrough into a permanent bonanza? The conventional wisdom has led far too many managements to give themselves the wrong answer. In the summer of 1988, Smith-Kline Beckman ran into a severe sales setback for its Tagamet antiulcer drug. The *Financial Times*, commenting on the problems weighing down chairman Henry Wendt, said that he had "followed a textbook strategy with Tagamet's cash flows."

The textbooks, not unusually, were wrong: in particular, Wendt paid $1 billion for Beckman, a medical instrument company that is now probably worth much less. And too little of the cash flow was diverted to protecting its major source: Tagamet, with its seven-year-long monopoly of the market. By the time of the 1988 crisis, its U.S. market share was down to under 38 percent. Before the onslaught led by Glaxo with Zantac, the market pioneer would certainly have been forced to give ground in any event—but surely not so much.

SmithKline had taken one courageous decision at the start of the saga—building a large plant in Eire in advance of a wholly uncertain market reaction. But that was a decision born of desperation, out of desperate need for a new product: Tagamet was the only new drug in the kitty. When its unimagined success turned despair into delight, the decision makers didn't realize that one day they might face a new and even more difficult decision: how to preserve market dominance in a market where product dominance had been lost.

Tagamet, said one medical expert in 1988, had become "kind of a stale drug." That's the same word—*stale*—that Abegglen and Stalk used to explain how Honda out-gunned Yamaha by making the latter's models seem out-of-date. What really goes stale, though, is the management of those immensely profitable superproducts. When successes sell themselves, all decisions and all managers look brilliantly successful. That is precisely the moment when the truly brilliant decision maker takes a fresh look at the potentially stale success, and takes fresh decisions to renew, to reinvigorate, and to revive. If companies don't get around to asking the question until after the rival miners are taking their gold, or never ask it at all, the right answer will only arrive if the gods are on their side. Man won't be.

5. THE HIDDEN HERO OF SCM

It's natural, when disaster strikes, to be stricken: natural, but sinful. Surrender is only acceptable when, as in the Japan of 1945, there is no alternative. In business, that ultimate destruction seldom arrives—hence the many cases of down-and-out companies, usually under new management, moving sharply up and up: an Apple Computer, say, rising from under the mighty weight of IBM and its clones to become a serious contender in the U.S. business market (and one of 1987's ten fastest rising equities, thanks to a 22 percent compound growth in sales since 1983).

The same phenomenon was repeated many times in Mrs. Thatcher's Britain, as the companies battered in the recession of her opening years—when factory output fell by a horrendous fifth—came back strongly with the U.K. economy. The comebacks followed a pattern of decision so similar as to constitute a universal recipe for success in an age dominated by Japanese competition. As one man, dozens of chief executives decided to:

1. Reduce head counts by . . .
2. rationalizing factories as they . . .
3. rationalized product lines to . . .
4. concentrate on niche markets where they could become internationally competitive by . . .
5. developing the technology of product and process so as to . . .
6. aim at world markets with world-class costs and performance . . .
7. achieved by redeployed and retrained work forces—including managements given financial incentives to outdo their own pasts and their competitors in the present.

Now, although this formula is evidently effective, and can be adapted to revitalize or reinforce any business of any size and any condition, it isn't exactly the equivalent of Einstein's $E = MC^2$. Rather, it's the equivalent of the Second Law of Thermodynamics. Any decision maker able to read should have known that, as surely as a kettle boils on a fire, a company can't stay hot in a competitive age unless it's competitive. Why did it take crisis, and usually the arrival of a turnaround management, to put the kettle on the fire?

Before answering that question, it's vital to note that all the companies concerned—businesses such as ICI in chemicals, Jaguar in cars, Rolls-Royce in aero-engines, Courtaulds in textiles—had deep inherent strengths on which they could draw, despite the terrible external buffeting they had received from forces such as the overvaluation of sterling and the superior competitive energies of the opposition. Internal deficiencies had compounded the external damage. But that's the difference between making awful or excellent decisions.

The great decision maker doesn't concentrate on the *weaknesses* in the company but on the *strengths*. That may be desperately hard when bombs are raining down upon your head (though Winston Churchill was doing precisely that, thinking about victory and its aftermath, during the worst nights of the nearly lost Battle of Britain). But the story of the American typewriter manufacturer, Smith-Corona, perfectly illustrates the virtue of looking for virtue: the pitiful past is only valuable for the lessons of failure, for pointing in unmistakable clarity to what went wrong as a sure-enough guide to what is right.

The Japanese onslaught had not destroyed four of Smith-Corona's basic advantages:

1. It could match or surpass any technological advance made by the competition.

2. It could finance ambitious programs in R & D, production, and marketing.

3. It had strong design traditions.

4. The reputation of the brand had not fallen along with its market share—indeed, it was to all intents and purposes unscathed: underexploited, but intact.

Put like that, the only response to such a list of strengths is What are we waiting for? But this is the question that should always be asked when the fortunes of a company are sliding away into an abyss as profound as that at Smith-Corona. After five profitless years, it bathed its parent, SCM, in $55 million of red ink in 1984/85. What Smith-Corona was waiting for was G. Lee Thompson, a chief executive recruited from Singer, who adopted the following program:

1. He *reduced the head count*—by over half, to under 2,000.

2. He *rationalized factories*—six were combined into one.

3. He *rationalized the product line*, concentrating on a new range of electronic models that were . . .

4. *internationally competitive*, even with 85 percent of the work done not in the Far East but in Cortland, New York. That was done by . . .

5. *developing the technology for product and process* so that the number of parts fell to 700 (compared to 4,000 in electric typewriters), and direct labor tumbled to two hours per machine—a 60 percent fall in overall labor cost since 1983.

Thompson told *Business Week* proudly: "The Japanese worker is not the be-all and end-all." Nor is he. But note how the Smith-Corona program matches precisely the key steps that Britain's battered giants took to achieve world-class standards in their chosen sectors. You might think that the turnaround was a triumph for an unbattered Briton, Sir Gordon

White of Hanson North America, which won SCM after a protracted takeover battle in March 1986 (see Part V, section 3). Not so: Hanson planned to sell the typewriter business (as did SCM). The turnaround ("Fabulous, fabulous," gloated a Hanson man) turned out to be an uncovenanted bonus of a rich takeover that, after other disposals, cost the Britons not a dime.

It's plainly an unwise strategy, though, to wait for a wonderman to turn up before you turn around. The cost and danger of delay are too great. It requires, true, a real mental and emotional effort to change from being a once-comfortable corporate insider into someone with the frame of mind of a keen and hungry outsider/appointee who still has his bones to make. But the effort becomes much easier if you start by asking and answering a few simple questions.

First, what are the company's strengths? That's the basic question whose answer, at Smith-Corona, showed that Japanese competition was not unbeatable. It is rightly the first question in the celebrated SWOT analysis that, by establishing Strengths, Weaknesses, Opportunities, and Threats, has been the foundation of many a marketing breakthrough (and many a Japanese corporate plan). Realistic appreciation of strengths is the crucial starting point—it's positive, forward-looking, energizing: the opposite of wailing and gnashing of teeth.

You're only interested in weaknesses so that you can correct them positively—in order to exploit those strengths positively. The positive approach is to think, question, and then act like a trained man called to your own company's bedside as a doctor. The physician's approach involves asking questions such as these:

1. Who would you keep, and who would you move (including yourself in your present role)?

2. What activities would you drop, expand, initiate, invigorate?

3. What aspects of the performance would you criticize?

4. What practices and philosophies in other companies/ industries might usefully apply in this business?

5. What, under the heading "we've always done things this way," should be radically reformed, or at least reexamined?

6. What management layers or pieces of the corporate structure could be removed without any effect on the company's present or future?

7. What additions in expenditure or organization would contribute most to the future prospects of the company?

8. What objectives would you form that are not already in the corporate plans?

Of course, if there aren't any plans, the last question becomes impossible to answer. Lack of plans equates with lack of thought, which is the usual reason large companies, like the typewriter company's SCM parent, fall into the morass in the first place. The large companies of the West are stacked with subsidiaries with records as dismal as the old Smith-Corona's; often, their parent's own overall records are little more inspiring. Is there a reason? Obviously there is—but it's a cause that, like the losses of Smith-Corona, can certainly be cured.

6. BUYING OUT THE CORPORATION

There was sensational news from the car industry in the spring of 1988. Toyota had decided to shelve its plans to recapture its leading share of Japanese car sales in the U.S. from Honda. In future it would aim to maximize its profits at "roughly current sales levels," instead of seeking to return to its traditional position on top of its rivals: in 1980, Toyota had 6.5 percent of the market and Honda 4.2 percent, against 1988's 6.1 percent and 7.2 percent. Senior Toyota officials said the company would also reduce capacity and costs and limit investment so that by 1992 all plants would be operating at 100 percent capacity on the basis of "a volume outlook that is realistic."

You don't believe it happened? Nor should you. But substitute General Motors for Toyota, and the Japanese for Honda, and you get exactly what the *Financial Times* reported in late April after "a series of presentations to Wall Street analysts by GM managers." It matters not that GM chairman Roger B. Smith a couple of days later sought to repaint the picture, averring that GM, which twenty years ago had half the market, was still intent on climbing back from the current relatively measly 37 percent in cars and 35 percent of cars and trucks to 45 percent of the latter. That was only another example of the remarkable talent for bumbling confusion that marked Smith's regime at the world's largest manufacturing company.

In his self-defense, Smith repeated his argument that the problems of the later 1980s were only a little temporary difficulty and that he and his decisions would stand vindicated a decade on. This implies a positively Japanese time perspective, but, as the first paragraph above made clear, what is unthinkable for a Japanese company had become so thinkable for GM that Wall Street promptly pushed up the shares for three consecutive days on the news of its retrenchment.

There was more at stake here even than the future of the U.S. car industry. GM is the place where modern management began with the unprecedented achievements of Alfred P. Sloan, and where it was first analyzed in Peter Drucker's greatly influential book, *Concept of the Corporation.* Is the wheel about to complete a full circle? Will the saga of the Western economic giant end where it began? The dismaying aspect of GM's "temporary" problems was that the company seemed so slow to change, even though the efforts to move the mammoth were quite strenuous. Just as the wonderful success of Sloan's creation was based on organization, so the probability was that GM's sickness was structural in origin.

This has nothing to do with the massive and unproductive reorganization by which Smith swept the old independent companies such as Chevrolet and Pontiac into divisions covering several marques. One consultant who had been working in GM reported that eleven layers of hierarchy separated the shop floor and the chief executive. That compared with five at Toyota. What, you may ask, did the other six layers do? Get in the way of the rest, in all likelihood, slowing down decisions and rendering them less effective.

Even GM's apparent successes raise doubts over its decisions. In 1987 the European companies made a bumper profit—and a very welcome one, considering that GM overall yet again lagged (by $1 billion, no less) behind the profits of the substantially smaller Ford. The European profit almost exactly equaled the losses of the previous few years, during which GM had been investing at about $900 million annually to modernize its plants and its product range. Subsequent to that, GM started to cut back investment to $500 million a year; according to GM's European chairman, that was to drop still further once the new Vectra range had been launched into the mid-market.

As in its layer upon layer of hierarchy, so in its European command structure GM harked back to management norms that should have been long gone: key roles were occupied by expatriate Americans whose provenance, given the parent's domestic record, wasn't exactly encouraging. In fact, much of the cumulative loss in Europe was the result of buying market share through aggressive dealer programs. When that stopped, the profit consequently started, but with GM still only fifth in Europe and stuck with a hard choice similar to its American dilemma of decision: either to compete in the marketplace at all points, or to concentrate on profit, in which case it would get no more competitive power and no more market share.

The lesson for lesser managements (lesser, that is, in the size of their responsibilities) is that underinvestment and overmanagement lead inevitably to no-win choices like the above—and

GM's decision dilemma is by no means unique among the world's great companies. Their stability, the rock of management in the postwar era, has become their weakness. These supertankers of the world economy used to sail steadily on; occasionally becalmed, every few years executing one of their cumbersome changes of direction, they were seldom shipwrecked, and never disappeared in the Bermuda Triangle. But the acutely destabilizing forces unleashed after 1973 have disturbed that stately progress—though mainly in the United States and Britain, where the corporate raiders and the investment bankers have been so dangerously unleashed.

In Western Germany and in Japan, the supertankers stayed afloat for very different reasons: the German causes, which arose from managerial and structural rigidities, explained much of the old *Wunder*economy's wobbling growth; the Japanese causes, which reflected continuous and amazingly swift adaptation to competitive necessities, just as fully accounted for the new *Wunder*'s relentless rise in world markets. British big-time management lies somewhere between the two extremes, neither as hidebound as the German nor as thrustful as the Japanese. But British compromise has won no prizes: the supertanker fleet's sorry voyage is shown graphically by the *Management Today* Growth League published in June 1987.

The top fifty names included only six that held any significance when the magazine started in 1966: four of this select half-dozen were retailers, a disproportion that tells its own tale of the irresistible rise in Britain's consumer spending and the equally unstoppable decline of her manufacturing supertankers. The general tale is one of great opportunities bungled and often-misplaced ambitions imperfectly pursued, with the result that basic strengths became weaknesses at worst, undervalued at best. The vulnerability of the confectionery firm, Rowntree Mackintosh to Nestlé's takeover, for example, was blamed by its defenders on the City's failure to appreciate fully the sovereign worth of the brands that the Swiss found so toothsome. But brands can't be meaningfully separated from the businesses that make and market the product: if brands are undervalued (as they have been in both the United States and Britain), they must be underexploited—in terms of generating their inherent profits and growth.

It's low nonsense to suggest, as some have, that a new accounting convention, placing a Nestlé-size value on a company's cherished brands, would somehow support the share price. Since when did the stock market pay any attention to balance sheet assets? The door swung open for the raiders on both sides of the Atlantic when the stock-market prices of the supertankers fell far below book value. The raiders' subsequent success in selling the constituent businesses at real market value—what other boards were willing to pay—is merely evidence of how central ineptitude made corporate wholes worth less than their parts, inverting the once-popular synergy theory that two and two add up to one whole management miracle.

Far from adding value, the decisions of supertanker managements have subtracted it. The defense could try to argue that, when two and two make three in the share price, the fault lies with the investors, not the management. But the argument collapses on the long roll call of severed divisions that have performed far better, and that right promptly, after escape from the supertanker. Nor is this merely a question of the buyout's financial incentives, juicy carrots though they are. The critical leverage—as the story of Smith-Corona and its typewriters also shows—comes from the independent power of decision, the elimination of bureaucratic tiers, and the strong sense of direction that the liberated management can generate: the Great Liberator is not the takeover expert, it appears, but his opposite, the divestment artist.

To hold back the potential of the severed divisions, other corporate aspects of the supertankers must have had the heavy, clanking effect of balls and chains. *Chain* is the right word, for long chains of command, winding down and around the organization, are the villains of these pieces. *Command* is the wrong word. Along that winding line, the ability of leaders to lead, of decision makers to decide, gets diffused and diluted. The former stately progress of the supertankers was self-propelled, not led. Few ostensible commanders followed Peter Drucker's formula for decisive leadership, as given in *The Wall Street Journal*: "thinking through the organization's mission, defining it and establishing it, clearly and visibly." His leader "sets the goals, sets the priorities, and sets and maintains the standards": in other words, he is truly in charge.

Effective leaders, as Drucker notes, are rarely "permissive." But "when things go wrong—and they always do—they do not blame others." That isn't because the others are of no account: the true leader "is not afraid of strength in associates and subordinates." Drucker's "final requirement of leadership is to earn trust." The crucial word in that sentence is *earn*. The supertankers' automatic journeys are lubricated by automatic trust. But an essential difference between Japanese and Western management is that the Oriental trust, while vast, is contingent on performance—and not, as is the case too often in the West, on promises.

Performance, in turn, rests on that readiness to change, to do new things in new ways, that is now the only guarantee (and by no means an absolute one) of corporate stability. The reason nobody would easily believe the opening paragraph of this section is that Japanese managers would never dream, even to Wall Street analysts, of sacrificing long-term market position for short-term financial rewards. These days, the business bureaucracies are doomed to take suboptimal decisions, and the bigger the corpocracies are, the harder they are going to fall.

It follows that, to get better, stronger, optimal decisions, leading to stronger, better, competitive performance, the corpocrats need to take lessons from their own severed divisions. They require, so to speak, to "buy out" businesses that remain and thrive inside the corporation. The formula is simple enough.

1. Construct operating companies in the coherent form they would need to adopt to stand on their own fast-running feet.

2. Reduce levels of management to the lowest possible number, with the fewest possible reporting requirements.

3. Give operating management true independence of decision and insist that the people concerned use it.

4. Encourage them to think ahead to ambitious long-term goals for their businesses and to embody those aims in their decisions and their management styles.

5. Link financial reward as strongly as possible to the performance of the individual businesses—and spread the rewards as far down as you can.

6. Encourage a high level of public visibility for the individual operating businesses.

7. Don't second-guess the operating managers: if that becomes imperative because of their errors, change the managers.

These seven decisions, while the most important internal ones corpocrats could ever take, are psychologically difficult for them, and might seem to represent an abdication of leadership. Not so: they mean leading excellently on the full Drucker definition. They are the way to breed "strong associates and subordinates," and, by earning their trust, to earn the ability to influence their decisions for the better without second-guessing, looking over their shoulders, slowing them down, or fighting endless internecine struggles. The alternative is to retain total control of the supertanker and all who sail therein. But the decision makers below decks won't then compete effectively, and if they don't compete, the whole supertanker will sink.

7. THE COMEBACK OF KODAK

Right across the Western world, the leaders of major corporations in all manner of industries and markets took the same decision in the early 1980s—the decision to compete. It sounds ridiculous. Hadn't markets always been competitive? Wasn't that intrinsic to the workings of capitalism? If companies hadn't been competing before, what had management been up to?

Not managing too well, according to figures published in *Business Week.* Even in mid-1988 U.S. manufacturers were carrying up to nine months in working stock and inventory—against under two months for Japan. On the vital measure of the time taken from order to shipment, the U.S. machine tool industry, once the wonder of the world, took five to six months; the Japanese two months at most. In the electronics industry, where Silicon Valley has set the pace in nonstop innovation and IBM has long lorded it over the largest market sector by far, U.S. quality defects and rework were averaging 8 percent to 10 percent; the Japanese figure is 1 percent or less—and you can't get much smaller than that.

Nor is there any doubt over how these large gaps have arisen. One is sheer firepower. In 1975 dollars, the Japanese in 1988 were investing $6,500 per worker, a 90 percent rise since 1975, against the American figure of $2,600: that was an increase of only a quarter. In consequence, the average age of U.S. equipment, at seventeen years, compared very badly with the youth of Japanese plant and machinery: only ten years.

Obviously, the Americans (like many Europeans) have found it tough to jack themselves out of the noncompetitive trough—for the above figures (and this is a grisly thought) represent a considerable *improvement* on earlier U.S. performance.

Large businesses based in the U.S. have been cushioned by the significant position in the global market they acquired by virtue of one uncomplimentary fact: in business after business, the U.S. home market still accounts for 40 percent of world sales. So it's been easier for U.S. managements to pull their punches and to resist a full-scale assault on their lack of competitiveness.

But there's a deeper explanation. The pressure of competition has demanded the fundamental and continuous change that comes hard to an old-line company, of which Eastman Kodak can stand as an example. Like IBM in computers, Kodak to all intents and purposes *was* the photographic market. It used its muscle to prevent competitors from breaking into its near monopoly. It made only the products management wanted to make, and used the quasi-monopoly to exercise a hammerlock on the whole chain of distribution.

Given half (or even a quarter of) a chance, most managements would try to achieve the same dominance today—and would call it successful competition. But behind such quasi-monopolies, their own immune systems are working against them. Internal innovation gets resisted as strongly as external, and sometimes even more fiercely. Management comes to rely on the longest production runs and highest volumes to obtain economic costs—which means that new processes and products get passed up. Maintaining the profitability rather than the progress of the company becomes a dominant mind-set.

In a word, the management becomes fundamentally uncompetitive. The consequence in Kodak's case was a six-year collapse in profits as Fuji Photo Film Co. drove coaches and horses through the gap that the giant had allowed to yawn open. Kodak was forced into a TINA decision: there was no alternative to radical shake-up. On the negative side, middle managers were axed, wage costs were trimmed, millions were taken out of budgets and overheads, whole operations were closed, the organization was restructured; more positively, R & D spending was increased, and quality and cost control were improved as the platform for a plethora of the new products that were so few and far between in the era of quasi-monopoly.

But *Business Week* still noted in February 1988 that the nub of critics' concern was that "the company has yet to inspire confidence that it can conceive, develop and market new products that aren't closely related to its office-copier and traditional photography businesses." The magazine quoted a string of flops in information technology, videos, electronic publishing, and batteries.

No doubt fortunately, the management under Colby H. Chandler didn't have to rely on those new ventures: Chandler could decide to buy growth and diversification in the traditional, deceptively easy way—by acquisition. Kodak's decision to purchase Sterling Drug for $5.1 billion is no different from scores of deals made every week by companies big and small. Effectively employed, acquisition can add greatly to a company's strength and radically accelerate its real growth—but it doesn't make an uncompetitive business competitive.

In many cases, management simply doubles up its problems—Sterling, in fact, is a competitive laggard: "While other companies are pumping out a steady stream of innovative prescription drugs," wrote *Business Week,* "Sterling has just one that tops $100 million in sales." The true test of competitive dynamism, very obviously, is not the ability to purchase other companies but the power to generate new growth by the exploitation of existing and new market opportunities. And there is a real and plainly active danger that, just as quasi-monopoly allowed that dynamism to degenerate, so, behind the screen of acquired pseudogrowth, the real relative strengths of the corporation will continue to be eroded.

8. DECIDING TO COMPETE

Why had the grand Western decision to compete been born, or become so universally necessary? The answer points to the nature of management's previous behavior, which had been uncompetitive in several senses. As technologies changed and developed, previously inviolable market shares such as Kodak's became threatened. Companies from Japan proved far more effective than Westerners at exploiting the so-called strategic windows opened up by technological shifts. The latter in turn helped both to create and to meet even more rapid and disruptive changes in consumer preferences.

By the time that slower-thinking and slower-acting Western decision makers had awakened to the challenge, huge competitive gaps had been opened up in the most direct area of all: basic efficiency in making the product. In the old days (whether they were good old days or bad is irrelevant—they're gone forever), managers could unwisely shut their eyes to lower Japanese costs by blaming the higher Western wage levels that were beyond their control.

The new days are worse—worse, that is, for the traditional market leaders—because the competitive gap has been created largely by superior technology and management. It's a gap that, if the underdog does nothing, will widen—unlike labor cost differentials, which tend to be narrowed by exchange rate movements and by domestic pressures on the successful competitors. Second, the gap, because of the nature of modern processes and design technology, is reflected in product quality and attributes as well as production costs. Third, leadership in production and product technology rapidly translates into market leadership in conditions in which protectionism is increasingly ineffective.

The fact that 45 percent of manufactured goods imported into the United States came under some kind of voluntary or involuntary protection didn't prevent the largest trade deficits in American history from piling up. Some of the lost markets have gone forever: consumer electronics is only the most conspicuous area where the United States, once world leader, found itself no longer in the race. There but for the grace of God went everybody else, so the decision to compete is easily explained.

But the stark contrast between Japanese firms such as Fuji and Western firms such as Kodak is not only the way in which the former brought down the costs of production. The Easterners have given their opposition painful lessons in innovation, cost-effectiveness, and aggression in existing markets, such as color film. They have also shown much greater ability to generate major new businesses from scratch. Honda, for outstanding instance, has, since the early 1960s, created a major car manufacturer out of nothing—using no assets save its engineering genius and reputation as a maker of motorcycles. In a series of strikingly brave decisions, Honda not only went into cars, but, squeezed into a small domestic share by the competitive strength of Toyota and others, decided to seek its future in the United States.

In the 1980s the Japanese company opened three plants in North America, upping its U.S. market share from 4.2 percent to 7.2 percent—as noted in this Part, easily ahead of Toyota. Such investment decisions are far harder, not only to take but to implement, than a decision to buy or be bought. The financial risks are (often deceptively) less apparent in the latter case, while the management risks (and work load) are far greater in the former. Also, the time scale is much shorter: when British Aerospace's chairman decided with the boss of Rover Group, the last survivor of British-owned mass production of cars, to pursue a merger, the initial contact took hardly any time at all—against the four years required to bring a new car from idea to reality.

It was, of course, the inability of Rover's predecessor managements, over many more years than four, to develop a successful competitive strategy that led to this final act in its deeply troubled history. The relatively easy decision to acquire or be acquired is not a truly *competitive* strategy. That takes (as in the Honda case) a whole series of decisions that are bound together tightly by an overwhelmingly important decision about what kind of company management wants to run.

The classical competitor was introverted, concentrating on becoming lowest-cost producer, and using its control over distribution channels to take maximum advantage of its productive power. The modern competitor is an extrovert, concentrating on the provision of highest relative value and highest relative quality—as perceived by customers who are not a homogeneous mass but a widely fragmented collection of needs.

This demands far more flexibility and far greater responsiveness than large companies are accustomed to show. So great are the obstacles that so wise an observer as Peter Drucker now says that big companies are irrelevant. The competitive, innovative pace is being set by smaller firms: large ones aren't needed for the job. Yet it's still a task that every management must have at the front of its preoccupations: to build the strategic capacity that in turn builds a business.

If management cannot build better businesses than it can buy, either it is not trying or it lacks abilities that are becoming more and more decisive as the pressures of competition mount. These pressures have their pains, but the reverse side shines bright. Today's public, in industrial and consumer markets alike, is far readier to accept new ideas—and to desert old suppliers for any better deal on offer. The decision to compete, therefore, has to hinge on keeping customers not by muscle and inertia but by constantly producing the best—on every dimension of the product and the service.

The decision to compete, in sum, is not a single decision at all. It is not a monocular vision of the present and future of the company but more like the multifaceted view through an insect's eye, not only because there are at least seven crucial dimensions of strategic decision but because each of the seven raises so many decisive subsets of its own—subsets that are best expressed, and tackled, in the form of questions and answers.

Study of the companies that have best mastered (in both the West and the East) the strategic decisions of the Age of Competition shows these seven crucial dimensions of success:

1. Compete.
2. Lead the market.
3. Think big.
4. Be professional.
5. Innovate.
6. Defend your base.
7. Welcome change.

Nothing, though, can guarantee success in times that are changing so fast and in which the challenges come from many directions. The challenges are not all external. There is the constant internal challenge of achieving the strategic efficiency from which good decisions flow and without which effective implementation is impossible. It isn't enough, for example, to tell management that competition is the essence of today's markets. Everybody knows that. *But do you know your sales as a proportion of those of your key competitors? How the ratio has changed over the past year? And how you're going to raise it this year—and next?*

Second, the essence of competition is to achieve a higher market penetration by obtaining a higher perceived ranking in the eyes of the customers who make up that market. *Do you know—not think, know—what customers think of you and your products or services, in relation to the competition? If you don't know, will you spend your money to find out?*

Third, the evidence is overwhelming that the race goes not just to the swift but to the management that aims highest, that thinks biggest. *Do you have plans for (a) developing existing businesses, (b) building new ones, and (c) acquiring other firms that will, if successful, have a radically large effect on sales and profits?*

Fourth, there's a rising premium today on professional management. That means knowing what you're doing, knowing how to do it, doing it, and working all the time to improve performance on all three factors. *Have your people all been through some form of valuable training in the past twelve months? Have you personally read any management books, attended any management seminars, taken any action on anything you've learned from any such source?*

Fifth, innovation has become a more fashionable theme even than competition, of which it is obviously a key ingredient. These days the new, or what's perceived as new, can create profitable supergrowth in the most unpromising situations— such as the way, previously mentioned, in which Minolta zoomed to the front of a static giant-dominated market in single-lens reflex cameras with its autofocus Magnum. *In the past year, has there been an important innovation in (a) internal procedures and processes, (b) the products and/or services offered to the market, (c) the way in which they are offered? Will there be any in the next year?*

Sixth, defending the base is basic. That's the one place where you must hang on to your customers with all your strength, by beating out the competition. *Have you compared your performance in your staple business with others, and are you convinced—by facts—that you are equal to or better than the best on all key aspects? If not, do you have plans to raise yourself to the best standards?*

Seventh is change. "The only permanent thing in life is change," said Heraclitus, and that was five centuries before Christ. *Have you in the last twelve months looked at any important aspect of the business with a critical eye—and, if you found defects, have you instituted reforms?* An example is the sales force: when did you last look at its recruitment, training, remuneration, organization, and performance? If any company, examining its sales effort across the board, finds nothing that could be improved, it deserves congratulation—and amazed congratulation at that.

The seven questions could just as easily have been seventy, because modern management and modern business have an infinite number of facets, just as modern markets have an infinite number of opportunities. The task of the manager, as decision maker and executive, is to reduce the complex and infinite to the simple and particular—a task that applies to the choice of opportunity and to the organization of the corporate machine that will exploit those choices, to the integration of modern technology into all processes, and to the management of human beings in the ways that best unleash their potential.

Such high ambitions won't be achieved by slogans. There's been no mention so far in this discussion of the word *core* or the fashionable concept of the *core business.* The idea of deciding which businesses deserve concentrated attention and which should be discontinued is a useful way of organizing the corporate mind. But it adds little new to the old (relatively speaking) ideas of Theodore Levitt or the Boston Consulting Group. Analyze most "core" businesses, in any event, and they fragment into many businesses that are not especially coherent. Moreover, since managements are free to decide on a total switch from one core business to another—such as the British company Reed International, ditching paper and other interests entirely to concentrate on publishing, and turning over nearly $4 billion in the process—the idea has no permanent value.

The true strategic core of a corporation isn't the business it happens to inhabit at any given point but its philosophy, its driving principles, its ethos, its ambitions and the way in which those ambitions are pursued. That concept, now going under its fashionable name of "culture," has a very long pedigree, stretching back to the between-wars creators of companies like National Cash Register, General Electric, and Procter & Gamble, if not before them to Du Pont. Like cores, cultures can be changed. The truly competitive culture, however, is built on that knowledge and so constantly evolves. The process of asking and constantly answering questions like those above will inevitably bring evolution in its wake. The triumph of truly competitive strategic decision making is to achieve revolutionary results by evolutionary means.

9. THE MIGHT OF MATARAZZO

One key decision is common to nearly all great businesses and mighty fortunes. That decision is wonderfully demonstrated by one Francisco Matarazzo. In 1892, he was an insignificant Italian from Castelbate, an insignificant place near Naples, who had arrived in Brazil with (so history has it) something like 700 francs knotted into his handkerchief. He intended to use this capital for a trading enterprise. But using his eyes and his head, the insignificant man spotted a most significant aspect of the Brazilian economy: in a backward land emerging only at that moment from a basis in slavery, all manufactured goods were imported, paid for by the export of the country's abounding raw materials.

In those circumstances, naturally, the Brazilians were paying their American suppliers of manufactures through every nose in the country. Matarazzo reckoned this gave him the perfect opportunity—no competition at home, huge margins guaranteed by the greedy suppliers from the north, and the whole immense market of Brazil (a territory the size of the continental United States) at his disposal. He chose lard as his first venture, opening a minute factory in rented premises in a town called Sorocaba—a place as insignificant as the infant entrepreneur—and began to succeed.

Matarazzo, though, decided to move to São Paulo, a town of little more significance than either Sorocaba or the man from Naples. When lard lost its magic, Matarazzo decided on another move—into flour; from flour, he moved up to macaroni, sacks, chemicals, glassware, and supported his now vast number of factories with plantations, a private rail system, cargo boats, a bank. On his death at age eighty-three, just before World War II, Matarazzo was employing 20,000 people in seventy businesses. At their zenith, under the leadership of the twelfth of the old boy's fourteen children, the 300 factories of the so-called Industrial Organization of Latin America were employing 30,000 people and using as much electricity as a single Latin American country, Peru.

What was the first Matarazzo's key decision that is common to most great businesses? There were several remarkable steps along his way.

1. He decided to seek his fortune in a wide open territory where by definition there were more opportunities.

2. He spotted a gross anomaly and decided to exploit it.

3. He decided to move out of a declining market before he also went into a decline.

4. He decided to diversify his product line wherever he saw an opportunity.

5. He decided to adopt vertical integration, getting control over his distribution, raw materials, and finance.

6. He decided to back the future of São Paulo, in which he was triumphantly right. Back in 1957, when the Matarazzo empire was riding at its highest, the great city on its plateau was a wonder of that part of the world, with 3 million inhabitants. Thirty years later there were four times as many people living among and around the city's skyscrapers and banks.

The still-larger element common to all six big decisions is that they are steps: each followed naturally from the other as Matarazzo ascended to one of the greatest fortunes ever made in Latin America. The great decision maker knows in his bones that one successfully completed advance opens the gate to another even greater opportunity. He develops an irresistible momentum—and that never stops until he does.

10. RESISTING THE IRRESISTIBLE

Walk down any smart Paris street and you'll see a Japanese restaurant or a shop sign in Japanese, or both. Go into two of the top hotels in Matarazzo's city of São Paulo, Brazil, in early 1988 and you would have found one staging a Japanese gastronomic festival and the other with a permanent Japanese restaurant. Walking around Brazil's megacity, the Japanese would seem omnipresent; waiting at the airport, every arrival would seem to offload another contingent from Japan—and this phenomenon has deep significance.

The Parisian influx, after all, could be at least partly explained by tourism. Thanks to the risen yen, the Japanese became the world's nouveaux riches, and the French have always had an eye for a fast franc. But nobody has ever visited São Paulo for the sights, although the upward and outward surge of this vast industrial and commercial center since Matarazzo and Company set it going has remained among the wonders of the world. That, of course, would explain the interest and presence of Japanese management and its entourage of waiters and chefs: Brazil has plainly been selected by Japan's decision makers as the prime target for their apparently irresistible expansionism.

The test of any Western competitive decision is that it must resist the irresistible, which doesn't sound too promising. Why the Japanese decision landed on Brazil is understandable: Japan needs alternative sources of the raw materials in which Brazil is rich, and there must be huge potential in a teeming market, larger in population than Japan and bigger in landmass than the continental United States. True, a country where, in the late 1980s, inflation could easily beat double figures in a month isn't the acme of economic or political stability. But does that matter if, like Hitachi, you are managing on a 2,000-year time horizon?

This readiness to take decisions on the longest of long views is one of the obvious strengths that helped Japan's top companies into their ascendancy. *Obvious* is the word. The management mystery is why Western decision makers have been so slow to recognize and imitate the methods that have worked magic for Eastern rivals, many of whom (as Westerners too easily forget) were once in dire straits. Take Toyota. The world's most successful car manufacturer was a highway wreck in 1949; strapped for cash and stuffed with unsold cars, Toyota laid off workers and suffered a strike that idled the desperate company for two months.

What saved Toyota was the work of an extraordinary inventor, Taiichi Ohno. He made the wonderful decision that a machine or a man producing defective goods isn't working; ergo, they must be enabled to work by the system. To this end, he devised some world-beating inventions: they included *kanban*, the brilliantly simple system of colored cards that travel with the parts to regulate the flow of just-in-time deliveries from suppliers; and *jidoka*, which roughly means "automation-plus." The plus consists of machines that stop themselves if malfunctions appear, and of workers who are encouraged to stop the line in similar circumstances.

Where Western factory managements concentrated their decisions on keeping the line going at all costs (and often too much cost), Ohno was only interested in producing perfect goods. The Toyota production system's elegant principles, which rapidly extended throughout Japan, have lately been spreading quite fast in the West. But it took thirty years to get from Ohno's wonderful decision to the perfection of his ideas: What were Western manufacturers doing (or not doing) all that time? Had the system been developed in Detroit, home of the traditional, mechanical, obsolete assembly line, would the Japanese have hesitated so long to follow suit?

During those three decades, the conventionally wise decision maker didn't weigh Japanese *management* too seriously. American managers and methods were assumed to rule; the essential decision—to match the Japanese blow for blow, system for system—was ducked by head-in-the-sand executives. The ostriches smothered themselves with the false comfort that Japan's successes all sprang from transient tricks such as the undervaluation of the yen. By the time that myth was finally deflated by the yen's superperformance of the 1980s, it was too late to save many American industries and companies.

The long-term power of Ohno-like decision making lay behind the deflating achievements recorded in the London *Financial Times* in early 1988 under the title "A Year of Stunning Adjustment." A survey noted the "remarkable agility" with which companies had responded to the challenge of the yen. Second-quarter corporate earnings were up 30 percent, factory output was growing by 5 percent annually, not a single significant bankruptcy had occurred, and sharply boosted investment had spawned a flood of new products. These innovations are one product of the long view; another is the Japanese genius at cost reduction (they call it "cost-down"). Thus Hitachi's giant VCR plant at Tokai, which once needed three whole minutes to make a set, cut the time to ninety seconds—for which the entire plant required just four workers.

The other prongs of Japan's answer to the yen challenge are to exploit new markets (hence Brazil) and (like the Americans before them) to export production as well as producers. The telling difference is that the Japanese stars started from a far stronger export base than the postwar American invaders of Europe. Nor is it easy to visualize the Japanese relinquishing their market holds after overseas plants have been established. Not for them the humiliation of a Volkswagen, forced by market failure to abandon American manufacture. The joint plant that Toyota established with General Motors at Fremont, California, rapidly became a legend as the most efficient in the GM empire (which, alas, meant less than it should have).

The more than meaningful results that Japanese managers have won with American workers in deadbeat factories like those surrendered by Firestone to Bridgestone of Japan have brought the challenge into America's front yard. There's no hiding place from the threat, unless companies decide to be more Japanese than the Japanese: more ambitious, more professional, more competitive, longer-sighted, more imaginative, more innovative, harder-working. That sounds about as promising a task as resisting the irresistible. But the Japanese didn't win their global leadership in, for just three examples, production systems, consumer electronics, and random-access memories solely through their own decisions and actions.

The inaction of the West's decision makers has been a crucial factor in what in many fields amounted to showing the white flag. But the subsequent harsh awakening may not have taught all the right lessons. It could be that even today's best corporate decision makers are running down the wrong strategic road. A new, strong, conventional wisdom grew up in the 1980s—the creed of competition. This set of accepted ideas has profoundly affected management's behavior and decisions in what are the most competitive markets ever seen. But the fate of conventional wisdom and accepted ideas is to be wrong—and the end-century conditions are the very ones in which error is most likely to be catastrophic.

Conventionally wise Western companies "rationalize" their product lines, business portfolios, and factories to achieve the lowest possible costs in the "core businesses" on which they concentrate and that qualify for this attention by the "attractiveness" of their markets and the company's ability to win a large enough market share to be at best a world-class (at least, a strong national) player. The clearest result of this wisdom has been wave upon wave of acquisitions and divestments, as companies seek to restructure their portfolios and strengthen those "cores." But there's a vital missing element—and all business history, including that of the turbulent present, teaches that this element is the most vital of all.

This crucial omission is shown up sharply in the book *Strategies and Styles* by Michael Goold and Andrew Campbell (see Part VI, section 10). In their study of well-known companies, the critical difference was the amount of top management time devoted to achieving planned "organic growth" in group businesses. The "financial control" companies, which concentrate on extracting the highest possible returns, achieved only a 3.5 percent organic growth rate over the years 1981 to 1985. The "strategic control" companies, which seek to have the best of both worlds (financial orientation and planning), grew organically by no more than 5 percent. For the out-and-out strategic planners, who place less emphasis on immediate financial returns, more on long-term growth, the figure was 10 percent.

All these numbers were pathetically beaten by the financial control companies' record on growth through acquisition—up 27 percent. Here the strategic control companies had *negative* growth because of the spate of divestments by managements struggling out of recession. Since, as was noted earlier, many of the businesses sold, especially the management buyouts such as Premier Brands, have gone on to perform excellently—far outgrowing their former parents—it must be true that under the previous ownership businesses were being managed well below their true potential.

Undermanagement is the real reason for the relatively sluggish record on "organic growth"—one that contrasts shamingly with that of Japanese companies, which hardly ever use the weapon of acquisition and even more rarely decide to abandon a business. The true measure of management is not its brilliance in finding and consummating acquisitions, it is its ability to achieve exceptional profitability and growth from its businesses and markets. The word *achieve* tells the essence of the task far better than *organic*, which suggests that, like the growth of plants and animals, business expansion is natural and (given the right diet) follows automatically.

That only applies for a limited period in the life cycle of any business. A far better analogy is "athletic" growth. Athletes constantly improve their performance and raise their sights by training, bodybuilding, and coaching; businesses are defended and improved similarly by the positive development at which the Japanese have proved expert. What's more, markets can be improved likewise. It is not completely true that there are no bad markets, only bad businesses. But even the worst markets usually contain at least one good business—a company that earns consistently high returns and achieves solid growth even though it may have only a small share of a market any strategic planner would decide to be highly "unattractive."

The concept of the "good business" sounds old-fashioned. So did the idea of running a company to generate cash, before recession made it a dire necessity. Then it proved to be a dynamic force for growth as well as an elementary and essential control. Creating or sustaining a good business places heavy demands on management, however; it may mean deciding to make a market bigger and better, enlarging the pie rather than struggling to carve out a larger slice. That may not be as tough as it sounds, for when a new competitor enters an apparently saturated market, the latter's total size (even if the new entry fails) almost invariably increases. What's the explanation?

The answer is obvious: the new entry stimulates the market; the old-stagers weren't stimulating it enough. Relatively small markets have often been turned into worldwide bonanzas (as happened with antiulcer therapy when Tagamet appeared), and seemingly dead markets have often been injected with wonderful life. The compact 35-mm camera seemed a lost cause until a consultant established why it wasn't being bought. When the client decided to redesign the camera to eliminate the obstacles to purchase, the segment started to grow by 50 percent annually in a world market whose "maturity" made it look anything but "attractive."

Market "attractiveness," in other words, can be powerfully influenced to create a good business. Another definition of "good business" is one you'd dearly love to own yourself (which successful buyout managers actually do). Proprietorial managers in the West, on the whole, have been far better than professional managements at making businesses grow organically—or athletically. That's no coincidence. The proprietor is in the business from personal decision, and it grows because he personally believes in the business and its market. He doesn't look at his company from one or even two angles but sees it as it really is: in the round.

By far the most successful challengers to IBM, in main-

frames, minicomputers, and personal computers, started as
proprietorial companies led by men such as Gene Amdahl,
Ken Olsen, and Steve Jobs; the professionally managed competitors, by and large (and most were very large), made miserable decisions and executed them as badly. The conventional
wisdom is helping to ensure that the professional managers will
go on failing to make their strategic decisions in proprietorial
manner and with proprietorial success. Refer back to the model
of the conventional wisdom, with its emphasis on "rationalization," "core businesses," "attractiveness," and "market share,"
and it's clear why the conventionally wise can't learn the proprietorial lessons.

The decision maker's real task is to develop and stimulate
lasting enterprises that, taking one year with another, will grow
profitably into a foreseeable future that stretches far ahead.
And this means doing much, much better than half of Britain's
one hundred largest companies, which, according to *Finance*
magazine, failed to match the rate of inflation in the return on
their plowed-back capital over the entire decade to 1987. Chief
executives certainly want real, athletic, organic growth. But
they probably won't achieve that truly enterprising expansion
without changing the ways in which they conventionally think,
decide, and act—and that achieved a sorry payoff from plowback that mirrors the murky U.S. performance.

It's fascinating to compare the postwar plowback of that
nonexistent but pervasive company, Japan, Inc., with the six-
point decision formula that made Matarazzo his millions.
Japan's decision makers went for the wide open spaces in expert markets for their products. They spotted anomalies such
as the quasi-monopolies accorded to companies such as Eastman Kodak and Xerox by slack Western competitors. They
moved their emphasis out of declining markets such as ship-
building into fast-growing ones such as electronics. They inte-

grated their production machine right back to raw materials in other lands. And consistently—in diversification, R & D, and selection of new markets such as Brazil—they sought to back the future.

More than that, they went beyond Matarazzo in implementing the seventh, most important, decision—to establish and maintain an unstoppable momentum. Many Western decision makers have still not comprehended the full meaning of Japanese corporate strategy, which in its latest phase is plowing back the massive capital surplus thrown up by earlier vast successes in order to establish a strong manufacturing presence in the West and a dominant position in its capital markets. Those Western ostriches need to take their heads out of the sand and contemplate not only the present but the past—including the fate of the Matarazzo empire.

The old boy had two weaknesses. First, that essential long-term vision didn't extend to providing an effective long-term succession. Mismanagement by his heirs reduced the Industrial Organization of Latin America to less happy straits, which left a later generation to try to restore the family fortunes. But the second long-term weakness was just as deadly. Outside Brazil, who's heard of Matarazzo? Almost nobody. Outside Japan, who's heard of Matsushita? The whole civilized world.

That's because old Konosuke Matsushita, unlike old Francisco Matarazzo, looked outward, beyond his own frontiers to the world, and went outward to build a global business around the concept of organic, athletic growth, expanding in ever-larger circles or climbing in ever-higher steps. Decision makers who stop short will never resist the irresistible. As the Japanese themselves have shown the world, it can be done.

To summarize some of the main points I've made about the competitors:

1. Nature abhors a monopoly or a complacent market leader: where either exists, there lurks an opportunity for an outsider to snatch.

2. When a success is selling itself, the great decision maker takes a fresh look at the success and makes fresh decisions to renew and reinvigorate its competitive life.

3. The second-stage development of brilliant breakthroughs may lack the brilliance, but will pay off even more brilliantly in long-term competitive strength.

4. Someday somebody will compete with you all too effectively unless you have a crucial internal strength that can be preserved or an external arrangement that protects your position.

5. The great decision maker doesn't concentrate on the weaknesses of the company but on its competitive strengths.

6. The successful buyout competes more effectively—less through the power of financial incentives than through independence, elimination of bureaucracy, and a new sense of direction.

7. Behind the screen of acquired supergrowth, the real competitive powers of the business are often being sapped.

8. The triumph of the truly competitive management is to achieve revolutionary results by evolutionary means.

9. Rationalization is usually another word for the closing or selling of businesses that have been managed far below their true competitive potential.

10. Decision makers who stop short of nonstop development and stimulation of lasting enterprises will never resist the apparently irresistible momentum of the Japanese—who have themselves often shown that the impossible can be done.

THE WAY OUT
OF THE JUNGLE

The six explorers who faced the forked path in the jungle and the Indian with the forked tongue are in all of us. Decision makers are by turns impetuous, intuitive, overconfident, rational, sheeplike, and unable to make up their minds. We come to the choice of path, often the correct choice, by shaking this kaleidoscope of conflicting drives until the pattern seems perfect, possible, or good enough. Even simple yes-no alternatives can place heavy mental stress on the explorers. But today, and not only in business, fewer and fewer decisions are simple.

More often than not, the decision maker, like an examination candidate, faces multiple-choice questions: only, the alternatives may be more than those listed on the paper; and, very probably, there's no single right answer. For instance, this book points uncharitably to sins of commission and omission by two mighty industrial managements: those at General Motors and IBM. In charity, these executives faced decisions of a complexity that their great predecessors were spared.

At GM, models could once be planned with perfect security, in the knowledge that American customers were content with broadly similar American-made gas-guzzlers given annual skin-deep face-lifts and marketed under brands (Cadillac, Buick, Oldsmobile, Pontiac, Chevrolet) to which the purchasers were inextricably attached. The path out of the jungle was safe, and it had no forks.

At IBM, a more sophisticated company than any in Detroit, a postwar generation of managers could expand across the world, secure in the knowledge that an immense customer base guaranteed the demand for excessively profitable leases of whatever mainframe computers the company's engineers chose to make. There was only one path out of the jungle, and it belonged to IBM.

When their paths suddenly forked, and the cannibals, tigers, swamps, and crocodiles appeared, the security and vested interests of the past blinded these decision makers, and many others, to the full significance of the changes. But even wide open eyes would have found no easy way to new safety. Threats such as Japanese productive efficiency, personal computers and their clones, the switch in taste toward smaller cars, or the pressure for universal software standards could not be met without complex decisions and equally complex changes in organizations that had become set in the ways of the earlier simplicity.

The decisions were complex. But the mistakes made by decision makers, many of them recorded in this book, were mostly simple. The explorers stepped straight into the swamp. The general cause was emotional and intellectual inability to confront and master change. The explorers either couldn't believe that their well-trodden path had forked so perilously or, believing in the fork but ignoring the peril, they plunged into the unknown without much care or merited attention.

The case of Kraft's John M. Richman can stand as a monument to the changing complexities of the end-twentieth-century world. As reported in Part VI, section 1, "The Divorce of Dart & Kraft," he first merged Dart and Kraft to gain the supposed benefits of scale and diversity, then demerged the pair to gain the supposed benefits of a concentrated food business, which also meant selling Duracell's batteries; but that deal laid Kraft wide open to the $11.5 billion takeover bid from Philip Morris.

The man-eating tigers had got it.

The modern decision maker, facing many forks and multiple perils, will get nowhere if the threats overwhelm him: the sixth explorer's indecisive waiting under the tree is no answer in an age when the opportunities are far more impressive than the threats. These pages have chronicled many of the brilliancies by which decision makers, from the mighty to the minor, have unerringly dealt with the two-tongued Indians, found the right paths, and changed their worlds by becoming allies of change.

In a world of swift, uncharted change, the way of the great explorer is the way out of the jungle. The man-of-action qualities of curiosity, adventure, boldness, preparedness, and determination have to be married with the scientific thinker's knowledge, know-how, analysis, forethought, imagination, and thoroughness. Convinced that he is right, the explorer/decision maker wastes no time when shown that he is wrong: he changes his mind. What else can you do in changing times?

The crocodiles, tigers, and cannibals make their own decisions, true, which increases the complexities for decision makers whose dietary habits are more wholesome. To believe that reason and courage will always find the right fork in the path takes a third noble human attribute: faith. With reason, courage, and faith on your side, though, the jungle should hold no lasting terrors.

Selected Bibliography

Since all business management revolves around effective decision making, any book on or by practitioners and their practices can provide useful insights into how the deciding mind works, for good or for ill. The following list is of works that have contributed, in one way or another, to my own thoughts on decisions and decision makers in general, and to the contents of this book in particular.

ABEGGLEN, JAMES C., and STALK, GEORGE, JR. *Kaisha: The Japanese Corporation.* New York: Basic Books, 1985. Nobody knows Japanese business better than Abegglen, a consultant and management professor, who is an excellent guide to Japan's decisive thinking.

DEMING, W. EDWARDS. *Out of the Crisis.* Cambridge, Eng.: Cambridge University Press, 1989. The contribution of this exceptional American thinker and practitioner to management East and West has been immense: his fourteen points are the key to the continuous decisions that result in improved quality and performance.

DRUCKER, PETER F. *The Effective Executive.* New York: Harper & Row, 1967. The only problem with the works of the master of modern management writing is which one to choose; but in the context of decision making, this is my pick for starters.

ENRICO, ROGER. *The Other Guy Blinked: How Pepsi Won the Cola Wars.* New York: Bantam Books, 1986. Written with Roger Kornbluth, this book contains an enthralling, though hardly impartial, account of how the most conspicuously wrong decision in marketing history justified the subtitle.

FALLON, IVAN, and SRODES, JAMES. *Takeovers.* London: Hutchinson, 1988. Written before the mergers-and-acquisitions mania reached its apogee, this book describes the processes that led to and executed some of the most expensive decisions of the era.

FAY, STEPHEN. *Portrait of an Old Lady: Turmoil at the Bank of England.* London: The Viking Press, 1987. An exceptionally well written account of why the subtitle has so often been an apt description of the results of the bank's decisions and indecisions.

GOOLD, MICHAEL, and CAMPBELL, ANDREW. *Strategies and Styles.* New York: Basil Blackwell, 1988. Deserves to become a classic on the subject of the role of the center in managing diversified corporations, which lies at the heart of corporate decision making, for better or (all too often) for worse.

HARVEY-JONES, SIR JOHN. *Making It Happen: Reflections on Leadership.* London: Collins, 1988. In a class of its own as a practitioner's "reflections on leadership," it provides a nonchronological account of how Britain's largest industrial corporation got turned around.

HELLER, ROBERT. *The Age of the Common Millionaire.* New York: E. P. Dutton, 1988. Although I wrote the book myself, it is still my most valuable source on many of the most valuable decisions made across the whole field of money-making.

JAMES, BARRIE G. *Business Wargames.* New York: Penguin Books, 1986. In demonstrating the relevance of military thought to management decision, this book provides many excellent analyses of decision making, right and wrong.

JOFFROY, PIERRE. *Brazil.* London: Studio Vista, 1965. Translated by Douglas Harman. This brilliant and beautiful short book was my source for the section on the fabulous rise of São Paulo and its most famous entrepreneurial decision maker, Francisco Matarazzo.

MAJARO, SIMON. *The Creative Gap*. London: Longmans, 1988. An invaluable and full account of how the crucial process of making innovative decisions can be improved and fostered in a supportive climate.

MORITA, AKIO. *Made in Japan*. New York: E. P. Dutton, 1986. The best known of all Japan's decision-making geniuses has produced an account of Sony's masterful development that is as useful as one of his company's multitudinous devices.

NAYAK, P. RANGANATH, and KETTERINGHAM, JOHN M. *Breakthroughs!* New York: Rawson Associates/Macmillan, 1986. The more I refer to this study of "How leadership and drive created commercial innovations that swept the world," the more I am impressed by its research and strength of analysis.

NIERENBERG, GERARD I. *The Complete Negotiator*. New York: Nierenberg & Zeif, 1986. The "father of contemporary negotiating training" has written a comprehensive and invaluable guide to making decisions in the hottest—and often most decisive—arena.

PINCHOT, GIFFORD, III. *Intrapreneuring*. New York: Harper & Row, 1985. An entertaining journey penetrating the corporate minefield, which, alas, enterprising incompany innovators must negotiate in the effort to turn their own decisions into action and get others to make any decisions at all.

WATERMAN, ROBERT H., JR. *The Renewal Factor*. New York: Bantam Books, 1988. The co-author of *In Search of Excellence* has thought deeply about how to cure the corporate sluggishness that induced the bad decisions that brought many *Excellence* heroes low.

Acknowledgments

Proving one of its theses (that one decision always leads to another), the decision to write this book led me on a fascinating journey through a vast terrain of sources for both accounts and analyses of decision making and decision makers. I am in consequence greatly indebted to the publishers of the books named in the bibliography for permission to quote—especially from the books by James C. Abegglen; W. Edwards Deming; Stephen Fay; Michael Goold and Andrew Campbell; Akio Morita; P. Ranganath Nayak and John M. Ketteringham, the last-named authors wrote *Breakthroughs!* under the auspices of the Arthur D. Little consultancy, although its main thrust is innovation, I found the accounts equally valuable in the context of how good decisions are made and obstructed; and Gerard I. Nierenberg.

The *Harvard Business Review*, as always, was a constant source of inspiration and information. I am grateful for permission to cite the articles referred to in the text by Michael Porter, Johny K. Johansson and Ikijuro Nonaka, Frank F. Gilmore, C. C. Markides and N. Berg, and Ben C. Ball. Several articles in *Fortune* magazine provided especially rich material, as did features in *Time*, *Business*

ACKNOWLEDGMENTS

Week, *The Wall Street Journal*, *Chief Executive*, the *Chicago Tribune*, and *The Journal of Business Strategy* in America; *Senior Management* in Bangkok; and, in Europe, *Reader's Digest*, the *Sunday Times*, the *International Herald Tribune*, *Finance*, and the *Financial Times*, whose reports on companies as far apart geographically as Asahi and Perrier were invaluable. I owe many thanks to all the editors, publishers, and writers concerned.

My thanks also go to the editor of *Management Today*, Lance Knobel, who kindly invited me to write a column for the magazine, another constant source of enlightenment: some of the material has provided the basis for chapters in this book. Nor can I ever forget the contribution made by my conversations with management leaders such as Sir John Harvey-Jones, whose speech to the President's Conference at Venice in 1986 I found especially inspiring; Fred Buggie, the expert on strategic innovation; Paul Judge, when chairman of Premier Brands; Ryuzaburo Kaku, president of Canon; the industrialists, especially Sir John Egan of Jaguar and Denys Henderson of ICI, who were interviewed for my BBC series and book *The State of Industry;* and Peter F. Drucker, whose work constantly sets an impossibly high target at which to aim.

The manuscript could not have been produced without the aid of my immensely competent sister, Jacqueline Edelman, and our combined Apple Macintoshes. But I must especially thank my publisher, Truman Talley, not only for his usual unfailing and expert support and guidance but also for first planting the seed of this book in my mind. The responsibility for the decision tree that grew is all mine—but the inspiration was his, and my gratitude is great.

Index

INDEX

"Attractiveness" of markets, 356–59
"Attractiveness" test, 38
Audemars Piguet watches, 271
Austin cars, 16
"Automatic" decisions, 120
Automobile industry
   Japanese, 16, 19, 40, 70, 160, 181,
     264, 297–300, 303, 322, 324,
     334–36, 345, 346, 353–55
   Korean, 80, 84–85
   U.K., 15–16, 166, 259, 261–71, 301,
     331, 345–46
   U.S., 16, 17, 52, 70, 80, 85, 158–62,
     164–67, 185–88, 192, 215, 233, 261,
     296–300, 303, 306, 335–37, 355,
     362–63
   West German, 16, 60, 245, 246, 265,
     269, 301, 355
   See also specific manufacturers
Avon Products, 170, 211
Azidothymidine (AZT), 80, 82, 84

Balance, principle of, 69–70
Baldwin, Stanley, 248
Ball, Ben C., 302–303
Bank of America, 249
Bank of England, 260, 288–90, 292–94
Banking, 17, 19, 71, 112, 167–68, 178,
   249, 250, 260, 288–94
Bartles & Jaymes wine coolers, 136
Bass family, 177, 178
BAT Industries, 144
Batteries, 1–2, 80, 84, 211, 343, 364
Battle of Britain, 331
Battle of the Bulge, 213
Bean, L. L., 90, 95
Bean, L. L., company, 90
Beatrice Foods, 139, 142, 145, 176
Beaverbrook, Lord, 59
Becherer, Hans W., 17
Beckman Instruments, 2–3, 329
Beer, *see* Brewers
Benedetti, Carlo de, 5–6
Benetton textiles, 233
Berg, N., 277–78
Berkshire Hathaway Company, 60

Berry, Anthony, 5
Berry, Tony, 106–11
Beta-blockers, 78
Betamax VCR technology, *see*
   Sony—VCRs
"Better-off" test, 38
Beyner, André, 273
Black, Sir James, 72, 74, 76–78
Black & Decker, 163
Black Monday, *see* Crash of 1987
Blind Watchmaker, The (Dawkins),
   218
Blue Arrow employment agency, 5,
   106–107, 110
Bluhdorn, Charles, 38, 140–41
BMW, 266, 269, 301
Boards of directors, 245–52
   change and, 189, 190, 248–52
   and company's self-perception,
     245–48
BOC group, 253
Boeing corporation, 302, 322
Boesky, Ivan, 56
Bonoma, Thomas V., 116, 119
Borg-Warner company, 170
Boston Consulting Group, 241,
   245–47, 349
Brain/body scanners, 311–12, 323, 325
Brand names, role of, 122–23, 129,
   229–30
"Brands," defined, 102
Brazil, 3, 7, 350–53, 355, 360
Breakthroughs! (Nayak and
   Ketteringham), 36, 40, 72–75, 81,
   82, 322–23
Brewers, 207–208, 220–23, 225, 226,
   240, 243, 319
Bridgestone tire company, 355
Britain, *see* United Kingdom
British Aerospace, 345–46
British Petroleum (BP), 253
Bronfman, Sam, 130, 144, 149
Brooks Brothers, 183
Buffett, Warren, 57, 58, 60, 61, 219
Buggie, Frederick D., 63–65, 67, 70,
   71

INDEX

INDEX

International Business Machines,
(IBM) (cont'd)
Akers's 1988 shake-up at, 157,
193–97, 203, 306
Boca Raton (Fla.) group of, 196,
202
in PC market, 3–4, 7, 23–24, 77,
118–19, 193–97, 199, 201, 202, 217,
222, 225–30, 232, 300, 301, 318,
330
"Seven Pillars of Wisdom" of,
198–202
International Herald Tribune, 118
Internationalism as one of "Seven
Ins," 230, 232–33
Intrapreneuring (Pinchot), 36, 117
Introduction as one of "Seven Ins,"
230, 232
"Investment grade" rating, 55
Investment as one of "Seven Ins,"
230–31
Iran, 2
ITT Corporation, 37, 38, 47–48, 58,
140–42, 146–48

Jaguar, 16, 259, 261–71, 331
Japanese, 18, 23, 245, 246, 268, 312
automobile industry of, 16, 19, 40,
70, 160, 181, 264, 297–300, 303,
322, 324, 334–36, 345, 346, 353–55
at battle of Midway, 62–63
and Brazil, 352–53, 355
competitiveness of, 311, 313–16,
320–21, 326, 329–32, 334–35, 339,
341–45, 352–56, 359–61
corporate leadership style of, 181
corporate planning by, 219–21, 223,
234
crash of 1987 and, 57
decision-making style of, 2, 29, 30,
40–48, 63, 82, 191, 359–60
expansionism of, 101–102, 112–15, 145,
352–53
and improvement/quality control,
161, 164–66
as innovators, 51–52, 64–67, 79, 82,
86–87, 90

long-view decision making of,
352–55
"motorcycle wars" of, 311, 314–16,
320–21, 329
as negotiators, 287–88
office layout of, 304–305
planning by, 219–21, 223, 234
U.S. advances copied by, 81–82
watch industry of, 259, 271–74,
277–79
JCB construction equipment company,
162
Jensen, Michael C., 143, 149, 150
Jidoka, 354
Jobs, Steven, 359
Johansson, Johny K., 64
Johnson, Robert Wood, 94–95
Johnson, F. Ross, 5, 121
Johnson, Samuel, 288
Johnson & Johnson, 94–95
Johnson Matthey Bankers (JMB), 260,
289–96
Jones, Reginald, 38
Journal of Business Strategy, 243
Judge, Paul, 235–39, 242, 243
"Judge-and-jury" decision making,
34–39
Japanese *ringi* system vs., 42,
45–46, 48
Junk bonds, 54–56, 58, 60–61
Juran, Joseph M., 163
JVC VCRs, 3, 41, 74, 322, 324–25
J. Walter Thompson (JWT) company,
101, 104–107, 109, 111

Kaisha (Abegglen and Stalk), 314, 315
Kaku, Ryuzaburo, 66–67, 71–72
Kawashima (president of Honda), 315
Kellogg's Corn Flakes, 65, 233
Kelly, Donald P., 139, 141
Kentucky Fried Chicken, 17
Ketteringham, J. M., 36
See also *Breakthroughs!*
Kidde, Inc., 141, 142, 169–70
Kirin brewers, 220
Kluge, John Werner, 56
Kodak, *see* Eastman Kodak

INDEX

Mergers and acquisitions, 101–12,
    138–51, 167–78, 187
  buying on basis of assets/market
    share/earnings, 173–78, 187
  competitiveness and, 346, 356, 357
  conglomerate-style, 138–41
  corporate raiders, 141, 155–56,
    167–74, 242, 338
  "de-mergers," 207, 210–12
  entrepreneur's four basic rules for,
    172–73
  Japanese and, 101–102, 112–15, 145
  strategic benefits of, 141–42, 149–51
  yes/no decisions and, 22
  See also specific companies
Merrill Lynch, 112–13, 168
"Me-too" decisions, 78–79, 226
MG cars, 16
Micro Channel technology, 301
Microwave ovens, 36, 39–41, 81–82,
    86–87, 323, 325
Midland Bank (U.K.), 71, 250, 294
Midway, battle of, 62–63
Miles, Michael A., 17
Milken, Michael, 51, 54–56, 60–61, 111
Miller beers, 240, 243
Milliken textile company, 327
Minnesota Mining & Manufacturing
    Company (3M), 37, 91, 302, 322
  Post-it Note Pads, 36, 74, 75, 322,
    324
Minolta corporation, 64
  Magnum camera, 65, 348
  single-lens reflex (SLR) camera, 65,
    79
Models, economic, 214
Monopoly, 311–12, 317–18, 342–44, 359
Montgomery, Field Marshal Bernard,
    19, 21, 267–68
Moody's ratings, 54
Morgan, J. P., 249
Morgan, J. P., & Co., 302
Morita, Akio, 3, 7, 102, 121–29, 229–30
Morris cars, 16
Motorcycles, 311, 314–16, 320–21, 329
MRB market researchers, 104–105
Murdoch, Rupert, 59, 149

Murphy's Law, 26
Myth destruction, innovation and,
    74–75

Nabisco, 5
  See also RJR Nabisco
Nader, Ralph, 16
National Cash Register (NCR),
    226–27, 229, 230, 234, 350
National Union of Mineworkers
    (U.K.), 20–21
Nautilus gym machine, 74
Nayak, P. R., 36
  See also Breakthroughs!
"Needs," Nierenberg's theory of,
    281–87
Negotiation, Nierenberg's theory of,
    280–88
Nestlé, 145, 337–38
Netherlands, 23
New Japan Radio Corporation
    (NJRC), 40, 41, 87
New York Stock Exchange, see Crash
    of 1987
Nicoll, Eric, 145–46
Nierenberg, Gerard I., 281–88
Nike running shoes, 74, 85, 323, 325
Nikon cameras, 65
Nippon Mining company, 2, 212–13
Nissan corporation, 299–300, 303
Nobel Prize, 78, 84
Nomura Securities, 102, 112–14, 122,
    145, 146
Nonaka, Ikijuro, 64
Nonperforming loans, 216
Nordhoff, Heinz, 60
North American Philips Corporation,
    24
Northcliffe, Lord, 130
Northern Telecom (Canada), 194
Numerical quotas, 162, 166

Objectives, 237–38
  management by (MBO), 92–93
Obsolescence, threat of, 67–72
Office layout, 304–305
Offshore manufacturing, 277–79

INDEX

Tagamet (drug), 2, 52, 72–78, 311–12,
  322–23, 328–29, 358
Taguchi, Genichi, 164
Takeover (Fallon), 167
Takeovers, *see* Mergers and
  acquisitions
Tappan company, 86
  See also Raytheon microwave ovens
Taylor, Alex, III, 297, 298
Teamwork, 162, 166
Technological breakthroughs, defined,
  85
Teledyne, Inc., 140–41
Texas, 216
Texas Instruments, 230
Thatcher, Margaret, 21, 156, 330
Third World debt, 215–16, 294
Thomke, Ernst, 273–74
Thompson, G. Lee, 332
Thomson, S.A., 140
Thorn lighting company, 81
Thornton, Tex, 140–41
Thorazine (drug), 73
Thriving on Chaos (Peters), 300–301
Thunderbird wine, 133
Time lags, innovation and, 70–71
Time (magazine), 114, 197
Timex watches, 271
"TINA" decisions, 21–22, 28, 97, 163,
  343
Tire companies, 242, 355
Tisch, Laurence, 148
Tisch brothers, 123
Titanium dioxide, 317
Tokyo stock market, 57
Toshiba microwave ovens, 41, 81,
  86–87
"Toughness" of decisions, 16–19
Toyota, 300, 324, 334–36, 345
  GM joint project with, 166, 355
  production system of, 16, 40, 160,
    322, 324, 353–54
Toys and games, 52, 80, 83
  obsolescence and, 68
Toys 'R' Us, 83
Trade unions, 21–23

Trafalgar House, 59–60
Training, employee, 162, 165, 166
Transferable successes, 85
Trans World Airlines (TWA), 143, 149
Triangle publications, 147
Triumph cars, 16
Tropicana juices, 60
Trump, Donald, 307
Tupperware, 211
TV Guide, 147, 148
Two-forks problem, 11–15, 362–64
Typewriters, 312, 332–34, 338
Typhoo Tea, 235

Ultra Pampers disposable diapers, 80
Unavoidable decisions, defined, 25, 28
Unfilled needs, 84
Unilever, 138–39
United Biscuits Brands Division, 145
United Brands, 145
United Kingdom
  automobile industry of, 15–16, 166,
    259, 261–71, 301, 331, 345–46
  banking in, 71, 250, 260, 288–94
  chairman-CEO doubling-up in, 304
  expansionism in, 101, 104–12
  Fleet Street, 59–60
  miners' strikes in, 20–23
  1980s business turnarounds in, 156,
    162–63, 166, 330
  PC market in, 217–19, 231, 301
  "supertanker" companies in, 337–38,
    359
  U.S. advances copied by, 81
U.S. government, 2
United States Lines, 4–5
U.S. Mint, 80, 84
United States Steel, 327
United Technologies Corporation, 38
Unorthodox decisions, defined, 96
UPI Group, 174–75
USX Corporation, 327

"Values" in stock market, 57–58, 213
Vaseline, 138
Vauxhall Motors, 166